AS Film Studies

Jo Harland
&
Nick Timmons

Nelson Thornes

a Wolters Kluwer business

Published in 2006 by:
Nelson Thornes Ltd
Delta Place
27 Bath Road
CHELTENHAM
GL53 7TH
United Kingdom

06 07 08 09 10 / 10 9 8 7 6 5 4 3 2 1

A catalogue record for this book is available from the British Library

ISBN 0 7487 9030 6

Illustrations by Angela Lumley, Harry Vennings and Dave Russell
Page make-up by Pantek Arts Ltd

Printed in Great Britain by Scotprint

Acknowledgements

The Publishers would like to thank the following for material used in this book.

Oliver Paine, Emily Mason, Darren Mallows, Simon Sandford and Jeffrey Courtenay for permission to use their work as exemplar material.

Extract on page 56/57 from a review by Pumpkin on *From Dusk Till Dawn* at www.ciao.co.uk/From Dusk Till Dawn Review 5423316

Extract on page 57/58 from a review by Adrian Horrocks on *From Dusk Till Dawn* at www.dso.co.uk/fr22.htm. Reproduced by kind permission of DSO.

Chronological arrangement of *Pulp Fiction* on page 74 based on *Pulp Fiction* by Neville Langley (York Film Notes, York Press, 2003). Reproduced by kind permission of Balberry Publishing.

Screenplay format information on pp 88–92 adapted from www.exposure.co.uk/eejit/script/#slug. Reproduced by kind permission.

International Box Office information on page 115 reproduced by kind permission of Screen International.

Time Warner Corporate Timeline on pages 117–119 reproduced by kind permission of Columbia Journalism Review.

Top 10 UK films and Top 10 US films charts on pages 129–130 adapted from *The Guardian*, originally produced using information provided by Exhibitor Relations.

Sources of film finance on pages 141-142 from www.raindance.co.uk and Raindance Producers' Lab Lo-To-No Budget Filmmaking by Elliott Grove (Focal Press, 2004). Reproduced by kind permission.

Exam question on page 150 adapted from WJEC AS Film Studies exam (January 2003). Reproduced by kind permission.

Extract about UK cinema ownership on page 167 reproduced by kind permission of Phil Hubbard.

Leaflet on page 170 reproduced by kind permission of The Plaza Community Cinema.

The four distinct elements of a star on page 184 from Christine Gledhill (ed.) *Stardom: Industry of Desire* (Routledge, 1991). Reproduced by kind permission of Taylor and Francis Group.

Photo credits

Fig 2.1 Sourced by the BFI; Fig 2.2 Dig Broadcast Co Ltd; Fig 2.11 © Royalty-Free/Corbis; Fig 2.12 [top] Paul Versalo/Rex [bottom] Courtesy of Universal Studios Licensing LLLP; Fig 2.14 akg-images/MGM/Bull, Clarence Sinclair/Album; Fig 2.15 Sourced by the BFI, Fig 2.16 Universal/The Kobal Collection; Fig 2.17 akg-images/Paramount Pictures/Album; Fig 2.18 Warner Bros/Dreamworks/Amblin; Fig 2.19 Courtesy of Universal Studios Licensing LLLP; Fig 2.20 Universal/Dreamworks; analyse this page 31 [left] Live Entertainment/The Kobal Collection [right] Danjaq/Eon/UA/The Kobal Collection/Hamshere, Keith; analyse this page 32 [top] akg-images/Columbia Pictures/Album [bottom] Courtesy of FilmFour and Assasin Films; Fig 2.22 Sourced by the BFI; Case Study page 71 Seven © MCMXCV, New Line Productions, Inc. All rights reserved. Photo appears courtesy of New Line Productions, Inc.; analyse this page 108 SNAP/Rex; Fig 5.3 Warner Bros/First National/The Kobal Collection; Case Study page 136 Columbia/The Kobal Collection; Case Study page 149 Sourced by the BFI; analyse this page 150 [left] Seon-ik Films [right] Dreamworks/Everett/Collection/Rex Features; Fig 8.2 BBC/Film Council/The Kobal Collection; Case Study page 172 [top] Dreamworks/Everett/Rex; Case Study page 172 [bottom] TopFoto; Fig 9.1 © and ™. Aardman Animations Limited. 2005. All Rights Reserved. Wallace and Gromit (wordmark) and the characters 'Wallace' and 'Gromit' © and ™ Aardman Wallace and Gromit Limited; Fig 10.1 IMP/The Kobal Collection; Fig 12.1 Woodfall/Kestrel/The Kobal Collection/Barnett, Michael; Fig 12.2 © Sixteen Films Ltd, photo by Joss Barratt. Photo appears courtesy of Sixteen Films Ltd; Fig 12.3 TopFoto/KPA.

Whilst every effort has been made to trace the copyright holders, in cases where this has been unsuccessful or if any have inadvertently been overlooked, the Publishers will be pleased to make the necessary arrangements at the first opportunity.

Contents

Introduction   iv

Part 1   FILM: MAKING MEANING (FS1)

Chapter 1	Film form and language	1
Chapter 2	Micro elements: film style	5
Chapter 3	Macro elements: narrative and genre	55
Chapter 4	Practical application of learning	85

Part 2   PRODUCERS AND AUDIENCES (FS2)

Chapter 5	The historical development of the Hollywood film industry	99
Chapter 6	The development of the contemporary film industry	115
Chapter 7	Film production	133
Chapter 8	Film distribution	145
Chapter 9	Film exhibition	161
Chapter 10	Stars	179

Part 3   MESSAGES AND VALUES: BRITISH AND IRISH CINEMA (FS3)

| Chapter 11 | Topic study: the swinging sixties | 189 |
| Chapter 12 | Close study: Sweet Sixteen | 207 |

Conclusion		217
Glossary		219
Index		223

Introduction

This book is aimed primarily at AS level students of Film Studies, with particular focus on the Welsh Joint Education Committees (WJEC) AS specification, but is also designed to be used in conjunction with other film and media-based courses. The WJEC AS level course breaks down into modules FS1, FS2 and FS3 and the text will deal with each of these under their specification headings, 'Making Meaning', 'Producers and Audiences' and 'Messages and Values'.

The book is designed to complement classroom study and as a resource for extra reading, as well as giving practical tips and exercises to aid understanding.

On a less formal level the book will, we hope, bring alive the subject of cinema and provide a fascinating and detailed insight into the world of film from initial idea to end product.

Watching and 'reading' film

Do you remember your first visit to the cinema? The hustle-bustle of the foyer giving way to the hushed, reverential tones of the auditorium? Even today, when some of that cinema etiquette may have disappeared, there is still something special about the cinema experience and we inadvertently learn a lot from the images and happenings that we watch on screen. Similarly, watching films in a different context, for example at home, has both similar and different pleasures and makes access to the medium easy and part of our everyday life. Consequently, as a result of a lifetime's viewing we are all incredibly experienced film-watchers and have become 'experts' at 'reading' films and making sense of them.

Beacuse of this previous knowledge, which you all have, it is not the task here to 'introduce film' to people who are already well acquainted with it, but to introduce the *study of film*. This is something more complex than merely viewing and commenting on films we have seen, and will allow us to explore film beyond the level of cultural pastime. The *study* of film will enable you, probably for the first time, to take apart and look in detail at that which you already know about cinema.

The pleasure of going to the cinema is not to watch people on screen laugh, cry or be fearful and so on, but to have these feelings ourselves. But exactly *how does* film draw out feelings and emotions in us? How do we 'make sense' of such a complex technical and creative process? How do film-makers enable us to forget our everyday world and transport us elsewhere? In short, how do we *make meaning* from cinema and what do we learn from it?

Making meaning (FS1)

Film-making and film viewing is an interactive two-way process. It is a *language* through which we communicate ideas and messages. The film-maker speaks in the language, which we, as viewers of many years, are able to understand and (importantly) respond to. This response can be professional (critics) or it can be personal. It can be collective (audience) or it can be individual (spectator). This *film language* and the subsequent *reading* of film, is where we will start our studies.

Film is an art form and one which, like other art forms – for example, fine art and literature – requires the 'reading' of various texts. By the term 'reading' we not only mean that you are able to make sense of the films set before you but also that you are able to extract further information at a deeper level of analysis. In this way the study of film is exactly like any other arts subject; you wouldn't expect to pass English Literature without poring over many books to gain a deeper appreciation, and you cannot pass Film Studies without watching many films! Even if certain films seem not to appeal to your personal taste this should not deter your academic appreciation or critique of them, and you may find that they contain many more levels of communication than you initially thought. As a consequence you may come to *like* them, or if not like them, you may come to *admire* them.

Producers and audiences (FS2)

Aside from being an art form, film is also an industry, and in the case of Hollywood, a multi-million pound industry that employs classic business strategies to maximise its profits. Different films cater for different audiences and just as the viewer is manipulated by the creative 'language' of filmmaking so they are also affected by the marketing and distribution of such films. Any study of the roles of film-watcher and filmmaker has to take into account the film industry as a powerful institution. Developments in technology and in media ownership have changed the way that we consume films and we need to understand what the impact of this is, not only on our own personal viewing habits but also on the film industry as a whole. This then will make up a further part of the study of film with particular emphasis given to the British film industry and the way it is funded.

Messages and values (FS3)

Beyond the technical/creative and business aspects of film there is the cultural value of film that affects all of us. The *messages and values* contained within different types of film, possibly in different contexts, are what make films such a vital tool of social comment. We learn a lot about our own and others' cultures through this medium, and the debates and discussions which arise from these depictions teach us a lot about history and the values of society. What do films from other eras tell us about those eras? What do films of today tell us about now? How does cinema reflect social and cultural change? The answers to these questions will require a cultural and ideological analysis of film and this will complete this introductory level of study.

The final part of the process is to bring all these factors – creative, technical, business – together, as it is only when they are combined as interdependent components of a whole piece of work that we can say that we fully understand the nature of film.

Above all, as stated at the outset, the aim is not to 'introduce film' in some kind of prescribed way but to build on that which you already know. Allow your own individual tastes and thoughts to prevail while keeping an open mind to film's endless possibilities. Use the tools and terminology you will acquire throughout the book to analyse and express those ideas. You will find no 'answers' in this book, for one person's all-time classic is another's all-time turkey! What you *will* find, however, is all the information you need about how the films you enjoy work to engage, educate and entertain you.

From the Publisher: note on 2006 specification changes.

Since the time of writing, WJEC have made changes to the AS Film Studies specification for FS1 Film: Making Meaning. We have updated the content of this book in line with these changes with the exception of a new micro cinematic code called 'performance'. This is covered briefly in Chapter 2 in 'figure expression' under the micro code 'mise en scène'. For more information on 'performance' please ask your tutor or visit www.wjec.co.uk where you'll find a list of further reading on page 114 of their Notes for Guidance document.

Film form and language

This chapter introduces the basic concept of film form.

Film form is an overview of the different components that make up film studies and, put simply, refers to elements that make film distinctive from other art forms in terms of style and content.

Film form breaks down into two distinct but interrelated parts: **micro** and **macro** elements. These are introduced here but explored further in subsequent chapters.

Film form: an overview

When the moving image was first introduced in the late 1890s people were understandably intrigued, amazed and shocked by its capabilities. An early film famously shown in France by the Lumière Brothers was entitled *Train Arriving at the Station*, and that, unbelievably to a modern audience, was exactly what happened on screen (see illustration on page 102). Reportedly, the audience leapt from their seats and fled in panic at the approaching train, such was the shock at seeing this amazing spectacle (and this was without sound!). As funny as this may seem, the ability of film to convey life-like images so convincing that we believe in them, still happens today.

OK, so we may not run in terror from the cinema any more but we still become submerged in the world on screen; this is the enjoyment of watching a good film. But ask yourself this: how *are* we drawn into the world of the film? How are we able to make sense of what we see on screen? How is the projection flickering before us in the cinema able to draw out the most personal of responses from us? To cry, to laugh, to be frightened; we experience all this temporarily through film and often in the company of strangers who are similarly and simultaneously inhabiting the same make-believe world.

analyse this Imagine a person coming from a different society, where there was no film or television. All the film 'language', which we so easily interpret, would be unknown to them. Ideas such as cutting between different locations, disembodied dialogue occurring as voice over, special effects, leaps in time and space – all this would be confusing and might make no sense at all.

Discuss and write down the various ways, apart from dialogue, that film communicates its message to you.

As children we quickly learn to 'read' the 'language' of film. That is, we learn to make sense of that which is presented to us on screen even if it is set on a strange planet or has an array of different characters. We can follow the film as it switches from one location to another, back and forth – sometimes going forward in time, sometimes going back – and still understand and believe what is going on. We can tell what the characters are feeling and thinking without any dialogue, not just through their body language (which is how it would be indicated in traditional theatre) but also because of the way the camera moves or the sound alters. Unlike the reading of words on a page we are never given formal instructions in this 'language' of film but by being exposed to it frequently from a very young age we learn how this way of communication works and subsequently how it creates meaning.

Case Study

The Wizard of Oz, made in 1939 (Fleming), used black and white film to show the 'ordinariness' of Dorothy's existence in Kansas. When she dreams of being 'over the rainbow' the film-makers use 'special effects' to create an imaginary world and switch the film stock from black and white to colour (at one point trying to merge the two in what would have been at that time an amazing special effect). As an audience we know instantly, as does Dorothy, that, 'this is not Kansas!' Without the use of anything except cinematic language we understand that we have been transported over the rainbow! For an audience in 1939 (remember there was no such thing as TV, let alone colour TV), this would have been magical.

However, understanding the technical process of film-making that 'transports' the audience is not the end of the experience in terms of film study; the next questions to ponder are, how does it affect the viewer and does it have further meaning?

Since those early days, cinema, like its audience, has become sophisticated. Keeping pace with advances over the last one hundred years of film-making in all the technical areas (camera, editing, sound, special effects, etc.) has developed our skill of 'reading' a film to a very high standard and film-makers can now 'play' with our knowledge and expectation of what a film should be. Mainstream cinema (which will be our focus at this introductory level), is essentially about story-telling and the presentation of those stories is becoming as complex as the technology itself. Understanding the *construction* of film stories is one part of our study while analysing their meaning is another.

analyse this

Think of a film you saw recently. Discuss it with someone – teacher, fellow student, friend or family member. Write down the comments that you both make about it (whatever they are). Then, and only then, read on and see how your comments compare with the notes overleaf.

It is important to note here that although we can all technically 'read' films there is never *one* reading of a film. One person will tend to read a film slightly differently from the next person depending on his or her own cultural values and experiences. **Cultural codes** make up a large part of the on-screen world and it is only when these cultural codes are combined with **cinematic codes** that we get our own unique interpretation of a film.

Film form: micro and macro components

Film form has two basic component parts. When we discuss film, whether it is in an informal environment or in an educational setting we tend to divide our 'analysis' into:

● What is it about? (*Content*)
● What does it look/sound like? (*Style*)

(Another question commonly asked is, 'Who's in it?' We will address this later.)

In film studies we can translate these ideas into what we call *macro* and *micro* elements.

An initial study of how film makes meaning involves looking at these elements closely.

FILM FORM	
Content **WHAT IS IT ABOUT?** **(MACRO)**	**Style** **WHAT DOES IT LOOK/SOUND LIKE?** **(MICRO)**
NARRATIVE	CINEMATOGRAPHY
IDEOLOGY	EDITING
THEMES	LIGHTING
CONCEPTS	SOUND
GENRE	MISE EN SCÈNE

Table 1.1 ▲ Micro and macro elements.

These two categories of 'micro' and 'macro' make up *film form*.

The micro elements, you will notice, are the *technical things that construct the film's 'style'*. The macro elements are the wider concepts that apply to the content of most art forms and concentrate on the messages in the story of the film. It is through the *combination* of these things that meaning is constructed.

It is important in film studies to have a solid understanding of what these things are and how they are used in conjunction with one another to 'create meaning' (the focus of one piece of coursework), so let's take a look at them individually.

Technical codes, often known as 'cinematic codes' are the techniques by which the *style* of the film is *physically* constructed. These are the micro elements of cinema and form one-half of a film analysis. As viewers we 'read' these codes and interpret them automatically into ideas. This chapter will deal with the five cinematic codes: **cinematography**, **lighting**, **mise en scène** (including performance), **editing** and **sound**. By deconstructing each element and analysing it we can identify how it works to create meaning. Of course, none of the following codes work in isolation, they are all dependent on one another (and also the macro elements) to create the finished piece and this must always be considered in a full analysis.

Cinematography: painting with light

This is the term for film camerawork, and the film cameraperson is known as the *cinematographer*. Cinematography is the most important of the cinematic codes as without the camera (see fig. 2.1) there is obviously no cinema. Developments in camera technology have been rapid in recent years with the introduction of digital technology and DV cameras. As with all technological advancements, this has had an impact on film-making for a variety of reasons and will be discussed later (see talking point on page 7). However, it is important that you understand that mainstream Hollywood production still relies (at the time of writing) heavily on the medium of film and the difference in technique between the two formats is vast.

Figure 2.1 ▶

key terms

Digitised
when media (images) are converted electronically from one format (e.g. film) and stored in a digital edit suite.

Most of the films that have been made over the last 100 years have been created, as the medium suggests, on *film*. 35mm film is the most common format for mainstream feature films (although some on smaller budgets have used 16mm). 35mm film is the kind of film that until recently (with the advent of digital photography), you would have loaded into your normal stills camera when you went on holiday. Cinematography is related to photography, which is when something is produced by or connected with light. The cinematographer will have in-depth photographic knowledge regarding film stock, light quality, lenses and focus.

Working on film is not an 'instant' medium like video/digital video (DV). You cannot re-record over what you have filmed and reuse the stock once it has been exposed. This is one of its drawbacks when compared with digital formats. Of course directors, on set, will have 'video playback', a monitor of what can be seen through the lens while shooting. However, this acts only as a monitor and variations in light and focus will only be confirmed (and controlled) once 'prints' have been produced from the negative. These first prints, which are rushed through to the director on a daily basis, are called 'rushes' in the UK and 'dailies' in the USA.

Film is also a very different medium to videotape or digital tape. Video is the format used up until now for many domestic cameras; however, there is a world of difference between a film camera and a video camera. Video is tape-based and 'instant'. It also has reusable stock (meaning you can re-record over the same piece of tape over and over again) and it runs at 25 fps (frames per second) as opposed to film, which runs at 24 fps, hence the two are incompatible when it comes to digital editing systems. Therefore a film cameraman and a video cameraman are not the same thing.

Digital camerawork

Figure 2.2 ▶

6

Digital technology has created a lot of debate in the film industry as to the future of 35mm film, and within the TV industry it is already widely used. With better DV cameras there is less of a reliance on film and all its associated developing costs. The DV camera (see fig. 2.2) does not capture light on film but translates and stores this information onto a computer chip. Therefore there are no 'negatives' as everything is stored digitally (electronically). The digital camera has the benefit of being 'instant', cheaper and more portable and is ideal for lower budget/independent productions. Its 'instant quality' saves time and therefore money but it does not have the photographic capabilities and quality that 35mm cinematography has (yet). There is also the problem of 'distribution' for digital work (getting it seen in mainstream cinemas), as most cinemas can only project film. Digital cinema or 'e-cinema' is forming but is still in its infancy. Its emergence raises lots of debate around what we value in our viewing experience.

Case Study

Danny Boyle's *28 Days Later* (2002) was shot and edited digitally but ultimately had to be transferred to film for projection in cinemas. When blown up to a large scale like a cinema screen, deficiencies in the quality of the image are highlighted.

The Blair Witch Project (Myrick and Sanchez, 1999) is also an example of a horror film using DV technology effectively and creatively, putting the 'amateur' quality of this type of camerawork to its advantage.

talking point

Digital cinema or 'e-cinema' is cinema which is not only shot digitally but also shown digitally, either disk-based (like DVDs) or 'live' (like downloading from the internet) and means that cinemas would no longer show the medium of 'film' as we presently know it. There are several benefits (lower costs, fewer prints for the industry, etc.) and disadvantages to this, (image scale and quality of images not generated digitally and the huge expense of a switchover to digital projectors). It also means that film distribution could become 'centralised' (sent as digital files) like TV programmes and that films across the country could be 'transmitted' simultaneously instead of shown individually. Some have suggested that it could also mean that cinemas are not just used to screen films but also 'events' like rock concerts or sports matches.

▶ How do you feel about this?

▶ Do you mind what size of screen you watch films on?

▶ Do you think cinemas could be successful as 'large TVs'?

▶ Do you think it will boost cinema attendance or bring about its downfall?

Common camera techniques

As film students, it is important that you understand not only the film industry's future but also its past. Having knowledge of the process by which some of the most famous films ever directed were made, will enhance your appreciation of them and the people who made them. By the same token, considering the possibilities of the future will also widen your scope of study. This combination of past and future will help you understand, and perhaps participate in, some of the debates that are taking place in the film industry at the moment.

Despite the different formats there are various, common things that are relevant to all cinematographers, and these are the ways in which they use the camera to create meaning.

Static framing

When we frame something we are making a conscious decision about what to include within that frame and what to exclude.

Deciding where to place the camera and what to include/exclude in the shot produces what Bordwell and Thompson call 'a certain vantage point' (D. Bordwell and K. Thompson, *Film Art: An Introduction*, McGraw-Hill, 1990). It is incredibly powerful in creating meaning as the camera does not merely record that which is in front of it (even in documentary this is true) but can be placed skilfully to create the required impression or identification. This means considering *distance*, *angle*, *height* and *level* of the camera.

key terms

Format relates to the different types of material that are used to create films or TV programmes, e.g. film, videotape, DVD, etc.

analyse this

1

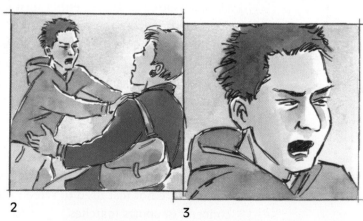

2   3

See how the different framing of the same shot above can create an entirely different 'reading' or meaning.

Frame 1 shows the youth pushing the woman out of the way of an oncoming car.
Frame 2 makes it look like the woman is being mugged.
Frame 3 shows the youth as angry and not the hero that he is.

Distance

analyse this   Look at these basic shot types.

Long shot (LS) – the whole person

Close-up (CU) – from the chin up

Medium long shot (MLS) – from the knees up

Extreme close-up (ECU) – detail

Medium shot (MS) – from the waist up

Medium two shot (M2S) – two people at medium distance

Medium close-up (MCU) – from the chest up

Over shoulder shot (O/S) – shoulder in foreground

In which kind of scene might it be appropriate to use each type of shot? (Ignore the specifics of the content, which are deliberately vague.) When might you use a close-up for example?

Angle

The distance combined with the use of angle can create further meaning. For instance, the same shot filmed from different angles can create a very different effect (see fig. 2.3).

Figure 2.3 ▶

Notice how the power and dominance of the person changes. And this is without the added signifier of lighting! Making someone appear small in the frame by use of a high angle shot can reduce his or her authority on screen. Similarly, filming from a low angle can make them seem more authoritative or terrifying.

This use of angle is by no means written in stone and film-makers will often subvert these 'rules'; therefore each shot has to be considered individually and placed in the context of the whole film and the character, but as a guideline it is a good place to start.

Height

Not to be confused with angle, the height of the camera is also valuable in creating meaning. Keeping a straight angle, the height of the camera can be adjusted for effect. You may wish to film something from a low height but still keep the angle straight on, for example, someone's footsteps (see fig. 2.4).

Figure 2.4 ▶

Similarly, having the camera at a high height can create a specific effect. For example, a comic effect can be created if you have two characters of opposing heights and you keep the camera on the taller one, cutting off the smaller character, or vice versa (see fig. 2.5).

Figure 2.5 ▶

Level

The level of the camera is the technique that is used the least, and can only really be explained by example. If the level of the camera is 'canted', (sometimes known as a Dutch angle), the image on screen will appear rotated in some way. It is an effect that is generally achieved through hand-held manoeuvre and creates a stylised look. It is more common in TV production than film, as this lends itself more easily to handheld work, and can often be seen in 'youth' programmes to give a sense of the unconventional. Take a look at fig. 2.6 below.

Figure 2.6 ▶

FILM: MAKING MEANING (FS1)

The moving frame

All the techniques referred to so far consider the framing when the camera is static. However, as you will be well aware, cinematography is rarely static in film and the framing outlined above will work in combination with movement. The distinguishing factor of film as a visual art above all others is that unlike theatre or painting, the frame has the capability of fluidity and change, which is able to take us into and around the make-believe world that is created. This movement of the camera relies on some basic, common techniques, which you must be able to identify correctly in conjunction with the framing if you are to describe and analyse film effectively.

The panning shot

The word 'pan' comes from the abbreviation of 'panoramic' as this shot can survey the whole scene with its movement from left to right or right to left (see fig. 2.7). (It was often used in westerns to capture the magnificent panorama of the imposing desert landscape.) With a panning shot, the camera tripod stays in the same position and only the camera head moves from side to side, or in some cases the whole 360 degrees.

Figure 2.7 ▶

A pan can be slow or quick depending on the required effect. If the pan is very quick and appears to blur the image it is referred to as a 'whip-pan'.

Common use: Often used in an *establishing shot* (a shot which opens a film or a scene) to allow the audience to take in the details of the setting or character. For example, the interior of a teenager's bedroom: the camera may pan around and linger on details that will tell us something about the character before we have even met them.

The tracking shot

In this shot the camera is mounted on a *dolly* (a device with wheels or runners), which is then mounted onto a track. The whole camera is then able to move along the track, either from left to right/right to left or backwards/forwards (see fig. 2.8). This is either done manually, and is pushed along by the *grips* (people who take care of all the rigging on-set) or it is done by remote control. The cinematographer will usually sit upon the dolly to control the shot and focus. A similar effect can also be achieved through other means and as the setting up of tracking shots takes a long time and is therefore expensive, on low-budget productions the camera may be attached to any device with wheels to obtain the 'tracking' motion. Again, tracking shots can be quick or slow depending on the desired effect.

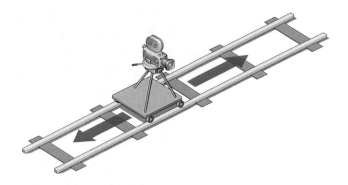

Figure 2.8 ▶

Common use: To convey speed in a chase sequence when tracking alongside a running character, or to convey shock in a static character as the camera tracks quickly towards them. Used slowly it can follow a character as they move through a scene.

The tilt

In this shot the tripod or base of the camera remains still and only the head of the camera moves (see fig. 2.9). The movement is up and down only, creating an angle on the subject being shot. If the camera is tilted down it will obviously be above its subject and if the camera tilts up it will be below.

Figure 2.9 ▶

Common use: The tilt is commonly used slowly, often to *reveal* something. For example, when a character arrives at the edge of a cliff or precipice the camera will often tilt downwards to reveal the danger. Similarly the introduction of a key character is sometimes marked by a tilt. Starting with the character's shoes and tilting slowly upwards the character is slowly revealed to the expectant audience. (See Martin Scorsese's *Goodfellas* (1990) and the first sight of the grown-up gangster and star of the film Henry Hill.)

The crane shot

A crane shot is when the camera (and cinematographer) are mounted on a crane and are lifted high into the air to get a grand overhead shot (see fig. 2.10). The crane can move in all directions (aided again by the grips), and this can achieve a 'swooping' effect like a bird. Cranes come in various sizes with the smallest ones being called 'jibs' which may just be above shoulder height (basically a little too high for a tripod shot). Crane shots are complicated and expensive because of the equipment necessary and the time they take to set up. Hence very low-budget films tend to have fewer, if any, of them and the best examples are from high-budget Hollywood studio films.

Figure 2.10 ▶

Common use: Can often be seen on high-concept films in the establishing shots. Because of the widespread, overhead view they are useful in establishing setting. Also used commonly to convey movement and speed like flying or floating; generally give a film an 'expensive' look and are employed a lot in effects movies.

Aerial shots

In an aerial shot, the cameraperson (usually a second unit or specialised crew) will shoot from a helicopter or small plane. These shots are always shot mute (with no sound) as the noise of the transport and the wind would render the sound unusable.

Car-mounted shot

The camera can be attached either to the side or windscreen of a moving car when the car is in shot. In this way speed can be exaggerated or a conversation between two front seat characters can be filmed without cuts. The camera can also be mounted to a different car (or boat or other vehicle), which travels alongside the vehicle in the film to follow the action.

Handheld shot

Even though a shot may look handheld, with film it often is not. In the 1970s a piece of apparatus was developed which is worn by the cinematographer and onto which the camera is mounted. This is called the 'Steadicam' (see fig. 2.11).

The apparatus acts as a 'shock absorber' as the cameraperson freely moves around while filming, avoiding sharp jarring movements and

Figure 2.11 ▶

allowing a certain stability even when running. True handheld shots are jumpy and hard to focus with a film camera (remember this is not video) but are sometimes used for the effect of chaos. One example is in *The Blair Witch Project* where the camerawork is deliberately supposed to look amateurish and shaky.

Common use: Documentary film obviously employs this technique, as unscripted pieces have to be flexible and spontaneous. That is why 'spoof' documentaries often try to mimic the action. The use of handheld shots gives a sense of urgency and disturbance when used sparingly in an otherwise smooth production.

Zoom

With this type of movement the camera itself does not move at all but instead it is the lens on the camera that creates the effect. Different types of zoom can be used to create different meaning. A slow zoom can be an indication of realisation, as in the slow zoom of a letter as it is being read or the slow zoom into a character's face as an idea dawns. It can also indicate a growing intimacy with the character(s) as it draws the audience in. A fast zoom can also indicate realisation but with an unsettling effect. When combined with the moving camera, and the quick pulling of focus it can create a disturbing 'trombone' effect (see the famous beach shot in *Jaws* or the balcony scene in *La Haine* where the background appears to rush forwards).

Don't forget the camera can zoom out as well as in to have the opposite effect.

Special effects

The special effects department on a large film works as part of cinematography and post-production (editing). When a scene is being shot the cinematographer will know which shots are going to have special effects added and will shoot accordingly. Sometimes this will mean shooting in a studio against a 'blue screen' or 'green screen' where action will be added later to the shot. For example, in a scene where someone is hanging over a cliff, the actor will be shot 'hanging' in a studio against a green screen and a shot of a real cliff will be filmed elsewhere. The two shots will then be merged optically to create one combined shot. Other special effects shots may mean shooting on location knowing that most of the actual location will be 'painted' out or will have new scenery added by the use of CGI (computer generated imagery). Film-makers can therefore add or delete unwanted imagery. However, this process is very expensive and time consuming and is therefore usually reserved only for large-budget productions. Each frame of the shot has to be 'composited' (altered slightly differently, somewhat like the process of animation), and there are 24 frames in every *second* of film! The film *Gladiator* famously used extensive CGI to recreate the coliseums of ancient Rome (see fig. 2.12).

Figure 2.12 ▶

Despite this, it is worth remembering that 'special effects' do not just refer to dramatic events using explosions and rockets etc. Many films that look as though there would be no need for special 'effects' often contain scenes that have been altered. For example, period dramas, where elements of the contemporary skyline have to be removed to create authenticity.

Other technical terms

DoP (Director of Photography)

This is the person in overall control of the cinematography on a film. On large feature films there may be a couple of camera operators or different 'units' to deal with the vast amount of work. The DoP will supervise and organise all this camerawork cohesively as well as carrying out the main body of work themselves.

Depth of field/ pull focus

The depth of field is a photographic term which refers to the amount of focus in the shot. If everything in the shot is in focus then the depth of field is 'deep'. However, it is common to 'pull focus' to one object or person and keep the background out of focus. In this case the depth of field would be 'shallow' and the focus foregrounded. There is a credit on the end of feature films for 'focus puller'; their main job is to assist the cinematographer and to align focus.

Aspect ratio

This is the shape/size of the screen and is determined at the outset with the choice of lenses that the DoP and the director choose to use. A TV screen and a cinema screen used to be very different shapes. However, to mimic 'widescreen' viewing which has been around in cinema since the 1950s, TV is now opting for an aspect ratio of 1:2.35 which is the typical 'letterbox' shape of the cinema screen. The ratio refers to the dimensions of the screen. For example, for every one part measuring up the side of the screen there will be 2.35 parts across the screen. With a ratio of 1:1.85 the screen would obviously be less wide until you reach 1:1, which is the perfect square.

The choice of aspect ratio could be important in analysing production values (it could have an impact on the message being conveyed). A great effects movie that expects a cinematic release would want to 'show-off' its work in widescreen but a piece of social realism (about real life) may compromise its ideals and messages if it were to opt for such Hollywood glamour, and would retain its 'grittiness' by keeping to a more TV-like aspect ratio. Social realism and documentary also often work on a lower budget with less opportunity for distribution in cinemas, therefore the aspect ratio of TV is suitable for its most likely screening 'platform'.

Activity

Identification of shots is a necessary element of film analysis but is only part of the required knowledge at this level. Once confident with the types of shots it is even more important that we understand why a certain type of framing is used at a particular point in the film and what effect it creates. This is how we develop film language. There is no point in knowing what a close-up is, if we cannot say when its use is appropriate or what meaning it conveys. With this in mind, and using the shot descriptors that you have just learnt, watch a sequence from any film and try to explain what the shots are and why they were chosen. How are the shots creating meaning and helping to convey the story?

Cinematography, then, is just one of the cinematic codes, and although this chapter has sought to look at it in isolation, a full analysis of any film requires that *all the cinematic codes combine to create meaning*. It is only when cinematography is considered in conjunction with lighting, editing, sound and mise en scène that we have the full range of film language and expression, and therefore the most information on which to base a 'reading' or interpretation of meaning. With this in mind it is important that the next cinematic code that we study is the one most closely linked with cinematography: lighting.

questions

▶ What are the five cinematic codes?
▶ What is the main difference between a film camera and a digital camera?
▶ Why is framing so important?
▶ A shot, which shows a person from the knees up, is called a what?
▶ What kind of movement is a tilt?
▶ What does DoP stand for?
▶ In what instance might a canted angle be used?
▶ What does ECU stand for?
▶ What is the apparatus called which is often used in 'handheld' shots?
▶ All the cinematic codes are collectively known as what?

Lighting: mood and atmosphere

Cinematography and lighting work closely together for obvious reasons; the shot has to be lit so that we can see it properly and all good photography, not just cinematography, gives considerable attention to its lighting. However, lighting is not merely functional. Illumination of the scene is of course vital if the audience are to see anything but it also has an artistic and creative purpose. Cinematic lighting serves as part of the film language much like all the other cinematic codes. The way a shot is lit can radically alter the meaning of a scene and have an impact on the audience. The cultural codes of real life dictate our expectation of lighting; a brightly lit place indicates safety and happiness, while a shadowy place will make us feel more apprehensive. (See the Case Study on *The Godfather* below.)

Certain settings are *expected* to have certain types of lighting to reassure us; the office generally has fluorescent, bright lights, the romantic restaurant will be candlelit, and the children's playground will have natural daylight. This is what we expect. However, as in all aspects of cinema (and especially with genre, which we will look at later), where we have *expectations* the director can 'play' upon them and surprise us. Subsequently these conventional examples of lighting can be subverted to create different effects.

analyse this

Imagine the effect of:
- a candlelit supermarket
- a dark hospital
- bringing up the house lights in a nightclub!

Lighting (as you can see from the unexpected examples of it above), is very much part of film language and it is the lighting crew's responsibility, in conjunction with the cinematographer, to 'paint with light', creating *mood* and *atmosphere* on screen.

Case Study

In the film *The Godfather* (Coppola, 1972) the lighting is a distinctive feature, which the director has spoken about at length. In the opening sequences the interior shots of the Mafia doing 'business' in the office are very dark. This (along with other cinematic codes) has the effect of making the audience wary and expectant. The scene was deliberately shot in a way that would cast heavy shadows and the film stock was slightly underexposed to add to the effect. At times it is difficult to distinguish things among the shadows but this was the effect the director wanted. Why? So that the lighting complemented the themes of the film: concealment, dark intent, threatening, shadowy Mafia-men and the mysterious underworld. This 'office' sequence contrasts sharply when it cuts to the wedding sequence, which is joyous and presents the respectable 'legitimate' side of the Corleone family. This sequence is brightly lit with sunshine and makes the audience feel like they are safe outside in the bright, natural light after the oppressive shadows of the interior. The two sides of the family and their duplicitous lives are therefore perfectly established through lighting.

Here is part of a film review that refers specifically to the lighting:

The lighting of *The Godfather* could be the subject of a whole documentary. The action is set in dark interiors, shadowed streets; period settings bathed in amber, brown, taupe, sepia. The costume colours and the lighting are so subtle and beautifully done that daylight scenes with bright colours, like the wedding at the film's start, create the same effect as walking out of a matinee into a summer afternoon. We're dazzled, but in this case we're equally dazzled by the dim and faintly seen details and lovingly filmed rooms and hallways that make up the Corleone family's world.

It's a world of late-afternoon and evening light and tones. Consider how the lighting influences our first view of Don Vito Corleone. The leonine head, formal tuxedo, silhouetted air of leashed power. Now consider how it would be to first meet him sitting in the sun on a lawn chair. Not quite the same, is it? In so many ways, *The Godfather* is a master-class on dramatic and effective film-making.

Source: Lura Burnette, *The Godfather*, classic movie reviews, www.tampabaywired.com

Lighting: definitions and techniques

Film terminology refers to hard (bright) and soft (dim) light such as that in *The Godfather* example, as *high key* and *low key* lighting respectively.

The huge lights that were used on early film sets have a switch (or 'key') which when pushed up high, brightens the light, hence the term 'high key'. Similarly when pulled down low the light is dimmed, hence the term 'low key'.

These two definitions are obviously very basic and there is a wide spectrum between the two. Rarely is there just one light illuminating a shot, instead several lights are used to create different effects.

However, one thing is always the focus of the lighting department and that is the 'star'. The leading actors (male and female), who are often what the audience has paid to see, are always lit to attract attention. Some 'stars' even have special relationships with cinematographers and their lighting crews so that they are lit and shot just the way they like to be. This stems from the Golden Age of Hollywood (the studio era of the 1930s and 1940s) when lighting achieved amazing glamorous results on actors long before the invention of digital enhancement. (See Chapter 5 on the studio era.)

Classic Hollywood lighting

Sometimes known as the three point lighting system (see fig. 2.13), classic Hollywood lighting would light the subject from three different light sources:
- *key light*: the biggest and brightest light shining from the front, usually slightly above, bleaching any hollows or contours in the face but creating shadows behind.
- *back light*: would create a 'halo' effect and help 'wash' out any minor defects and bring back the balance disturbed by the key light.
- *fill light*: would literally 'fill' any shadows created by the first two. For example, shadows that were cast across the nose or under the eyes.

Along with specialised make-up, lighting could create a 'perfect' image (see fig. 2.14).

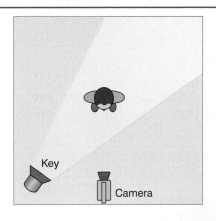 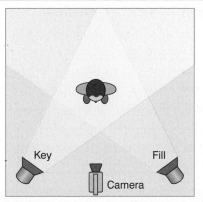 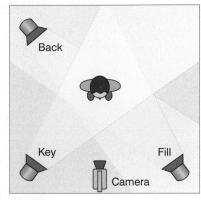

Figure 2.13 ▲

Figure 2.14 ▶

Quality, direction, source and colour

Lighting can be analysed by referring to four of its elements.

Quality

When referring to the quality of the light we are not referring to whether it is good or bad, but to its *intensity*. Lighting can be *hard* or *soft*. Hard lighting will be of strong intensity and will create strong shadows if it is the only light present. Soft lighting creates a more even tonality and is created with light that is less intense. Naturally each of these, hard and soft, is used appropriately to complement the scene. Bright, strong sunshine would provide intense light quality. A grey overcast day would mean the light quality was less intense but this may be the very effect that is required, suiting the nature of the character or the themes of the film.

Direction

From which direction is the light coming? This is possibly the most useful element in an analysis of a shot as it is this technique that enables a variety of moods to be created. Possible directions include:

- *Overhead lighting*: A single light from above will cast harsh shadows and create a sinister, unflattering look (see fig. 2.15). The effect will highlight contours of the face so if, for example, the film-maker was trying to make a male character look more masculine or hard this might be appropriate.

Figure 2.15 ▶

- *Under lighting*: The opposite to the above but having a similar, sinister effect. Under lighting will hollow out the eyes and emphasise every line and crease on the face (see fig. 2.16). Hence it is rarely used to light female stars unless they are playing an evil character. The horror film often makes much use of this technique, which people sometimes imitate by putting a torch under their chin. Try it!

Figure 2.16 ▶

● *Side lighting*: This will have the effect of casting a shadow across one side of the face, something that may be desirable in a thriller or mystery (see fig. 2.17). It is often used in conjunction with lights from other directions to soften the harshness of the light.

Figure 2.17 ▶

● *Back lighting*: As mentioned in classic Hollywood lighting, used alone it can create a 'halo' or silhouette effect depending on the context of the shot (see fig. 2.18). A silhouette will keep a character in shadow, building up expectation and suspense in the audience.

Figure 2.18 ▶

Source

What are the actual and perceived light sources in the shot? A scene may include table lamps or candles (known as practical lights) but the scene will rarely rely on these for all its lighting. You may have noticed in some films that a character will light a match, say in a cave, and the illumination is brighter than any match light you have ever witnessed! The match is the perceived source of the light although the actual light may be an off-screen side light. The effect of fire burning is another example of a perceived light source. The flickering of flames on characters' faces will often be an effect created through lighting.

Colour

The colour of the light is also important. In the example above a reddish glow would be necessary to convey the idea of fire but the colour of the light need not be realistic. Filters and gels can be used to add a certain 'wash' to the whole scene. A bluish or greenish look in science-fiction is typical (the coldness of colour often complementing the common themes of technology and lack of humanity) and a sepia look in period films may be used to convey a time long ago.

The colour may be used to distinguish between past and present; it may be warm or cold to complement the mood of the sequence. Whatever it is, it is always worth considering in your analysis of lighting as it communicates much to us in terms of film language.

Look at the examples of the use of colour in *Gladiator* (Scott, 2000). See how the lighting in this film serves to separate the past from the present, conveying the warmth of the character's family life (see fig. 2.19) and the coldness of the battle (see fig. 2.20). The character's dreams and memories are always bathed in a warm yellow glow and a similar effect is used in the scenes of combat to signify the heat and dust of ancient Rome.

Figure 2.19 ▶

Figure 2.20 ▶

analyse this

Look at the article on the website below for some fun tips on how to light low-budget films. The pages are informative and may help those undertaking practical video making as coursework. Note the use of some of the key phrases we have discussed in the section.

www.exposure.co.uk/eejit/light/

questions

▶ What is another name for classic Hollywood lighting?
▶ What are the lights used in this system?
▶ What effect would a single back light create?
▶ What effect does under lighting have? Give an example of where it might be used.
▶ Quality, colour, source and _____ have to be considered in an analysis of lighting.

key terms

Mise en scène (setting the scene). It refers to the four basic elements that make up the visual language of the scene: setting, costume (including hair and make-up), props and figure expression (or performance).

Mise en scène: setting the scene

The third of the cinematic codes that we shall look at is **mise en scène**. The term 'mise en scène' (pronounced 'meez on sen') literally translates as 'putting into the scene', but a less formal translation and one that is easier to understand is, 'setting the scene'. The mise en scène refers to *four* basic elements that make up the visual language of the scene aside from the other cinematic codes of cinematography, lighting, editing and sound. (Sometimes lighting is referred to as part of the mise en scène but, in cinema, lighting is so complex and such a large area, that in Film Studies we refer to it separately.) These four basic elements are setting, costume (including hair and make-up), props and figure expression (or performance).

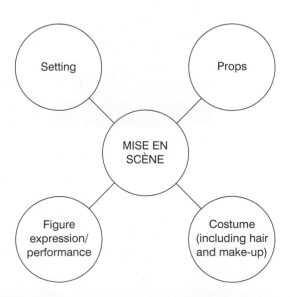

Mise en scène, like much film terminology which you will come across in Film Studies, is French, (*film noir*, genre, auteur, metteur en scène, etc.). This is because the academic study of film as we now know it, was initiated in France in the 1950s by a group of film-makers and intellectuals via a journal known as the *Cahiers du Cinéma* (Journal of the Cinema). Their aim was to raise the level of film study to that of the other arts like painting and literature. Up until this point film had been regarded 'merely' as popular entertainment and not worthy of academic debate, but the writers of the *Cahiers du Cinéma* brought a new approach to the subject – hence the reason we study it today. Their studies meant that the original French phrases that were used to describe film have remained.

Reading a scene

The mise en scène is vital in conveying information through 'visual signifiers' (things we see on screen). It is through the visual elements of the scene that we extract much meaning. Even when the film is mute (without sound), the setting, costume, props and figure expression (body movement or gestures of the actors) will tell us a lot. In silent cinema it was vital, with much emphasis on one particular aspect: figure expression. As a result, the performances in early cinema may seem over dramatic when compared to today's film-making.

Activity

Take a look at any sequence of silent cinema. How are you able to work out what is happening within the scene and who the characters are? If you are unable to access early cinema then choose a contemporary example and watch it mute (with the sound turned off).

What you have just done is a simple analysis of the mise en scène. It is likely that you do it every time you watch a film but it is probably subconscious. From the very opening of a film, you are assessing the information presented to you, filling out details of character and story (narrative) in your own mind, based on experience that you bring into the cinema with you.

Our cultural knowledge combines with our film knowledge when we 'read' the film stills, and we apply the same judgement to what we see on screen as we would in reality if faced with a similar situation or person. As well as this, because we are all experienced film viewers we can read typical 'iconography' (stereotypical imagery – see the next chapter on genre for further detail of iconography) that we have seen before. For example, the 'baddie' wears black or the 'goodie' wears 'white'. The 'baddie' is ugly and the 'goodie' is beautiful. The 'geek' will wear glasses and the 'jock' will be of a large physical stature.

Remember, these are *stereotypes* and, as with all the micro elements, the imaginative film-maker is free to play with them and your expectations of them. However, in mainstream cinema they are often a basic starting point for relaying information and therefore meaning.

Mise en scène: analysis

When we study film we are *consciously* analysing the art form. To do this with mise en scène it helps to break it down into its component parts and to consider not only the surface information but also the deeper 'symbolism' of the imagery in the film.

Setting and props

The setting of a scene is crucial to our understanding of time and place. We can locate ourselves in a certain place, town, country, planet or even galaxy! The setting will convey basic information like time and date (present day or historic) and perhaps whether the characters are urban or rural (city 'slickers' or country 'innocents'). It may convey isolation (horror) or claustrophobia (thriller) or it may indicate wealth, poverty or class as well as many other things. The information about the physical setting, which in a novel would be very detailed, with perhaps several pages being devoted to its description, has to, in film, be conveyed very quickly in visual language by skilled set designers and **prop** buyers who work alongside the director.

In a living room scene the props could be anything from pictures on walls to flowers or curtains. These things can be cleverly used to convey elements of story or character. For instance, subtle props like dying flowers or fading curtains may fit with the theme of change within a story or the state of mind of the character.

There also may be a *key prop*, which is something vital to the story. This is often given the privilege of a close-up because it is so significant and must not be missed by the viewer.

key terms

Props
is the abbreviated term for 'properties' and refers to all the items within a scene that are placed to 'dress' the set.

analyse this

Look at the opening sequences of several films and consider how the *setting* is established and how it conveys visual messages. These 'establishing' shots often set up the story that is about to begin.

Without a setting the audience would find it very hard to settle into the framework of the story.

Case Study

Consider the following scene from director David Fincher's hugely successful and critically acclaimed 1995 thriller *Se7en:* Note how the setting conveys 'surface' information but also thematic relevance.

Se7en: The City as Hell

It's night time and it's pouring rain. It is almost impenetrably dark. We see a seedy boulevard that looks vaguely as if it belongs on the Lower East Side of Manhattan. Detective William Somerset (played by Morgan Freeman) – a dour, weary-looking man in his 60s wearing a trench coat and hat – is shown dashing from the door of his apartment building, past a couple of grubby homeless men sharing a bottle, to hail a cab. He sighs upon entering the vehicle and gazes

Continued

out onto the street with a look of utter exhaustion on his face as the cab moves slowly into traffic. Through the backseat window we catch a passing glimpse – from Somerset's point of view – of some uniformed cops dressed in clear plastic rain gear bending over what appears to be a corpse sprawled out on a glistening, crowded sidewalk. We hear a siren. On the opposite side of the cab, a police cruiser pulls into view, its lights flashing. 'Where you going?' asks the driver glancing into the rear-view mirror. 'Far away from here,' responds Somerset still staring out the window. And the camera lingers for two or three seconds more on his furrowed, bone-tired face before cutting away.

As the sequence indicates, the makers of *Se7en* represent its unidentified, New York-style urban setting as a thoroughly noxious, menacing place, an allegorical Hell as full of suffering and anguish as the Inferno of Dante, on which it appears to have been modeled. This contributes to the film an oppressively despairing, apocalyptic mood. But the function of the urban environment in *Se7en* goes beyond providing a suitably expressive backdrop for the film's bleak story. In the course of the film, the city's nastiness and immorality – and the sense of defeated resignation it imposes on its residents – emerges as an explicit and recurring theme.

Meanwhile, the built environment projected by the film as the showcase for all this butchery radiates a definite aura of decay and despair. *Se7en*'s metropolis appears to be in an advanced state of decrepitude. Its buildings are filthy, weathered, crumbling, and mouldy, their walls full of cracks and holes, their paint peeling and stained, their floors creaking. The fat man's house, to cite a memorable example, has windows so heavily streaked with dirt that they barely admit light. The apartment building where the detectives find the man murdered for personifying 'sloth' has hallways and stairwells that are covered with litter and slick from rain that we are left to suppose has seeped in through fissures in the roof. Piles of overflowing black plastic garbage bags, disintegrating cardboard boxes, and abandoned pieces of furniture crowd the streets. There's trash strewn everywhere. Graffiti is present in nearly every outdoor shot; even the lampposts appear to have been 'tagged.' Those buildings that don't appear to be decomposing – like the police station or the lawyer's office or the library where Somerset hunts for clues – look old and exhausted.

Source: Steve Macek, 'Places of Horror: Fincher's *Seven* and Fear of the City in Recent Hollywood Film', *College Literature* (Winter 1999) 26 (1), p. 80.

It is important to understand that with mise en scène, nothing in the scene is accidental. Everything listed in the example above is deliberate and relevant. Therefore in an analysis of settings and props, careful attention to detail is necessary. Furthermore, always think how the details of the mise en scène add 'depth' to the film by symbolising that which is often not outwardly expressed; the themes.

Figure expression/performance

Figure expression refers to the body language, movement, posture and poise of the actors. We can read from this much about the character without any dialogue. The way the character walks, stands and performs facial expressions are all relevant. Even the physical stature of a character will be significant.

Case Study

The *Terminator* films, starring Arnold Schwarzenegger, rely heavily on both his physical stature and an exaggerated figure expression for which the actor himself has become famous. The robotic movements and emotionless gestures fit aptly with the characterisation of a Terminator.

Remember though, this is an extreme example of the use of figure expression and other performances in different films may be much more simple or subtle, indicating moods like happiness, worry or confusion.

Costume (including hair and make-up)

The way a character is dressed is one of the most important signifiers for the audience.

As in real life, there are associations made with different kinds of dress and these are utilised both stereotypically and atypically in film-making. Not only can costume indicate time period but certain 'uniforms' are also indicators of character. The geek, the office worker, the tramp, the gangster, the police officer, even the alien will all have an identifiable 'costume'. The level to which these costumes are customised to fit the individual role is varied and hence each film has to be considered on its own merit.

There may be a key element of the costume, which is synonymous with the character, such as a certain hat or a jacket, or there may be certain colours that are associated with that character or characters (in westerns it was typical for the good cowboy to wear white and the villain to wear black).

Hair and make-up are also significant in defining a character. Apart from taking a great deal of time casting a part, film-makers will often then ask that actor to change their hair according to the role. This can range from Demi Moore actually shaving her head in *GI Jane* (Scott, 1997) or dying hair a different colour, to wearing wigs to achieve the desired effect. Sometimes the hairstyle of a character will change throughout the course of a film to indicate the development of a character, and along with setting and costume, hair can indicate the era or the passing of time.

analyse this

Suits are used for both of these characters; what qualities do we attribute to each? How are they the same but also different?

Make-up is used in most film-making but is more significant in certain types of films than others. For example, horror films, fantasy and science fiction utilise it a lot to create imaginary characters. The use of prosthetics to utterly change the look of an actor into an alien, zombie or superhero is commonplace. *The Lord of the Rings* trilogy (Jackson, 2001), has many examples of this and along with a diverse range of costumes succeeds in creating a whole new world for us. The mise en scène in a film like this (fantasy), is therefore not only creative but also vital in the film's success, as we have no cultural references to relate to unless you have ever been to Middle Earth or met hobbits!

Comedy often also makes good use of make-up along with visual special effects (a subsidiary of cinematography and editing), and this can succeed in making characters likeable or funny. An example of creative make-up in comedy may be Eddie Murphy in *The Nutty Professor* (Shadyac, 1996), or Jim Carrey in *The Mask* (Russell, 1994), where much of the comedy is visual and relies on a skilled make-up department in conjunction with special visual effects.

FILM: MAKING MEANING (FS1)

Only when all the elements of mise en scène are considered and combined with the other cinematic codes can we gain a full and in-depth analysis of the meaning created by the film-maker.

analyse this

Now that you know the four components of mise en scène, look at the stills below and analyse them in detail for setting, props, figure expression and costume (including hair and make-up).

For example, what kind of character do you think they are? How can you tell? Can you tell what time period it is? How? Can you tell whether the characters are rich or poor? How?

Activity

Now create your own mise en scène

Using all the elements of mise en scène (setting, props, figure expression, costume) describe in detail how you would convey an urban street character arriving at the rural home of a friend he has not seen for a long time. Remember, visual signifiers only – no dialogue!

questions

▶ What does mise en scène mean?
▶ What are the four elements of mise en scène?
▶ What are 'props'?
▶ What is iconography?
▶ What is the term used to describe body language and movement?

key terms

Post-production
the phase in the process after production where the film is edited and music and effects are added.

Production
the phase in the process where the actual shooting of the film takes place.

Shot
is a 'set-up' within a scene. There may be many different set-ups (shots) to film a scene. For example, the same conversation may be shot from many different angles.

Scene
a succession of shots.

Sequence
a succession of scenes.

Editing: piecing it all together

Editing is the first of the cinematic codes which is part of post-production as opposed to production. This means it is a process which largely takes place after all the footage has been shot, and so in simple terms is about 'piecing it all together'. The editor's physical job is to join the end of one shot to the beginning of another in a way that will make sense (construct the story or narrative) and run smoothly. The editor is also responsible for putting together the initial 'rough' sound track. (On a large film the sound editor will eventually take over this role as the editor becomes mainly a picture editor.)

Director: Stephen Hail NSFTV			
A Red Cat – Shooting Schedule			
Date	**Scene**	**Actors**	**Extras**
5/3/99	5 Cliff Car Park	Mel & 4	poss.
	17a	4	poss.
	17b	All 8	
6/3/99	4 Benthams car	Mel & 4	No
	18	M, C, J	No
7/3/99	10 York Minster	E, T & L	Yes
	(int.)		
8/3/99	9 York Minster	E, T & L	Yes
	(ext.)		

Table 2.1 ▲ Shooting schedule

key terms

Take
a sample of one shot. A shot may need many 'takes' to get it right.

Cut
is the term used to mark the change of shot when editing. When editors worked on film they would literally 'cut and splice' the film with 'joining tape'. With digital editing, the same term is used as the shot 'cuts-out' or 'cuts-in' although the original footage is never actually cut at all, only a digital copy.

The process

Films are not shot chronologically (in story order). All the **scenes** from one location are shot together despite where they appear in the film. Take a look at the sample of a shooting schedule on the previous page.

Notice how the scene numbers for one location vary considerably. One scene may be from the opening of a film and the other from the end. There will have been much character development in the supposed intervening scenes. This could mean that actors begin shooting their final scenes *first*, having to imagine that other parts of the story have already taken place.

When the editor receives the material, he/she receives them in this shooting order and not story order, so must begin to piece them together. Placing whole scenes next to other whole scenes is only the beginning of the editor's job and constitutes a very 'rough assembly'. Rarely are whole scenes done in one shot (or set-up) and rarely are they simply placed next to each other, but instead have to be **cut** and interwoven to make an interesting way of telling the story. The story order will generally have been decided at the script stage but it can alter, sometimes radically, in post-production (editing).

In mainstream film 'classic continuity editing' devised in the early days of cinema is often used. This kind of editing is generally deemed well done if it is 'seamless' or 'invisible' and one shot leads smoothly into the next.

When we are watching a film we often do not notice the editing if it is done in this way as it is deliberately unobtrusive and allows the viewer to get engrossed in the story.

Activity

Try counting the cuts in a five-minute sequence of a mainstream film. It is very difficult to get the correct answer first time; you may need to replay it and to use the pause button to count exactly how many there are.

key terms

External cuts
are whole scenes joined to other whole scenes, e.g. a scene in a pub followed by a scene in a shop.

Internal cuts
are cuts within a scene, using the various different angles and set-ups within that one scene.

Continuity editing

Continuity editing offers us some basic rules about editing that have stood the test of time. The editor basically organises and has control over three important factors in the finished film:

- Space
- Time
- Rhythm.

The organisation of space on screen is vital if the audience are not to be confused. Much of what takes place in the world of the film happens off-screen and the off-screen space has to be constructed as well as that on-screen. When people on screen talk to one another it must appear as though they are doing exactly that even if they do not share the same shot. As film is not usually in a 3D format, making the flat screen work convincingly is important. The editor follows some basic rules to ensure that this happens.

Space

The establishing shot

As mentioned in the section on cinematography the establishing shot is the initial shot of a scene as well as the first shot of a film and the editor will employ it to help the audience locate the space they are being drawn into.

For example, if we begin a scene with a man standing at a washbasin we have no idea where he is supposed to be. His home? A public lavatory? Usually an establishing shot will preceed this shot to show the location of the washbasin and therefore tell us something about the character. A brief shot of the door to the gents' toilet in say, a department store, will immediately locate the audience in the space being created for them.

Match on action

Making sure that action matches across shots and scenes is vitally important if the film is to make sense and not jar. If a character lights a cigarette in one shot then they must be smoking it in the next shot. If a character's hair is parted on one side in one shot, then it must be parted on the same side in the next shot of them. It sounds simple but remember back to the shooting schedule; shots in different locations may be shot weeks apart, and if the character lights a cigarette and then in the film walks out into the street they are effectively entering a different location which may be filmed days later, by which time they have forgotten exactly when they lit the cigarette and in which hand they were holding it. This is called *continuity* and is the chief concern of the editor. We have all seen examples of bad continuity – in fact whole programmes are devoted to it – and to ensure it doesn't happen a 'continuity person' will often sit on set making 'continuity notes' which means writing down all the details of a shot so that if the shot is continued days later the scene can be recreated exactly as it was. However, if the lack of continuity is not spotted (only high-budget films can often afford the luxury of a continuity person), it may be too expensive to go back and reshoot, so it has to be left in if there is no way of cutting around it.

Matching the action to make the on-screen space work also means that when actors are not physically sharing the same shot it has to look as though they are sharing the same (off-screen) space. A character talking to another character off screen is only convincing if there is an *eyeline match* (remember, the other actor is often not there for those shots and a member of the crew will fill in the off-screen lines). Again the editor is responsible for matching this (although if it has not been shot correctly in the first place there is little he/she can do with it).

A common editing technique is the *shot-reverse-shot*, which may make use of the eyeline match. Again this organises off-screen space and makes the spatial relationships believable. An example of this could be a person looking at something off screen (shot). We are then shown what they are looking at (reverse), and then we cut back to the original person (shot). If we are not given the reverse or the reverse is delayed (as is common in horror or thriller) then it has a suspenseful or shocking effect.

Figure 2.21 ▶

Shot   Reverse   Shot

Matching the action to organise space can also involve a *cut-away*. A cut-away is a life saver for editors as it allows them to literally cut away while they remove the intervening footage of the original shot. For example, in a scene where a character (schoolboy) rises from his chair and leaves his desk, heading for the door, instead of watching the whole journey from desk to door we can 'cut away' to something (another schoolboy, the teacher, a clock etc. and then cut back to him as he opens the door and leaves. This is again a useful device in organising screen time and speeding up the action.

The action is also matched by direction. When characters or objects are all moving in one direction in one shot it makes spatial sense to have them moving in the same direction in the next shot. If the boy leaves to the right of the screen, he will emerge from the left of the screen in the next shot to create continuity.

One of the most important rules when it comes to the organisation of space on screen and continuity is the *180 degree rule*.

The 180 degree rule

The 180 degree rule dictates that the editor must not use, in a sequence, shots that cross an imaginary 180 degree line of action (sometimes known as 'crossing the line'). To understand why this is so, study the following illustration of four cameras shooting two actors. (Remember, in film-making only one camera is used for a scene like this so not all cameras would be there simultaneously; treat each camera as the same camera but moved into a different position).

Occasionally the line is crossed deliberately by film-makers to create confusion or disorientation. You may notice the line being crossed in fight sequences or chase scenes for example. When analysing how the editing creates meaning for the audience the spatial organisation is a major factor in any analysis.

analyse this

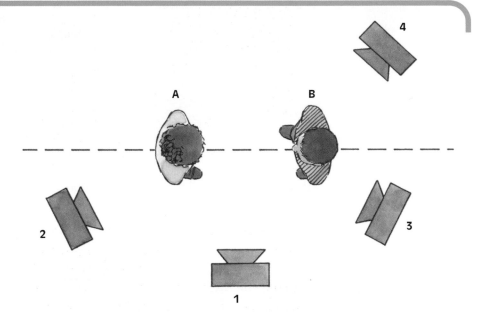

Look at the positioning of each camera separately and consider the viewpoint (what the audience will see on screen), from camera one, two and three.

It appears to be quite straightforward: over the shoulder shots as if the two characters are in conversation. But what would be the viewpoint from the fourth camera? When you have given it some consideration look over the page at the fourth camera which has 'crossed the line'.

B   A

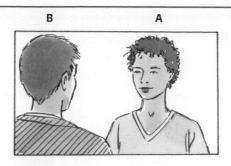

The actors have suddenly switched screen sides! This would be disorientating and jarring on the audience when the shot was cut in among other shots and the conversation would no longer be seamless.

Camera 1   Camera 2   Camera 4   Camera 2

Camera 4   Camera 3   Camera 2   Camera 3

The continuity is disrupted and the spatial relationship is disturbed.

To avoid this and to follow the action without this disturbance the camera must *move with* the action to always keep them on the 'correct' side of the line.

Time

As well as spatial relationships, the editor also has control over temporal relationships in the film. This simply refers to the organisation of time throughout the film.

By this we mean not only the physical running time of the movie (on average about two hours) but, more importantly, the timescale within the story of the film, which can be anything from an hour to eons!

Rarely is a film edited in real (actual) time where one minute on screen represents one minute in real life, although it is not unheard of. It often takes a lot longer in real life to do something than it does in the movies. Distances can be covered quickly and time can elapse at a fast pace in the film world.

This is called the *compression* of time.

As mentioned previously, match on action techniques can compress time by cutting out mundane and redundant footage.

Another technique which is often employed to compress time is the *montage* or *compilation* sequence.

This is where associated images are connected often by using a series of *dissolves*. One shot 'melts' into the other continually for several minutes. The meaning which we usually extract from this is that a considerable amount of time is passing. Over the top of the montage sequence there will probably be a soundtrack, usually significant music and when the track finishes so does the sequence.

Montages are stereotypically used in romantic sequences to indicate couples falling in love or in gangster films to indicate the maturing of the gangster or the serving of the prison sentence. (See *Angels with Dirty Faces*, Curtiz, 1938.) There are, however, many other examples of them. As well as compressing time the editor is also able to stretch time and make events take longer than they would in reality.

analyse this

Examples

a) The 'training' montage sequences in the *Rocky* films starring Sylvester Stallone compress time classically as they follow his training regime.

b) In *Notting Hill* Hugh Grant's character passes through the market place and as he does so the seasons change through a series of dissolves indicating that a year has passed in what in real time is approximately three minutes.

Now try and think of your own examples where this happens in films you have seen.

Case Study

A classic example of stretching time is the 'ticking time-bomb' sequence which often appears in Bond films where there will be a shot of the timer on the detonator indicating that there are only ten seconds left. Three minutes later, the scene is still playing and there is a second remaining on the clock as the hero diffuses the bomb!

In *Superman*, Lois Lane (the superhero's love interest), falls from a building and it takes almost a minute before she nears the ground. Superman manages to reach her just in time as we knew he would. In reality the fall would be over in seconds.

In both this instance and the ticking time-bomb example, the editor employs a technique called cross cutting. This involves cutting between the two characters, Lois Lane and Superman, or between the bomb and the hero, giving each just seconds of screen time before cutting back to the other. This has the effect of creating suspense for the audience, as the stretching of time delays the final rescue and adds to the audience's anticipation.

Parallel cutting is another way in which time is stretched. This is when two events are happening simultaneously in different locations. In effect the time frame is repeated each time. The editor will cut between one event and the other, which are usually connected, creating simultaneous action. This again creates a sense of build-up but also in some cases a sense of dramatic irony.

One of the most famous examples of parallel cutting is in the *The Godfather* (Coppola, 1972), where Michael Corleone is being made godfather at his nephew's christening. A brilliantly symbolic piece of imagery is dramatised further by the fact that the editor makes parallel cuts between the events of the christening and the massacre that Michael has ordered which is taking place at the same time; an example of the high impact that editing can have.

Rhythm

The rhythm of the editing, or the pace, is vital in creating different kinds of meaning and expectation for the audience.

Leaving a 'beat' at the end of a shot often adds a cinematic quality and a chance for the audience to breathe and sense the closure of the scene; for example, holding the shot of a door for a few extra seconds as it closes behind a character will often indicate reflection.

This is very unlike TV editing of say, soap operas, which, with their fast turnaround and strict time limit, cut very quickly from shot to shot.

To alter the rhythm of the scene the editor will use fast and slow cuts. This is determined by the length (the duration) of each shot.

A typical action sequence will 'build'. The editing immediately before the climactic car chase will have longer, slower shots which gradually get shorter in length and so quicker. At the height of the action the cutting will often be at a rapid pace with very short shots, although not too short. (Any shot which is less than 24 frames is less than a second long and although this may work on TV, on a cinema screen where the eye has to scan a greater area it is hard for the audience to determine the image. Of course, this 'rule' as with all the others may be broken deliberately to create a sense of chaos.)

Immediately after the climactic scene the shots begin to lengthen and slow, which indicates to the audience that they can now relax.

Graphic matching is also used to complement the rhythm of a scene. This is where shapes, colours and composition are matched to mirror or link one shot with another.

For example, the spinning of a ceiling fan may cut to the spinning of helicopter blades, creating a graphic connection between the two images; a series of different door slams in succession would constitute a graphic match. The connection is between the images rather than the action, and allows for a smoother or more visually stimulating transition.

Ultimately, if the rhythm of the overall film is not 'flowing' or does not feel comfortable, then the film will be uncomfortable to watch and the audience's suspension of disbelief will be interrupted and hence their viewing pleasure will be spoiled.

Transitions

In all of the editor's work with space, time and rhythm he/she uses a combination of transitions to get from one shot to another.

A straight *cut* is just one way to move from shot to shot. Here are the others:

- **Fade up** (or fade in): This is where the screen starts as one colour, usually black but it can also be white, and the image fades up through the black.
  Typical use: At the opening of a film or scene to indicate a new beginning.

- **Fade down** (or fade out): Exactly the same as above but in reverse. The image fades into black or white, hence the term 'fade to black' at the end of most shooting scripts.
  Typical use: At the closing of a film or scene to indicate the end.

- **Wipe**: Wipes can be vertical, horizontal or diagonal and the image on screen can be effectively 'wiped' either with black or with another image or with another character which is introduced over it.
  Typical use: Examples can be seen in *The Mummy* (Sommers, 1999), (diagonal wipe when the hero swings into the hidden cave) or classically, in *Star Wars* as a method of switching from one scene to the next, although this technique looks a little dated now. The wipe's use in contemporary cinema is often restricted to comedy rather than serious drama, perhaps because it is a visually obtrusive and a very obvious transition.

- **Dissolve**: This is where two shots overlap and create a double image with the second image gradually 'dissolving' through the first. This may involve only two shots or multiple shots which continue with each shot dissolving into the next (as in the montage sequence). Dissolves when done well can be very creative and well composed. A good example of this is the famous shower scene in Hitchcock's *Psycho*. When Marion lays dead at the end of the scene her staring eye dissolves beautifully into the rotating plug hole; the two circular shapes merging are also an example of graphic matching.
  Typical use: To indicate some sense of the passing of time. Where cover is thin and editing skill is poor there will be an over-reliance on the dissolve as a means of getting from one shot to the next. This method is very common in pop video production where there is no narrative.

key terms

Transition
a way of moving from one shot to another.

Cover
the amount of varied footage shot for one scene.

Narrative
a story or a description of a series of events. It is a word which is not specific to film but to other ways of storytelling also. (See chapter on narrative.)

Linear
in order or sequence.

Non-linear
not in order or sequence.

Parallel
simultaneous, at the same time.

questions

▶ What are the three basic factors that the editor considers when cutting?

▶ How does an eyeline match work?

▶ What is a cut-away and when might it be used?

▶ Give examples of how an editor might compress or stretch time.

▶ What is another term for the 180 degree rule?

Sound: the icing on the cake

Sound is one of the most important, yet one of the most neglected, of all the cinematic codes. A lot of people, in these days of domestic film-making, mistakenly believe that the sound will just 'happen' when you turn on the camera. With commercial film-making and film cameras the sound and the image are recorded, and subsequently treated, separately. Often, the original sound that is recorded at the time of shooting is later replaced with much 'cleaner' and often 'closer' sound which is recorded later under studio conditions. The process whereby the sound is edited, added to and mixed, is therefore the final part of film-making and it is not until this is done that the film really seems complete. In this sense the sound, as a cinematic code, is the icing on the cake.

The process

As the sound and image are recorded separately (but both at 24fps), they later have to be *synchronised*. To do this a clapperboard (see fig. 2.22) is used at the beginning of each shot (time code is also useful for this on other formats). The visual image of the closing clapperboard is matched exactly with the sound on the audio-track of the loud clap, and once matched, the two can now run, from that point on, in **synchronisation**.

Figure 2.22 ▶

There are three basic sound elements:
● Dialogue
● Music
● SFX (sound effects).
On the original **soundtrack** recorded at source there will be no music (unless it was playing on set) or sound effects as these are all added in post-production. As previously mentioned, the original sound will often act as a 'guidetrack' for the replacement of better quality sound. When

key terms

Soundtrack
refers to any sound which accompanies the picture. When we talk about 'music soundtrack' we mean music which is added to the film from various artists but not specially written for the film.

Score
the music specially written for the film.

dialogue is replaced this is known as *ADR* (Automated Dialogue Replacement); after shooting is over, actors will go into the studio and re-record some of their lines which are not clear on the original, or which have excessive background noise or to record extra lines which will be added off-screen. A *Dialogue Editor* will then cut these lines in over the original lines and the *Dubbing Mixer* will blend them into the finished soundtrack. A *Foley Editor* will do the same with footsteps and body movements and the *Sound Effects Editor* will do the same with sound effects, which may not always be aurally dramatic. (Like visual effects it can just mean heightening the reality of everyday things, e.g. the sound of a cup being placed on a table, or the flick of a light switch.) Music is the final thing which is added to the finished cut.

Film sound can be split into two categories:
● **Diegetic sound**
● **Non-diegetic sound**.

The 'diegesis' of a film is the entire fictional world that the film creates. This includes any events presumed to have occurred even if not actually seen. The diegesis would include any off-screen space that is created and anything that emanates from 'the world of the film'.

Case Study

Diegetic sound is any sound which believably arises from the created image.
   In a scene which takes place between two characters in the country-side, the diegetic sound may include:

● Characters' dialogue
● Bird tweet (atmosphere)
● Car wheels on gravel road
● Music playing on car radio
● Car doors opening and closing
● Tractor noise
● Faint aeroplane noise
● Animal noises.

Non-diegetic sound is any other sound that forms part of the overall product but is not emanating from the world created on screen.
   In the same scene the non-diegetic sound may include:
● Music soundtrack
● Voiceover.
Notice how the music playing on the car radio is diegetic but the music on the soundtrack is non-diegetic. Diegetic music must have a believable source and in this case the car radio provides that. The pitch and quality of the sound would also indicate the diegetic quality of the music whereas the soundtrack, even if it is the same song as the one on the radio, will have a different quality and level of production, and will hence form part of the non-diegetic sound. Other types of music, like orchestral score (music written specially to accompany scenes in a film), are almost always non-diegetic, unless there is an orchestra in the scene!

Notice also how there are creative sound effects added to the list to fill in the aural landscape even though those things may never actually appear on screen, like aeroplane noise or animal noise. This is because these sounds believably arise from this 'film world' and are not out of place in this scene.

Wild tracks are sounds recorded during production to provide 'clean' sound for the sound editor. Once a scene is complete the recordist will perhaps ask for quiet time to record certain sounds which he/she knows may be useful later in post-production. This could simply be a few minutes of the 'atmosphere' (the sound of the room or location), or it could be a particular car sound, door slam etc.

analyse this

Imagine a street scene in New York. It is the job of the sound editor to make the scene as aurally believable, but also creative, as he/she possibly can. List any sounds you would expect to hear in a scene like this (excluding dialogue).

Most of the sounds you list will be collected as 'sound FX' and mixed into the finished soundtrack. These sounds will be *diegetic* sounds.

Activity

Look at the introduction of any film and chart the different sounds. Which are diegetic? Which are non-diegetic?

key terms

Aural
relating to hearing/ears. Not to be confused with 'oral' which relates to speaking/mouth, as they are both have similar pronunciation.

Using sound creatively

As well as being able to deconstruct sound into its various descriptive categories it is important in an analysis of cinematic codes to assess *why* such sounds have been used at certain times in the film and what impact they have on audiences.

Again, as with the other technical codes, as experienced film watchers we are familiar with the way that sound is used in film and we have certain expectations of it. We know for instance that non-diegetic music which builds slowly usually means that something 'big' is about to happen and so makes us apprehensive. We know that sound effects will often accompany cuts in the image to give them more impact and we know that certain types of music indicate a certain mood; for example, 'romantic' music indicates falling in love.

Because of this knowledge we have expectation and because we have expectation we can be taken by surprise when those expectations are not fulfilled.

An *aural motif* is a phrase of music or a musical effect which keeps appearing in the film as a prelude to dramatic moments. Whenever the audience hears this they relate it to something in the story and read meaning into it. A very famous example of this is in *Jaws* (Spielberg, 1975). The famous bass notes of the approaching shark make one of the most well-known aural motifs in cinema history. Altogether now, 'Nnerr na, nerr na . . .'

The sound of silence

When analysing sound, do not forget that a lack of sound can have just as much impact as a complicated soundtrack. Silence in cinema is very disconcerting. This is for various reasons. The silence that pervades the cinema auditorium when the soundtrack is very quiet is itself very tense. This may not be the same experience with home viewing. Hundreds of strangers sat in quiet anticipation is an almost unique experience and has the effect of instantly quietening anybody who is talking.

In terms of cinematic codes the use of silence as opposed to the use of sound can work against expectation. If we are used to being 'warned' with non-diegetic music that a dramatic event is about to take place then we are shocked if the event takes place without such warning.

Case Study

In *Goodfellas* (Scorsese, 1990) there is a famous scene where Joe Pesci's character shoots dead a young boy who is there to serve drinks. Motivation for the killing of this minor character is minimal and there is very little build-up through character development except that Pesci's character is depicted as volatile (he previously shot the boy in the foot by accident). There is no non-diegetic music in the scene and therefore no indication that this shocking action is about to take place. In fact most of the diegetic sound is laughter. The unpredictability created for the audience by the lack of aural warning befits the uncertainty of the scene and the audience immediately feels the shock felt by the other characters as the boy is fatally shot. The loud gunshot effect which rings out, cuts through the relatively quiet soundtrack and creates dramatic impact, made all the more great because it is totally unexpected.

Pleonastic and contrapuntal sound

Another creative use of sound is by using it to create a pleonastic or contrapuntal effect.

Pleonastic sound is often non-diegetic sound which is added to give extra resonance to an action and which perhaps mimics the action itself.

One of the most famous examples of this is in the shower scene from *Psycho* (Hitchcock, 1960). The screeching violins that mimic the stabbing action of the sequence sum up perfectly the horror of what is taking place, and so famous is this use of pleonastic sound that the scene can be recognised from this alone.

A similar and more recent example of this type of sound can be seen in Tarantino's *Kill Bill* where the 'swooshing' of the sword fights is heightened by the creative use of pleonastic sound effects.

Contrapuntal sound is also often non-diegetic sound but instead of emphasising and complementing the image, this type of sound works in opposition to it. This creates disparity between what the audience can *see* and that which they can *hear*. This sound, when contrary to the picture, can have several effects. One is to allow the audience a true insight into the character's state of mind. For example, where a character's actions appear to indicate a certain way of life, the contrapuntal sound, in the form of a voiceover, may give us their true thoughts which are in contrast to the action the audience is seeing.

Music can also be used as contrapuntal sound. The music track may serve as a sharp contrast to the image, thus giving the effect of irony.

An example of this is in Terry Gilliam's science fiction film, *12 Monkeys* (1995). The tune *It's a Wonderful Life* is played over a dystopic view of the future, creating a poignant and ironic statement on the destruction of the planet.

analyse this

In the famous 'torture' scene in Tarantino's *Reservoir Dogs* where a policeman has his ear hacked off, the music track is a swinging and upbeat – *Stuck in the Middle with You* by Steelers Wheel – and hence contrapuntal. The effect of this is twofold. First, it serves to distance the viewer from the horrific violence that is taking place and give the scene a stylised, almost comic-book feel. Critics have even said that it makes the violence look 'cool' and is therefore unacceptable. Secondly, it acts as an added signifier of Mr Blonde's ruthless and psychotic character. The fact that the music is so upbeat and the crime so violent shows the audience how Mr Blonde relishes the deed.

Think now of films that you know which may use contrapuntal sound effectively. Try to explain the meaning that is created by the use of the contrasting sound.

Conclusion

As with all the cinematic codes, sound rarely works to create meaning in isolation.

Sound, whether in the form of dialogue, music or sound effects is often just one of the technical components that are shaping the overall meaning of the sequence.

Sound can indicate character, or time period, or mood and atmosphere, but it does this most effectively when combined with cinematography, lighting, editing and mise en scène. This is the same for all the cinematic codes, and any micro analysis should consider the interdependent relationship of all the film's elements.

▶ Explain the role of the clapperboard.
▶ What are the three basic elements that make up film sound?
▶ What is contrapuntal sound?
▶ Is the title music to a film diegetic or non-diegetic?
▶ What does synchronisation mean?

Cinematic codes: combining to create meaning in examples of micro study

Now that we have concluded our study of all the micro elements we have the tools and terminology with which we can approach any film sequence. Not only does a good analysis describe accurately what is happening on screen but it also draws its own conclusions about the meaning created and the response that follows. This section offers examples of analyses that explore the micro elements in a couple of fairly well-known films.

The micro analysis attempts to focus on a short sequence and analyse it in detail to establish the meaning behind the use of all the micro elements. A good approach is to remember that the way in which a film is shot, lit, cut, etc., is only *one* way of shooting, lighting and cutting it, so why did the director decide on *that particular way* of filming the sequence? How else could it have been done? If things like camera angles or editing were changed what difference would it make to the scene? How does the existing way of filming manipulate or 'direct' your reading of the sequence?

The micro analysis may begin with the identification of the meaning created, with the essay striving to demonstrate how this is done. For example:

● How does lighting and camerawork contribute to ET's sense of isolation in the opening sequences of the film?

The meaning has been established in the title and will now be illustrated.

An example which presents this approach of analysis follows:

Grade 'A' exemplar material

How do the micro elements mise en scène and cinematography establish characters and introduce the audience to the key themes of the film in the opening sequence of Richard Kelly's **Donnie Darko**?

The opening shot of the film is high up on a hillside in a canyon, in the early hours of the morning just as the sun is rising. It's a beautiful setting, the frame surrounded by trees and plants, with clear blue sky as far as the eye can see, tinted a shade of pink at the bottom of the horizon by the waking sun. The camera pans around this scene providing the audience with a perfect view of this utopian landscape.

The camera continues its pan around on to a twisting and turning road, where Donnie Darko lies, like a wounded animal in the middle of the road. This extreme long shot shows Donnie's isolation from the people and the world around him, and it is immediately clear that he is unusual and an outsider; after all, not many teenagers sleep in the middle of a road in the wilderness. The camera creeps slowly towards him in a tracking shot, swallowing up the road as he rises slowly looking over the edge of the hillside and down onto the world beneath. He stands there powerfully in a medium-close-up; with everything at Donnie's feet, this shot indicates his power even in isolation and shows the audience that he is a strong character.

In the next shot Donnie is on his bicycle (an old black racing bike with chrome spokes and brakes), soaring down the hillside elegantly and effortlessly, in a medium tracking shot. The sun now peers through the trees as it rises higher and higher as it awakes with Donnie, soaking the road in sunlight and decorating it in shadows. The camera is below Donnie looking up at him as he bears down upon it, emphasising his power. The time of day for this setting is important as it shows Donnie is at one with the world, rising with it, almost with it at his command. The tracking shot means that rather than merely observing Donnie, the audience is joining him on his journey and feels immediately attached to the main character; a static view of him from further away would make the audience feel unattached from the character.

The next shot is a point-of-view, as the audience takes Donnie's position on the bike and enjoys his view of the surroundings, another personal view from the audience allowing them to see the world through his eyes. This opening sequence shows the audience they will see the world of the film through Donnie's eyes and share his experiences.

In the next shot Donnie is nearer home and cycling through his neighbourhood, and we see a close-up of a sign reading 'Middlesex Halloween Carnival, Oct. 26th–30th' which provides the audience with a time of year and also, although they don't know it yet, a hint at the key point in the film. Halloween night is when everything changes and the film unfolds. This initially ambiguous sign provides some intrigue for the audience.

Donnie then cycles over a crossroad and into his own road; he passes morning walkers and observes but does not engage them with a friendly wave of 'hello', again hinting that he is isolated in his local community and somewhat the outsider. The audience will be curious as to why this is the case. He powers past and cycles past his house towards his back yard, the camera flowing away from him and across into the front garden, where Donnie's father is blowing leaves. The initial long-shot provides the audience with a view of the surroundings allowing them to acquaint themselves with the neighbourhood, before zooming in slowly and introducing them to his father. Donnie's eldest sister emerges from the house smiling, her father playfully blowing air in her face as she runs off, the pair laughing. The playful relationship between the two as opposed to Donnie who cycles straight past without acknowledgement yet again shows the audience that Donnie is an outsider, even in his own home. The audience will be intrigued to know why this relationship exists, having not yet been supplied with any evidence for it. Only three minutes into the film the relationship between Donnie and his family and community has been established without dialogue from the way the scene is set and filmed. The mise en scène and cinematography are extremely important here as with no dialogue this is the only introduction to the character profiles that the audience initially receives. The camera is always dead level with the other characters, providing an objective representation of them. The length of the flowing shots makes everything appear relaxed and natural. Along with the green scenery this hides the super-natural element to the film, as night and day seem to represent the natural versus the super-natural and the two sides to Donnie with all the sinister events in the film happening at night time, while all this is apparent now in the light of day is this utopian world.

Donnie heads in through the back garden, dumping his bike carelessly on the lawn as he wanders in. We see his sister bouncing up and down on the trampoline in a large garden surrounded by trees and bathed in sunshine, before the camera sweeps down in a crane-shot to focus on Donnie's mother reading a book while sitting in a garden chair. The camera cuts to a long-shot of his mother as Donnie walks across the scene and the camera pans round with him, following him into the house and towards the fridge where a sign reads 'where is Donnie?' In this sequence every shot flows into each other, and the depth of field becomes greater as additional characters walk into shot to reveal more and more of the same setting, first revealing the character to the audience and then establishing the setting. This provides the audience with a complete introduction to Donnie's family and where he lives and very quickly establishes his home environment.

The next scene is introduced with a long-shot of the family sitting around the dinner table in the evening; the room is softly lit by a chandelier and a table lamp, creating a relaxed and homely environment. Immediately Donnie appears out of the fold as he sits on his own around one side of the table, while the others sit closely together around the remaining three sides. The next shot is a medium-close-up of his sisters, the eldest speaks, and the camera then bounces around the table between these two and the mother and father, the medium-close-ups clearly depicting reactions and following the conversation, and Donnie remains anonymous for some time. The use of a medium-close-up shot allows the audience to get to know the characters more intimately from Donnie's point of view as we observe the conversation, as if we are too sitting around the table. The audience gains more insight into relationships and personalities, as reactions and figure expression are clear. When Donnie does enter the conversation with inappropriate comments, the rest of the family's reaction is telling, and the faster cuts between sister and mother make the audience feel small and intimidated from Donnie's position as an onslaught of criticism heads his way. As the argument gets heated and the insults fly, the cuts get quicker and quicker and as a spectator you're almost left feeling dizzy as the camera bounces around the table, the fast pace signifying the building tension. When everything dies down the shot length increases once again as an eerie silence falls over the table. Many of the shots in this sequence contain little or no speech and focus solely on figure expression.

The next scene has a more observational tone as we watch from above as Donnie's mother and sister quarrel about him in a dull hallway with white doors and woodwork and nothing but a table and lamp in view. We gain a little insight into their relationship from this scene, the camera acting as an eerie presence, watching unnoticed, again hinting to the audience's subconscious about the super-natural elements in the film.

We are then taken inside Donnie's bedroom, where unlike in many other shots we see a long-shot of Donnie on his bed, allowing the audience to also take in the mise en scène. This is done to further give us an insight into the main character's life and personality. A hand-drawn eye and various other pieces of artwork can be seen on the wall. The eye provides a symbolic link with the eerie presence in the previous scene, and provides a link to later in the film, where Donnie's visions enable him to save mankind. There are also shelves full of books and he is reading, and this shows that Donnie enjoys literature and art, and in fact later in the film he mentions that he would like to be an author or illustrator, showing intellect and creativity. While this may not be significant to the plot of the story it is there to make the audience feel closer to the main character and feel empathy for him, so that we are on his side throughout the film.

We then get a brief observational high-angled shot from inside the parent's bedroom, before cutting away to Donnie in the bathroom, this again providing an eerie presence in the room, watching. There is a close-up as he looks at himself in the mirror-cabinet, this symbolises the duality of Donnie's character which becomes ever-present as the film progresses. He then opens up the cabinet and removes a bottle of medication, also in close-up; he takes some pills, shaking his head, almost in disgust. The entire opening sequence is riddled with clues as to what will come later in the film, and there are many enigmas to be solved leaving the audience gripped and anxious. This last sequence reveals the questioning of Donnie's sanity, even by himself, and this is an important theme throughout the film. He must trust himself to make some brave decisions, as it is he who must save the world as an unlikely hero.

Another way to approach the essay is to work through the cinematic codes and explain how meaning is created by their use throughout the scene. See the following.

How do cinematic codes combine to create meaning within a sequence, from the film **The Italian Job** (F. Gary Gray, 2003)

I am going to discuss how cinematic codes are used in different ways to create meaning. I have chosen to look at the 2003 remake of the classic 60s film *The Italian Job*. The scene I am going to discuss takes place 25 minutes into the film, after the opening heist in which the team of smart crooks is double-crossed. The team is meeting to plan their revenge and they are introduced to Stella, the new member of the team.

The first shot of the scene is an establishing shot showing Stella driving to the meeting point. The scene's opening shots establish a clear setting in an isolated area completely separated from all other people. There is building work and signs of development but absolutely no cars on the roads showing that the area is secluded and not visited. This suggests that what the team is doing is suspicious and likely to be illegal, because in an isolated area no one can see what they are doing and the fact they are going there intentionally implies waywardness. However the scene has high key lighting because it takes place in daytime. Usually low key lighting is used when something illegal is being plotted but the high key lighting suggests that the characters are not dark and evil. Subtle things, like the lighting used in this scene, lighten up the mood and create a positive feeling towards the characters, making the audience side with them and instead of wanting them to fail the audience wants them to succeed.

We then cut to Charlie explaining to Stella who each member of the group is and providing a story about a part of their lives. This dialogue helps the audience get a closer insight into the characters, helping them to identify and empathise with them and creating depth and meaning to their characters. The stories are shown with external jump cuts to flashbacks. By using flashbacks we get a deeper, more detailed and more realistic insight into each character as the stories can be visualised; this also makes the scene more interesting. The flashbacks add comic effect and add a unique quality. They also help to create a better structure and pace to the scene. The transition between cuts into and out of the flashbacks are done using blinds rather than straight cuts as this show more clearly that the flashbacks are happening at a different time and place. This causes less disorientation to the audience.

The other elements used in the flashbacks show the period and setting. Non-diegetic music is used to good effect to help the audience understand the characters or period through the music. Charlie's flashback takes him to his early childhood and this is conveyed in the non-diegetic music. The Jackson Five song *ABC* is used. This upbeat pop song reflects the cheekiness of his character and how young he was when he was first stealing. Through Charlie's flashback we see that he is not an unscrupulous thief because he steals money from the school bully who stole the money from the other pupils in the first place, making him almost a Robin Hood figure. This conveys to the audience, just as the lighting did, that Charlie's team is who the audience should be supporting. Left-Ear's flashback uses 70s disco music, reflecting the period and also his smooth cool cat character. The diegetic sound dips and becomes distorted in Left-Ear's flashback at the point where he is losing his hearing so the audience hear what he would have heard at the time and can empathise with the character. Handsome Rob's flashback uses the song *Heartbreaker*, portraying him as exactly that. The flashback for Lyle (AKA Napster) uses heavy metal music showing the period in which it was set, the youth of his character and his slightly erratic yet complex personality. The use of diegetic sound and sound effects in the scene, such as the screech of Handsome Rob's car, adds realism to the scene.

Charlie knows his team members so well that it makes a nervous Stella feel intimidated. Because the group is so close she feels like an outsider. We see this by the group's figure expression and interaction with Stella when they are introduced. The boys greet each other with warm friendly gestures showing their bond as a tight group. Charlie introduces Stella and the other boys greet her with a civilised hello, but the lack of acknowledgement and interaction shows that the boys don't trust her yet. Also, they are anxious not only about having a woman on the team but also her lack of experience. Their anxieties are shown in their figure expression towards her; they are polite but suspicious. We see Stella feels like an outsider because throughout the conversation she is positioned outside the circle standing away from the others. Her posture is stiff and she looks anxious and intimidated by the fact that the group is so close and she isn't a part of that. An arc shot is used to show this isolation of Stella. The camera arcs round each of the boys and then cuts to Stella outside of the circle. This helps the audience empathise with the character, and this makes the audience more involved in the film.

The audience realises from this scene that Stella only feels comfortable with Charlie because she talks to him comfortably asking him questions, showing us that there is a good relationship between them. This is mirrored by way they are positioned in the frame in a medium close. They are positioned at eye line to show not only that they are equal but also to make the audience feel more involved because it's at eye level.

From this scene we see that Charlie is the leader of the group because the group all focus and gather round him. He also initiates all the conversation. Through the dialogue and figure expression we can see that Lyle is the youngest and most immature of the group because he's moaning constantly and when he falls off his motor bike Charlie asks him if he is all right. From this we can see that Charlie is also perceived as the father of the group taking care of the others. This is further reinforced through the dialogue 'That's Lyle, my computer genius'. Charlie also says it in an almost proud tone of voice showing he feels Lyle is the one he has to look after and almost father. He never refers to the others as 'my' because he knows they can take care of themselves.

This scene is also significant in creating meaning later on in the film, because the group's first reactions and behaviours is a complete contrast to later on in the film when Stella is simply seen as one on the boys. Stella is accepted and is just as close to the group as anyone, but because she is a woman all the boys actually become highly protective of her and she is cared for and appreciated. Stella becomes confident and happy, in contrast to in this scene in which she is nervous and uncomfortable.

The costumes in this scene reflect the characters' personalities. For example, Charlie's costume is smart and stylish which is reflected in his character. The props used by the characters also reflect and add meaning to their personalities. Lyle uses a motorbike (not very successfully). The bike represents his youth, speed of thought and slight immaturity. Left-Ear's classic car represents his smooth and individual personality and Handsome Rob's fast sports car reflects his personality as fast-paced and smooth.

The final part of my sequence follows directly from the last scene. The scene cuts externally to California with an establishing shot of Los Angeles, followed by cuts to the events that would have occurred between scenes like the change in time and location, the plane journey and travelling to their hotel. These are played in fast motion using only one shot for each event. This condenses time by removing unnecessary scenes in a way that is not disorientating. The audience still knows what has happened and to where the characters have moved. The non-digetic music played over the scene sets the scene for a relaxed Californian evening, reflecting the relaxed mood of the characters.

The team, equipped with new member Stella, gathers on the roof of their hotel to discuss plans. Stella is still trying to gain their trust and earn their respect. She is now acknowledged and included in the conversation but still the boys are wary of her intentions. This is shown through the dialogue and figure expression. Stella is more talkative and independent and has a more confident posture showing the audience that although the boys are suspicious, Stella is proving she can do everything the boys can thus gaining the audience's respect and adding more depth to her character. We are constantly seeing new developments in character creating meaning to the plot and characters.

Again the costume and props used help to reflect the individuality of the characters, providing meaning to the costumes because we understand their character and why they would be dressed like that. The costume, props and figure expression used in films helps us understand and predict character behaviour and in this sequence we can clearly understand and predict the characters' personality and behaviour based on the elements contained in the mise en scène.

The editing throughout the sequence is seamless continuity editing. The editing is not noticeable except when the flashbacks occur and even then the scenes are linked in a way that makes sense. Cuts are used between shots and remain seamless because they do not break the 180 degree rule, and no internal jump cuts are used that could disorientate viewers.

The sequence I have studied is effective in its combined use of cinematic codes to create meaning within the sequence for the audience.

Activity

Choose a short sequence from any film and analyse it for its cinematic codes. It may help initially to look at each code in the scene separately. Once you have done this in note form try to write up the notes in essay form as practice for your micro coursework.

● Remember to always give a brief description of the scene and where it appears in the film.

● Remember to think how the codes combine in an inter-dependent relationship instead of working in isolation.

● Remember to use the correct technical film terminology when describing shots.

● Remember to explain how these codes create *meaning and response* in the spectator, giving your personal impressions.

Summary

By using the information in this chapter on cinematic codes you should gain a complete understanding of the micro elements of film form. Refer back to the sections when writing up an analysis to remind yourself of the various terms and descriptions, but do not forget to apply meaning to the shots you describe. As stated at the outset, you are already an expert at extracting meaning from cinema but reading this will enable you to articulate and explain that meaning in accurate detail and with full understanding of how it is created.

Micro elements are only 50 per cent of film form (look back to the table on page 5). Apart from these *physical* elements of film-making, there is also the *content* of what we watch to consider. Together they provide a full understanding of cinema as an art form and as entertainment. The other 50 per cent, therefore, is made up of the macro elements, which we will focus on in the next chapter.

Macro elements: narrative and genre

T he macro elements of film form are distinguishable by the fact that, unlike the micro elements, they are not physical, tangible things (like cinematography or lighting), but concentrate on the content of the film. Macro elements are the ideas, concepts, messages and values within the film, and most of these are embodied in the *genre* and *narrative* of the work. These two macro elements give the film its 'form' or shape. The structure of the story and our expectations of that framework are manipulated by the creative use of these two things. Like all the elements of film so far discussed, they do not operate in isolation but combine to create meaning in the overall, finished product.

Genre

Film Studies theory is dominated at A/AS level of study by two major approaches. These are the genre approach and the auteur approach. Auteurism is something you will study in detail in your second year and focuses on the individual film-maker, their vision and personal creation. The study of **genre**, however, focuses on convention and collective meaning. The opposite of the individual approach, it relies on a film's conformity to a set of pre-existing conventions. Genre study groups together a large body of films according to the common attributes that make the film a typical example of its type.

A typical conversation about cinema between friends may go like this:

Francis: I went to the pictures last night.
Martin: Oh yeah, what did you see?
Francis: *I Robot*, a science fiction film.
Martin: Oh really. I don't like that kind of film . . .

The dialogue above may be one you recognise, in which case you may unknowingly already have some knowledge of the concept of genre and how it functions for a film audience. The conversation will usually continue to cover some other key areas of film study as Martin goes on to ask, 'What was it about?' (narrative), and 'Who was in it?' (stars).

Francis's reference to 'science fiction' as a type of film identifies its genre but this can be substituted for any other type of film and Martin, in response, will always use the information in the same way. He takes the genre (in this case science fiction), and assesses its attributes, then applies his personal taste and judgement. To do this Martin must have

key terms

Genre
French term meaning 'type' or 'kind'.

FILM: MAKING MEANING (FS1)

certain *expectations* of that genre and therefore that genre must have a certain 'formula' that Martin has come across before.

When Martin thinks of science fiction what does he associate with it?

> **Science fiction = Outer space as a setting. Futuristic technology. Robots or aliens. A battle of good versus evil. Themes of dystopia.**

Film genre, in this way, acts as shorthand for the 'formula' of this particular type of film.

analyse this

Look at the list of the following genres:
- Comedy
- Gangster
- Thriller
- Horror
- Romance
- Action adventure.

Without reference to specific films, what are the common attributes of each type? In other words, what would you expect to see in each of these kinds of films? List your answers and only then apply specific films to those attributes. Do they fit?

talking point

What is your favourite genre? Why?
What is your least favourite genre? Why?

When you find it difficult to slot a film into a specific category it may be because it is a *hybrid genre*. This means it is a mixture of more than one genre and therefore contains elements from each. For example, a romantic-comedy contains both funny and romantic elements (*Love Actually*, Curtis, 2003). The romantic-comedy has become a mainstream genre in its own right but other combinations of genre are not so easily accepted.

Case Study

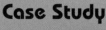

From Dusk Till Dawn (Rodriguez, 1996) received very different responses when it was released.

Look at the two reviews below:

From the sublime to the ridiculous

So here I am, happily ensconced in what I believed to be a crime thriller cum road movie, when suddenly the story descends into chaos: the inhabitants of the Titty Twister are not at all what they seem, and from this point onwards the movie turns into a vampire/zombie/horror gore-fest, with the kidnappers and their hostages having to unite to fight against the evil forces they have encountered in the bar.

Continued

If I had known what I was in for, I probably would have enjoyed the film a lot more. Despite the sudden change of mood, the gory section of the film is well done, with quite a few comic moments and some excellent special effects. However, I felt that far too long had been spent actually setting the scene and developing the characters, and I was thoroughly disappointed to discover that I would never really learn the outcome of the kidnapping and the Geckos' crime spree, as the ending of the film was clearly going to be somewhat absurd. Once again, if I had known more about the film, I would have taken the 'serious' opening section with more of a pinch of salt and not become too absorbed in the story (one occasion where a spoiler is actually a good thing!), but if there's one thing I hate it's a film with an unsatisfactory ending, and – for me, taken at face value – this was one. I do think that even if I had known, I would have struggled not to become too involved, as at least half of the film is taken up with a fairly serious and believable storyline.

Source: Edited from a review by Pumpkin on *From Dusk Till Dawn*, www.ciao.co.uk/From_Dusk_Till_Dawn__Review_5423316

From Dusk Till Dawn

Written by Quentin Tarantino, and directed by Robert Rodriguez, *From Dusk Till Dawn* changes mid film from a violent crime flick to a gory vampire pic. After a kinetic, pre-credits shoot-out in a convenience store, and a flashy title sequence, the film at first settles for being yet another Tarantino twist on the overworked theme of two outlaws on the run, driving across the wide, open, American spaces. This time, the criminals are the Gecko brothers (Clooney and Tarantino) who dress in black, *Reservoir Dogs* style.

In search of a way across the Mexican border, the brothers kidnap a faithless preacher named Jacob (Keitel), who is on a motoring holiday with his daughter (Lewis) and adopted son. After Keitel successfully smuggles the criminals into Mexico, there seems nowhere left for the plot to go, other than into a leering retread of *Straw Dogs*. Mercifully, the sudden switch to supernatural horror spares us this, but is itself little improvement.

The remaining screen time is spent in an endlessly drawn out battle. For its horrific half, the look of the film changes dramatically, eschewing the dusty road and dilapidated motels of the first part, in favour of a brightly coloured look that seeks to make a virtue of its unrelenting cheesiness. The Titty Twister itself, with its glowing neon sign, and gangs of bikers roaring around outside, seems to have come fully formed from the airbrushed cover of some arcane heavy metal album. The film does possess lots of dumb appeal, with its mixture of gangsters, vampires, excruciating dialogue, graphic

Continued

violence, and the shocking shift from one genre to another. But to preserve his cult cache, Tarantino will have to do better.

Source: Edited from Adrian Horrocks, *From Dusk Till Dawn*, www.dso.co.uk/fr.htm Reproduced with kind permission from DSO.

The reviewers above both cite their disappointment with the film. Key phrases like, 'If I had known what I was in for . . .' and 'Tarantino will have to do better' indicate this, their disappointment coming from the expectation that they had. The film obviously did not deliver what they expected. The first reviewer actually feels cheated that he was allowed to think that the film was something that it ultimately was not. He became engrossed by the developing characters and the setting of the scene only for those things to utterly change and become meaningless in the finished, overall product. He therefore states that the ending was 'unsatisfactory' and as a viewer feels frustrated.

The second reviewer, contradictorily, expresses tedium with the tried-and-tested formula of the first half but, at the same time, does not like the 'shocking shift of genre' in the second. Both reviewers are left with disappointment, which largely stems from the generic mismatch.

Genre, therefore, is a delicately balanced concept between the expected and the different. Too much of one or the other and it runs the risk of rejection. Genre dictates audience expectation, and once used to the idea of what a film of a certain genre 'should be' we are often not prepared to tolerate anything less.

From Dusk Till Dawn went on to achieve cult status (although still one of Tarantino's lesser known projects) as some people loved the very fact that it was so odd in its use of genre. Others hated it, but no matter what, the film makes an impression.

Expectation

Much of what we look at in AS Film Studies has to do with expectation. Having seen so many films in our lifetimes we are used to the way that film-makers use film language and we often enjoy the familiarity of the well-trodden path. At the same time, however, we are constantly looking to be surprised with *new* ways that film-makers use the language. This applies both to micro and macro elements. Just as a film-maker may find a new way to use the camera or to overlay sound, they may also find new ways to use genre (and narrative, which we will discuss later).

How many film conversations take place where we say, 'I didn't like that. I thought it was going to be (funny, sad, scary, etc) and in fact it was (funny, sad, scary etc.)', therefore unsettling us and spoiling our enjoyment of the film. Despite individual taste, we expect a comedy to be funny and a horror film to be scary and if this does not happen the film will probably fail at the box office (though critically this may not necessarily be the case).

On the other hand if you enjoy a film it may be the very fact that it is unlike anything else you have seen before and so far removed from what you expect that this in itself creates enjoyment. Many films work on this basis: adapting and mixing old genres in a new way.

This demonstrates that there is a market for new ways of adapting genre and this is how genre *evolves*, shifting and changing over time as film-makers experiment with new ideas while remaining within the same basic generic framework. Certain genres come in and out of fashion over time, having a resurgence when they are given a modern twist. One only has to look at the western or the musical to see this.

The generic study of film presents 'pure' genre as the 'standard' and other films in the same category are variations on this model. This is necessary for our viewing variety and pleasure when watching mainstream movies; after all, how would we recognise the *unusual* if we didn't have *the usual* to compare it to?

The paradox therefore, regarding the genre approach to film study, is that the films are *the same but different* each time.

Repetition and difference

The idea that films can be grouped together and are 'the same but different' relies on the concept of 'repetition and difference'. If we revert back to established genre (as opposed to hybrid), as the basis for our understanding, it helps us to analyse this concept.

Although we can define various types of films in a general way by referring to common attributes, if all films in one category were *exactly* the same then there would only be one film in each genre. This obviously is not the case and we can enjoy many films of the same genre because although their basic framework is similar, when it comes down to *detail* the films are different.

Repetition within a genre can relate to plot, characters, narrative structure and certain cinematic codes, but equally the *difference* between films of the same genre can also be created through the unusual use of these things. Imagine a science fiction film where the hero is sent to kill the alien (repetition; we have seen this before) but the hero is female (difference) The film *Alien* (Scott, 1979) was successful in 'reworking' the genre in this way.

Generic structures can therefore be seen in paradigmatic form, with each element interchangeable. A basic, common framework exists but components within that framework alter from film to film. Let us now work through the elements within genres that typify the balance between repetition and difference.

Repetition through iconography

It is often through the mise en scène that we really begin to recognise a film's type. Aspects of mise en scène may typify a genre so acutely that they take on iconic status.

AS FILM STUDIES

key terms

Iconography iconic signs (especially of mise en scène when applied to genre) which typify a particular place or thing visually.

Iconography refers to the elements within the frame that are synonymous with the genre.

Think of a film's setting for instance. It is often the first iconic detail of mise en scène that helps us identify the genre. If the setting is a 'flying saucer' or outer space we can hazard a guess that the film is science fiction. If the setting is a lonely, isolated house the chances are it is a horror film or thriller of some kind. And maybe not so much now, but some years ago, if the setting was the desert you could be sure you were in for a western.

Once again, like most things to do with the generic approach, it relies on formula, expectation and stereotype. Setting is just one example of iconography that is open to new uses for those film-makers who wish to play with their audience's expectations.

In the past, science fiction has made new use of the desert setting, for instance in *Star Wars* and the *Mad Max* films (some theorists say the science fiction film is the new western only with a different setting). Horror in the forest (*The Evil Dead*, *The Blair Witch Project*) is another example of a new setting for an established genre (although note that isolation is still the key) and the subversion of this iconography goes on as genres evolve.

However, the differences in one area will be balanced with familiarity in another, so that audiences do not lose their connection with the genre. Hence, in mainstream Hollywood cinema although the setting (or some other aspect of mise en scène) may be the unusual factor, the figure expression or props (for example) will remain familiar and will fit with our expectation of that specific genre.

In this way iconography extends beyond setting to other aspects of mise en scène that are regularly associated with a certain genre. Jill Nelmes's *Introduction to Film Studies* (3rd edition, Routledge, 2003) makes this point through the use of a 'typical iconography' chart (see analyse this).

The formulaic film

The audience cannot always rely on iconography alone to indicate a film's genre, especially (as mentioned before) as more and more film-makers are using iconography in different ways and with different meaning; science fiction could be set under water (*Waterworld*, Reynolds, 1995), or a Shakespearean adaptation could be set in the 1940s (*Richard III*, Locraine, 1995).

Other familiar elements also fuel our expectations and indicate the generic formula. These include:

- Title styles
- Musical signifiers
- Audio/verbal signifiers.

analyse this

Look at the chart below and see how elements of the mise en scène are iconic of that genre.

Genre	Costume	Weaponry	Transport	Character type
Western	Cowboy hats Chaps Holster Spurs Cowboy boots	Guns Bow and arrows Lassoo	Stagecoach Railroad Horses	'Hero' cowboy Outlaws Sheriff Saloon girls
Traditional gangster	Trilby hats Shiny shoes Trenchcoats Smart suits	Machine/tommy guns Revolvers	Expensive cars with blacked-out windows	Mafia don Trusted confidante Rival gang member Wife/moll Traitor
Sci-fi	Space suits/metallic costumes Strange facial features (pointy ears/green face, etc.)	Laser guns Light sabres	Teleporter Hi-tech modes of transport (hover-car) Spaceship	Mission leader (hero) Aliens Girl (love interest)
World War Two				
'Gangsta'				

What would be the typical iconography for the remaining genres?
Notice how each genre contains *different* detail of the *same* overall elements.

Title styles

As the first thing we see (often on posters that publicise the film, let alone in the first minutes of the film's opening), the title styles can again crystallise our expectation.

Titles are important, especially to producers, as the title sequence can attract or repel an audience in the first few minutes. How often, when a film comes on television, have you allowed yourself to see only the opening titles before deciding that it is not the film for you? The colour and shape of the letters themselves signify so much to us.

Some films have very elaborate title sequences imposed over the establishing shots of the film. In this case the average viewer may not even notice the credits, paying more attention to the clues in the narrative. But in other films the narrative clues are deliberately withheld and the title sequence itself takes on mysterious qualities. The audiences therefore have only this to work on in judging the film's content and genre.

Activity Look at the titles below. Which genre of film do you think they belong to and how have you come to your conclusion? Now work with a small group. Each of you should design a title for a film called *The Haunting*. Compare your designs. How similar are they?

analyse this The opening sequence of David Fincher's *Se7en* is particularly interesting and conveys the mood of the film accurately with its scratching, flickering titles. We know already by the end of this short sequence that this film will be disturbing.

Sometimes the opening sequences are just white lettering on a black background giving nothing away, in which case the audience will seek out other elements to identify genre.

Musical signifiers

When the titles offer us little in terms of confirmation of our expectation we turn to the music that usually accompanies the opening of the film (that is, assuming there is some). Directors who like to subvert expectation may leave the opening silent or may replace the music with some other sound.

analyse this Both Tarantino's films *Reservoir Dogs* and *Pulp Fiction* start with dialogue not music. This device is known as the 'pre-title' sequence, whereby a scene will be played before the titles appear giving the audience a 'taster' of what is to come. The James Bond films are famous for employing this technique.

Different types of music act as aural signifiers and often, just by listening to the soundtrack alone, we can identify the genre of the film. However, it is important to think back to the section on cinematic codes and sound; film-makers can use contrapuntal sound to unsettle us and create an ironic effect. Therefore the audio signifiers may be misleading.

---

analyse this

Stanley Kubrick was famous for the use of classical music in his films. *2001: A Space Odyssey* (1969) and *A Clockwork Orange* (1971) are good examples of how music which you do not usually associate with a certain genre (in both of these cases, a kind of science fiction), can have an unusual effect.

Verbal signifiers

Certain genres have their own verbal speech patterns. In other words we expect the characters to speak in a certain way depending upon the type of film.

The actual words (dialogue) and the tone in which they are expressed are again indicators of genre. By looking at excerpts from scripts without knowledge of the film you may well be able to assess the genre.

For example, a period costume drama will often have dialogue that has a literary quality, which is expressive or even poetic. You will rarely hear expletives or slang which would be common in a gangster or hip-hop film. Action-adventure films are famously sparse on dialogue using lines that often state the obvious (e.g. 'Quick, get out of the way, he's going to attack!' as the monster looms). The dialogue in this genre is often dramatic or functional (say, when the hero needs to explain his actions and speaks to himself out loud) which is in stark contrast to realist films, which attempt to make language as conversational as possible. Slapstick comedies on the other hand (as well as gangster films) have a tradition of fast-paced witty dialogue with characters' lines often overlapping.

Once again these are stereotypical examples and film-makers can opt to play with these expectations to create impact or dramatic effect.

Iconography, titles, music, and audio signifiers all help us to identify the genre and to sum up our expectations of it. This is why these key elements are used to great effect in film trailers, as it is often the identification of the genre that will tempt us into the cinema. An unusual use of these elements can have a similar effect.

---

key terms

Narrative
a story or a description of a series of events. It is a word which is not specific to film but to other ways of storytelling also.

Narrative and genre

As well as iconography being a familiar feature in generic film-making, patterns and formula are also evident in the **narrative** of these films.

What is narrative?

One of the most common questions in conversation about a film is, 'What is it about?'

AS FILM STUDIES

key terms

Plot

refers only to the actual events on screen including any non-diegetic material like titles or credits.

Story

refers to the actual events portrayed on screen *plus* those events which are not but which form part of the story. Events which do not appear on screen can be events which are implied or referred to and which we the audience need to know about to make the film make sense.

The film's content (or macro elements), is often the primary focus and we tend to view the stylistic or micro qualities as secondary to this.

Thus the sequence of events, which is the narrative, keeps us engaged with the film, and this forms a large area of our study.

So does narrative mean story?

For our purposes, not quite. In Film Studies we make a distinction between **story** and **plot** (see key terms).

Here are some examples where story is distinct from plot:

- In Scorsese's *Goodfellas*, Henry Hill is a young boy involved in petty crime for the Mafia. The film shows him going to juvenile court and getting his first 'pinch'. Subsequently we see the fully grown Henry Hill and through use of voiceover we know that he has progressed through the ranks of the Mafia to be one of their main players. We never actually *see* this take place but it is inferred that this is what has happened. Hence it is part of the story.

- In Cameron's *Titanic,* Rose survives the sinking and goes on to be an adventurous, independent young woman. We know this from a brief montage of shots of photographs of her throughout time, riding horses and flying aeroplanes. She also makes reference to her husband who was a good man but who died. Again this is implied and not seen and forms part of the story.

- The *Star Wars* films often open with captions detailing the action so far. These actions are not seen but also form part of the story and how it makes sense to us.

Cause and effect

Narrative therefore can be a combination of both story and plot and is the term used to refer to the *sequence of events*.

The sequence of events in narrative cinema revolves around the concept of 'cause and effect'.

As Bordwell and Thompson point out,

> 'A narrative is a sequence of events taking place in time and space, in a causal relationship. A sequence of random events does not make a narrative.'

Source: David Bordwell and Kristin Thompson, *Film Art: An Introduction* (3rd ed. McGraw-Hill, 1990).

This means that the viewer is able to make meaning from the associated images and sounds that are placed next to one another in a film. One event causes another to happen and so on and so forth as the narrative progresses.

analyse this

Look at the sequence below.

Although this is a very basic narrative we are able to make meaning from it as it tells its own little 'story'. Each image leads directly on to the next image and this is what we mean by 'causal relationship'.

However, if the images were abstract and unrelated we would have great difficulty in establishing cause and effect and therefore meaning.

This doesn't make sense to us as we are unable to see the connection. There is no narrative.

Narrative patterns

Just as we have patterns or formulae of iconography in generic films so we have patterns of narrative.

Each single genre tends to have a distinctive narrative 'shape' or form and just like with iconography, details within the narrative change but the overall framework often stays the same. If we study the formula of narrative in each genre a pattern emerges.

For instance, how many times have you been able to predict the ending of a film you have watched? How were you able to predict it? Because you had seen a similar pattern of events before.

Narrative patterns have been the subject of debate and analysis for a very long time and form part of the theories of **structuralists** like Vladimir Propp and Tsetvan Todorov.

In 1928, Propp (*The Morphology of the Folk Tale*) analysed the basic structure of folk tales and found a limited number of stories which were repeated over and over with simple variations. You may well have heard a similar theory applied to music: the limited number of chords means ultimately that there must be a finite number of tunes, however, with all the different variations in style, variety is maintained.

Propp declared that stories (and films, after all, are stories) all contained a combination of eight typical character roles and limited 'spheres of action' (certain situations would arise over and over again).

Propp's character types

- The *hero*, or character that seeks something. ('Hero' is an active way of carrying the events of the story and need not necessarily refer to gender.)
- The *villain*
- The *donor* who provides an object with some magic property
- The *helper* who aids the hero
- The *princess*, reward for the hero and object of the villain's schemes
- Her *father*, who rewards the hero
- The *dispatcher*, who sends the hero on his way
- The *false hero*.

Propp's functions/'spheres of action'

Preparation

- A member of the family/community leaves home.
- A warning is given to the community or its leaders/a rule is imposed on the hero.
- The warning is discounted/the rule broken.
- The villain attempts to discover something about the victim.
- The villain discovers the required information.
- The villain tries to deceive the victim to gain an advantage.
- The victim is deceived by the villain and unwittingly helps him or her.

Complication

- The villain harms a member of the family/community.
- One of the family/community desires something.
- The hero is sent out to find what is desired.
- The hero plans action against the villain.

Transference

- The hero leaves home.
- The hero is either tested or attacked; he meets the challenge and receives a magical agent or helper.

- The hero reacts to the donor.
- The hero arrives at or is transferred to the place where he will fulfil his request.

Struggle

- There is a struggle in a specific setting between hero and villain.
- The hero is branded.
- The villain is overcome.
- The state of disorder is settled.

Return

- The hero returns.
- The hero is pursued.
- The hero escapes or is rescued from the pursuit.
- The hero arrives at home or at some other place and is not recognised.
- A false hero presses a claim.
- A task is set for the hero.
- The task is accomplished.

Recognition

- The hero is recognised.
- The false hero or villain is unmasked.
- The false hero or villain is punished.
- The hero attains the princess and the wealth and power of the state.

The 'ingredients' for all stories, Propp argued, could be found in these lists.

Activity

To test how accurate Propp's findings were, pick a mainstream generic film and try to apply the above characters and situations.

Todorov

Tsetzvan Todorov similarly found that stories had a common structure. Basically, a story, he says, will often have a beginning, a middle and an end. In fact, his full theory describes five transformations of the story:
- State of equilibrium
- A disruption of the ordered state by an event
- A recognition that disruption has taken place
- An attempt to repair the damage of the disruption
- A return to some kind of equilibrium

These theories help us in understanding the formulaic nature of *mainstream* film-making but this is also where they have their limitations. As with all the other aspects of film-making the conventional rules of film language are there to be twisted and sometimes broken and you will come across many films where these theories do not apply. If music were the art form to which we were applying structure then a genre like 'jazz' might provide the exception as jazz attempts to subvert pattern to be 'freestyle', organic and unpredictable in shape. Films do this too, and there are many examples of exceptions to the 'normal' narrative pattern. Again, where convention exists rules will always be broken by innovators.

However, in our study of genre and collective meaning the structuralist theories of Propp and Todorov become very interesting.

They allow us to apply collective narrative structure to certain genres. That is, we can see similar stories being told over and over again with, of course, the necessary degree of variation to make them interesting. Consequently, if we can do this, we can identify not only the repetition but the difference in narrative.

How are generic stories the same but different?

This is best explained through a **paradigmatic** model similar to the one we looked at for iconography on pp. 59–60.

Most genres have a basic narrative pattern which remains the same but with the detail varying in each.

key terms

Paradigm
an example/ pattern/model with a *vertical* set of associations (from Saussure's theory of communication).

analyse this Look at the following chart that attempts to illustrate how stories in generic films operate within a formulaic structure.

Romantic Comedy			
A couple meet	dislike each other/ can't be together	overcome obstacles	and eventually end up together.
Young single parents at children's daycare	so used to being single	their children become friends	they get married.
Ordinary man and famous actress in his bookshop	worlds apart	he hides her from the press	then chases to catch her before she leaves for LA.
Wedding planner and groom at preparation for his wedding	he is to be married	his fiancée declares love for another	declaration of love for each other.

The initial description of the generic formula is the sentence across the top of the chart but see how each part can be substituted to achieve variety across a range of films. Using this recipe, you can make up your own romantic comedy.

The paradigmatic charts show the nature of repetition and difference of films within the same genre: romantic comedy – *One Fine Day* (Hoffmann, 1996), *Notting Hill* (Michell, 1999) and *The Wedding Planner* (Shankman, 2001).

Activity

Practise your own paradigmatic exercises using films you know from the following genres:
- Horror
- Action adventure

Other familiar narrative devices

The examples given show that genre relies to a certain extent on familiar story patterns many of which contain the basic beginning–middle–end structure.

However, other narrative devices exist and recur in other stories.

The way in which the narrative is told is an interesting variation from story to story. Many films have a *narrative agent*, which is a person or thing that 'carries' the story and leads the viewer through it. As an audience we align ourselves with the narrative agent who sometimes takes the form of *narrator*.

The narrator is the person telling the story and they can do this either by *being* a (main) character in the film and being the subject of it, or by telling the story of a character in the film, in which case their storytelling may employ the use of voiceover. When we have non-diegetic voiceover we tend to trust the voice as it speaks directly to us, the audience. This technique usually means that the narrative will be subjective – a highly personal account.

analyse this

In the opening sequences of *Goodfellas*, Henry Hill, the main character, is established as the narrator by a freeze frame and his non-diegetic voiceover saying, 'I always wanted to be a gangster'. From this moment on we know that he will lead us through this story. (As it turns out, his voiceover is testament from the witness box.)

When we are told a story from one character's perspective we embark upon a *restricted narrative*. The audience are only allowed to know what that character knows and will only be present in scenes where they are present. This has the effect of the audience 'discovering' the plot as it unfolds and perhaps having to work out and guess what will happen. This is where the viewing pleasure comes from. This narrative device suits certain genres in particular, for example, thrillers, or murder mysteries.

When a story is told from the point of view of many different characters (objective narration), we embark on an *unrestricted narrative*. The audience has access to information that perhaps the characters are unaware of. They see and hear the story from all sides. This has the effect of filling the audience with anticipation and making them wonder when the other characters are going to find out, and how. Genres which often employ this technique include romantic comedies where the audience can see the separate lives of the two main characters and wonder when they are going to collide.

Other stereotypical traits of storytelling in film include **action** and **enigma codes**. These form part of universal film language and are familiar signals to the audience.

Action codes are based on a combination of figure expression and editing and are when characters make significant moves or gestures to indicate that a certain action will take place. For example, in a scene where two characters are in battle and the weapon is across the room it is not unusual for there to be some significant eye movement, coupled with edited shots of the weapon, to indicate to the audience that they are about to make an attempt to retrieve it.

Enigma codes are narrative devices which set up little puzzles or mysteries for the audience to solve. For example, when James Bond is captured by his enemies how will he escape? (With Bond it is never a question of *will* he escape? More *how*?)

key terms

Action codes significant moves or gestures to indicate that a certain action will take place.

Enigma codes narrative devices which set up little puzzles or mysteries for the audience to solve.

Activity

Watch a sequence of more than five minutes from any generic film and attempt to establish if there are any action or enigma codes.

So far, then, we have established that single genres often have a formula or pattern within their visual style (iconography) and their narrative and that through analysis of genre we can determine the similarities and differences in any particular category. This is to assume a straightforward and classical approach to film-making but, as we know, not all film-makers follow this style.

We have already at the start of this section looked at the nature of hybrid genres and how the formula can be disrupted. The formula can also be disturbed through unusual use of narrative. In fact, increasingly sophisticated audiences are requiring increasingly sophisticated narratives to maintain their interest.

When the theories of Propp and Todorov cannot be applied

Many films do not fall into the neat categories of Propp and Todorov and so do not 'fit' the theory of equilibrium–disruption–restored equilibrium. For a long time, these kinds of films existed mainly outside of studio film-making, finding oxygen in the independent and experimental sectors, but increasingly Hollywood is catching on to the fact that some audiences like their stories to be complex and unresolved.

More and more films are being made that mix genre, fracture narrative and do not deliver the expected, and these films are equally, if not more, successful at the box office.

The lack of expected resolution

Case Study

David Fincher's *Se7en*

David Fincher's *Se7en*, which we have already discussed in terms of mise en scène (Chapter 2), is an unusual use of the familiar and the unfamiliar in terms of genre and narrative.

The film is a relatively classic crime thriller. A serial killer is on the loose and appears to pick his victims according to the seven deadly sins. The iconography of the film is very typical with its urban setting, use of conventional weaponry and costumes reflecting the old style detective (Morgan Freeman in suit, trilby hat and trench-coat) and the new rookie cop (Brad Pitt in leather jacket and slim black tie). This coupling of contrasting detectives as 'partners' is a classic narrative device in films of the crime genre and initially the film looks set to follow a traditional generic pattern.

Narratively, the film is restricted as the audience attempt to work out who the killer is alongside the two detectives and there is a certain expectation that the killer will be found in the end, providing us with our satisfactory 'resolution' to the story.

However, as Nick Lacey (*Narrative and Genre*, Macmillan Press, 2001) points out, the formula starts to unravel approximately two-thirds through the film as the narrative takes an unexpected turn.

Seven Copyright MCMXCV. New Line Productions, Inc. All rights reserved.

It is the point at which the killer hands himself in to the police that the audience become confused. Why is he doing this?

With this kind of genre and this kind of narrative we do not expect the killer to hand themselves in to the police because finding the killer

Continued

is the motivation behind both the narrative and the audience's interest. If the killer comes forward surely the story is over, concluded?

Lacey explains that the unpredictable nature of the film is indeed due in part to the fact that 'resolution' to the original problem (of finding the killer) comes too soon in the narrative – when the murderer hands himself in. The 'villain' (Kevin Spacey's character, 'John Doe') takes control of the narrative from this point, reflected in the fact that at one stage Morgan Freeman's character shouts, 'John Doe has the upper hand now'. The villain, although dead at the end, goes on to be successful in his mission to punish the seven deadly sins and our 'hero' (both as protagonist and as Brad Pitt) does not achieve success or reward and is, in Lacey's words, 'damned'. This narrative therefore goes against some of the last parts of Propp's theory where the hero returns and is rewarded with the 'princess'; in fact the 'princess' (Gwyneth Paltrow) is decapitated. This disturbance of narrative formula creates shock and excitement in the audience as it is a conclusion which we could never have predicted.

The director (David Fincher) therefore uses genre and narrative in familiar *and* unexpected ways (repetition and difference) to create something interesting and shocking.

Source: Nick Lacey, *Narrative and Genre* (Macmillan Press, 2001).

Non-linear and fractured narratives

Another way in which established genres and narratives break away from the formulaic is in the way in which the story is told.

The use of *non-linear narrative* is another way in which the expected narrative pattern can be disrupted and can create the 'difference' within a genre.

A non-linear narrative is a narrative which is not told **chronologically**. Non-linear narratives have always existed within Hollywood with the use of the 'flashback' to tell a story, but in more recent (postmodern) times the non-linear narrative has gained favour and fashionable kudos through the work of filmmakers like Quentin Tarantino.

key terms

Chronological arrangement of events in order of occurence.

Pulp Fiction **(Tarantino, 1994)**

Pulp Fiction is famous for its cyclical narrative. The narrative is fractured and episodic and makes the audience think very carefully about the time frame of the action. The beginning of the film is actually the middle and the end is not the end! However, despite its apparent innovation in temporal relationships on screen, is the actual narrative (the story) any different to conventional tales of this type?

In terms of genre it can be said that it contains some very familiar ideas as pointed out by critics:

'This idea is supported by those critics who find Pulp Fiction a rather conservative film, despite its multiple storylines and eccentric characters'.

Source: Kevin Howley, *Breaking, Making, and Killing Time in Pulp Fiction*
(DePauw University, USA, 2004).

'For all its interrupted storylines and surprises, *Pulp Fiction* is self-consciously conventional in content, just as Tarantino is a proud partaker of the mass-media fiction world of the pulp magazines, a genre of strict narrative conventions. The boxer whose honor won't permit him to throw the fight, the gangster's moll with a wandering eye, the camaraderie of professional killers – these are all subjects so hoary as to be clichés'.

Source: Pat Dowell, 'Two shots at Quentin Tarantino's *Pulp Fiction*',
Cineaste (1995) 21 (3), pp. 4–7.

Dowell suggests that elements of the film are very familiar to us but it is the presentation of the chronology (time) that is unusual.

To read more about the narrative structure of *Pulp Fiction* go to: **www.nottingham.ac.uk/film/journal/articles/making-breaking-and-killing.htm**

Activity

Other films which make an interesting study of narrative pattern within familiar genre are *The Usual Suspects* (Synger, 1995) and *Memento* (Nolan, 2002).

analyse this

Take a look at the chronological arrangement of *Pulp Fiction*. Kevin Howley (*Breaking, Making, and Killing Time in Pulp Fiction*, DePauw University, USA, 2004), argues that when the film's story order is rearranged we actually have a classic piece of Hollywood narrative, complete with happy ending!

He argues that although Vincent (John Travolta) is killed in a previous scene, the fact that we see him and Jules (Samuel L. Jackson) complete their mission provides the resolution for *that particular* story, and the escape of Butch and Fabienne in the 'final scene' provides the conclusion and 'feel good factor' that the audience require and that classic narrative structure dictates.

Monday
Vincent and Jules drive to Brett's apartment
They enter Brett's at about 07:22
Roger and Brett are murdered
Marvin is accidentally shot dead in the car
Vincent and Jules go to Jimmie's
At 08:40 Winston Would is contracted
At 08:49 Winston Would arrives at Jimmie's
After the clean-up Vincent and Jules go to the Hawthorne Grill to eat
At about 09:20 Pumpkin and Honey Bunny pull the hold-up
Vincent and Jules leave the diner
At about 10:00 Butch is being brided by Marsellus at Sally LeRoy's
Vincent and Jules arrive at Sally LeRoy's
Vincent confronts Butch at the bar

Tuesday
Evening. Vincent goes to Lance's house to buy heroin
Vincent picks up Mia for the date
The dance contest at Jack Rabbit Slim's
Vincent and Mia go home. Mia overdoses on heroin
Mia is revived at Lance's

Wednesday
Evening. Butch has a dream of Captain Koons before the fight
Butch wins the fight and escapes in Esmarelda's cab
Butch has rendezvous with Fabienne at River Glen Hotel

Thursday
Butch and Fabienne wake up and realise that Butch's watch has been left at his apartment
Butch goes back to his apartment to collect his watch
Butch murders Vincent
Butch heads back to the motel and meets Marsellus on the way. They fight
Butch and Marsellus are captured by Maynard in the Mason-Dixon pawn shop
Marsellus is raped by Maynard's friend Zed
Butch kills Maynard and rescues Marcellus
Butch returns to Fabienne and they escape

Themes and ideology (messages and values)

Particular genres, through their narrative, often deal with particular themes and ideology. Themes and ideology are messages and values that emerge through the characters, the storyline and the mise en scène of the film. These messages are subtle and underpin the wider context of the film.

For example, the science fiction genre often conveys messages about the dangers of technology that is out of control and the bleak vision of a future controlled by robots (variations on the Frankenstein model). Humanity's insistence on 'playing with nature' (usually in the name of greed) and its consequences form another of the recurrent themes along with alienation and how to deal with the 'other': a thing or person which is unlike ourselves. (See films like *Bladerunner, Jurassic Park, I Robot, 28 Days Later, ET,* etc.)

Other genres carry other messages and values.

analyse this

Look at individual films, identify their genre and try to establish what the wider themes and messages of the films are. For instance, what comment does the romantic comedy make on love and heterosexual relationships?

Once you have identified these wider 'messages' of the film, explore how common the same theme is in other films from the same genre.

The recurrent themes and ideology within particular genres often form the basis of the viewing pleasure that we get from them. They can act as 'comfort' to the spectator, by offering 'imaginary solutions to real problems' and creating 'myths'. This is the basis of the theories of Lévi Strauss and Barthes, who conclude that we derive pleasure from generic/narrative forms because they offer a solution to real social problems and we can 'control' the outcome, unlike in our real lives. For instance, if we are lonely we may get enjoyment from the romance film knowing that the outcome of the story will be love! If we are without money it may be nice to watch films that enable us to partake in an extravagant lifestyle.

Put simply, 'myths' which are created in film include:
● Sports movie – the underdog always wins.
● Romance – the boy always gets the girl or vice versa.
● War film – the hero always defeats the enemy.
Hence it is often extremely satisfying to watch genre films and imagine that life could be like it is in the movies!

Stars

Certain film stars also carry certain generic connotations as part of their image.

FILM: MAKING MEANING (FS1)

75

We associate individual stars or actors with a particular genre. This means that when we see that a film is to feature a certain star we expect certain things of that film and of that actor. For instance, Jim Carey is known for his comic acting, (especially visual comedy) and we expect any film of his to carry a certain comic element. He rarely plays 'straight' parts but has found a winning formula for his 'type'. Many stars have early careers where they find, or are assigned, niche roles only to find as their career progresses that breaking out of that niche may be difficult. Once an audience likes you in a certain role they, or the studio, are reluctant to let you change.

- *James Cagney* became famous for his gangster roles under contract to Warner Brothers and a long time after his death that is still how he is remembered. However, Cagney tired of these roles and longed to star in musicals (he was a trained dancer). He occasionally got his wish, despite much wrangling with his studio over his restrictive contract, but audiences years later rarely think of his musical numbers (*Yankee Doodle Dandy*, Curtiz, 1942 etc.) preferring to keep him as their favourite gangster.

- *Robert De Niro* who became famous playing gangsters and hard men has in later years turned his hand to comedy but again his fan base is resistant to the change. His success in comedies like *Analyse This* and *Meet the Parents* has only come about because he is able to make intertextual references to his other roles in his more successful films. In both of these comedies he still plays either a gangster or a hard man.

- *Sylvester Stallone* and *Arnold Schwarzenegger* both had successful star images as action heroes. This is still the expectation of these two stars. When they both tried to switch genre (Stallone, *Throw Momma from the Train*, 1987; and Schwarzenegger, *Junior*, 1994) they suffered some of the biggest box office flops of their careers and Schwarzenegger subsequently returned to action form in *Terminator 3*.

However, the shifting of genre and type for an actor can sometimes work well. When stars or actors are cast *against* type the audience's expectations of them is challenged. In the examples above this switch has not been particularly successful but in some cases it has relaunched careers.

- *John Travolta* was cast in *Pulp Fiction* as a slightly overweight, drug- using gangster. His most famous role before this was in musical-orientated films, *Grease* and *Saturday Night Fever*. His transformation to 'serious' actor was welcomed by audiences especially as Tarantino had the foresight to play on the intertextual reference to *Saturday Night Fever* in the scene where he dances with Uma Thurman in Jack Rabbit Slims diner.

- *Robin Williams* who started his career as a stand-up comic became known at first for comedy and then in the 1980s for his sentimental portrayals in dramatic roles. He was always the 'emotional' good-guy character. However, in recent times he has been cast against this expectation to appear as a murderer in Christopher Nolan's *Insomnia* and another dark role in *24 Hour Photo Shop*. Some of the pleasure of watching these films is that you really do not expect him to play the bad guy and the contravention of formula is enjoyable.

analyse this

Look at the list of film stars from past and present. What types of films and what kind of 'image' do you associate them with?

Reese Witherspoon
Gwyneth Paltrow
Goldie Hawn
Vincent Price
Will Smith
Al Pacino
Marlon Brando
Meg Ryan
Ray Winstone

analyse this

When doing an analysis of genre and narrative in a particular film try to consider the expectation you have of the stars playing the parts within it. Do they fulfil their image or do they go against it? Do you expect them to be in it until the end? What happens if they leave the narrative or are killed early on?

Genre and narrative: gangster films

Let us take a look at gangster films in an attempt to develop a macro study of this particular genre. By applying what we know already we can perhaps work out how films within this particular category are the same but different and where the pleasure lies in watching this kind of film. In any study of genre there must be a *collective* approach (looking across the spectrum of films within that category) which is illustrated by reference to the *specific* (an individual example). In this way broad statements can be made about the expectation of the range of films which make up the genre, in this case gangster films, and by reference to individual scenes we can perhaps identify either:

- a pattern or formula
- a disturbance in the pattern or formula
- both of the above.

It may help to initially identify typical iconography, typical characters and typical narrative patterns of your chosen genre.

Activity

Choose a genre and make a list of all elements of the mise en scène that is familiar to that genre. Look at the iconography chart in Chapter 2 to help you.

Then make a list of all the typical character types that you would expect to find in your chosen genre.

What kind of themes or messages do you expect the film to deal with?

Now think about the conventional narrative formula of your chosen genre. Does it always have a happy ending? Is there always resolution? What is the typical disruption? How is it normally solved?

Gangster genre

Our expectations of the gangster film include:

Gangster iconography

- Smart suits
- Shiny shoes
- Expensive cars
- Urban setting
- Guns/other weapons
- Nightclubs/controlled venues

Gangster characters

- The hero (sometimes of immigrant descent)
- The boss or 'Don'
- The right-hand man
- The double-crosser
- The moll (love interest)
- The rival

Gangster narrative

- The rise of the gangster
- The high life of the gangster
- The fall of the gangster
- The gangster's death or capture

Gangster themes

- Loyalty
- Community (family or group)
- Religion
- Ultimately crime never pays.

If we take three gangster films from different periods in history we may be able to see where the formula above exists across all three but also where it differs.

The films chosen to study are *Angels with Dirty Faces* (Curtiz, 1938), *The Godfather* (Coppola, 1972), and *The Road to Perdition* (Mendes, 2002).

From looking at specific films within the same genre it becomes clear how genre and narrative are formulaic and how disturbances to that formula can have great impact and provide viewing pleasure.

Activity

Watch the film *Angels with Dirty Faces* and attempt to apply the above attributes. Apart from being a classic of its type what elements make it unique or unusual?

Case Study

Angels with Dirty Faces

Angels with Dirty Faces was made by Warner Brothers at the height of the studio era in Hollywood in the 1930s and is the archetypal (or model) gangster film starring one of the famous gangster-associated stars, James Cagney. It appears to conform to all the points listed above including the narrative structure. At the beginning of the film we see our gangster hero Rocky Sullivan as a boy and it is explained to us how he got into crime. At the end he is executed by electric chair (which could be said to be one of the 'surprise' elements of the narrative), and hence the theme of 'crime never paying' is fulfilled.

Activity

Watch the film *The Godfather* and attempt to apply the attributes of the generic formula. At the same time record the differences and the instances where you were surprised.

Case Study

The Godfather

The second film, *The Godfather* shot in 1972 'made' a gangster of Al Pacino and appears to contain most of the common attributes above with some exceptions and some additions; these additions are what marks it out as different from other gangster films.

- The iconography is typical, although unlike *Angels with Dirty Faces* the weaponry used to kill becomes more creative, with a cheese wire being employed at one point and a horse's head being left as a warning.
- Expensive cars and clothes are evident and the idea of community is conveyed through the multi-purpose phrase 'the family'.
- The urban setting is familiar although the scenes set in Sicily make up an unusual aspect of the mise en scène.
- Themes of loyalty and double crossing abound.
- Explanation of the rise of the gangster exists. (Understanding *how* gangsters came to be so helps audience identification.)
- However, unlike *Angels with Dirty Faces* the narrative pattern is not neatly tied up. By the end of the first film, when the Mafia members come to kiss Michael's hand, we have only really reached the 'rise' of the gangster which is usually only half of the story! It leaves the audience without the 'fulfilment' or expected moral message that 'crime never pays' and taken out of context it appears to glorify the gangster. This may be one of the reasons why it is such a memorable gangster film. The 'incomplete' story leaves the film with a powerful ending and with audiences wanting more which the sequels will provide.
- For a gangster to not get his come-uppance is rare.

FILM: MAKING MEANING (FS1)

Activity

Watch the film *The Road to Perdition* and apply the attributes on p. 78 but also pick out the surprises in the film.

Case Study

The Road to Perdition

The third film, *The Road to Perdition* made in 2002, again contains many of the attributes from the list on p. 78 but with even more differences.

- The cars and suits are evident and because of the time period in which it was set it even has similar iconography to *Angels with Dirty Faces* and *The Godfather*, complete with trilby hats and traditional weaponry.

- Sullivan is doubled-crossed by associates (a theme in all three examples) and steps *outside* of the community to leave the gangster life behind. Usually characters who step *outside* of the gangster community are either captured or die and indeed this is his fate.

- One thing which offers a difference is that a large part of the beginning of the story is set in a small town (the mob's 'base') as opposed to an urban city. We see lots of rural areas, and a beachside setting opens and closes the story. This is very different from the traditional urban setting. The city comes into effect as a place of anonymity and escape from the gang.

- The gangsters 'moll' or love interest takes the form of Sullivan's wife to whom he appears totally devoted and loyal; there appear to be no girlfriends. When she is killed we get our expected theme of 'double-crossing' and we expect a 'revenge' narrative from the principal narrator (the son) but this is in fact fulfilled by the father (Hanks). Compare this with *Angels with Dirty Faces* and *The Godfather* and how Rocky and Michael Corleone 'get even'.

- It quickly becomes apparent that this is going to be different from other gangster films. The fact that Tom Hanks plays the lead role, Sullivan, is initially a surprise as he is not a star known for playing killers. Hanks is known for his all-American good-guy image and the fact he plays a murderous gangster requires some adjustment for the audience. However, our doubts are soon assuaged and the formula of his star image restored by the fact that although Hanks is a gangster he is a good gangster! The narrative revolves around the relationship of father and son as opposed to a concentration on action and this is familiar from other roles that Hanks has played.

- This film also differs from the other examples in that the 'high life' of the gangster is not overplayed. Sullivan's life does not appear extravagant or rich. He sees his work as a gangster as steady employment (see *Pulp Fiction* and other (post)modern gangster films for this) which provides a comfortable, not lavish, lifestyle. In fact he

- has a conscience, insisting when he robs a bank that the money is not taken from the poor.
- The 'rise' of the gangster is limited in this story. All we know is that Sullivan became a gangster because he was a poor Irish immigrant who the 'boss' (Paul Newman) helped out by providing a house and a job. The gangster's life is portrayed in this film through the eyes of his son whose innocence is lost as he discovers what his father does for a living. Like Michael Corleone before him in *The Godfather* he is reluctantly dragged into the 'illegitimate' business to protect what is left of the 'family' (common theme), only in this case it really is blood relatives and not just the extended 'family business'.
- Narratively, where this film is the most different from others of its type, is in the conclusion. Having been introduced to the gangster life the son does not take it up for himself as Michael Corleone does. He is spared having to fire the final shot and he does not pursue it to its ultimate conclusion, death or capture, ultimately rejecting it in his final voiceover. The gangsters' life being rejected means there will be no sequel, no return and Sullivan gets what he wanted for his son: a legitimate life. Where Michael Corleone in *The Godfather* decides to follow in his father's footsteps (despite his father Vito, like Sullivan, not wanting this) this boy does not and the narrative conclusion is peaceful. However, it offers the traditional gangster message (*see Angels with Dirty Faces*) that crime does not pay in the death of Sullivan at the end.

Macro analysis

Although the focus here has been the gangster genre, a study of *any* genre's macro elements (genre and narrative) will need to consider all of the points in this chapter. Some points may be more relevant to chosen genres/films than others. Some films may be entirely formulaic and predictable and others may rework typical generic elements and therefore be surprising. Remember always in your analysis to discuss your response to the film you have chosen to study. Just because we can predict a film's narrative does not make it any less good a film – in fact this is often the source of our enjoyment. Equally a film that does not follow a formula might evoke different responses: pleasant surprise or frustration for example. A full macro assignment will discuss all these elements and will work from the broad understanding of genre to the specific understanding of a particular film, illustrated by a sequence from it.

Grade 'A' exemplar material

To what extent are the films you watch formulaic? Discuss with reference to genre and narrative and illustrate with one or two comparative clips

Using two films from the horror genre, *Halloween* (John Carpenter, 1978) and *Scream* (Wes Craven, 1996), I will analyse to what extent the films we watch are formulaic.

The horror film is one of the staple ingredients of a varied movie-going diet, and as such comes with defined criteria as to what constitutes a successful representation of the genre. The first and most important audience expectation of a horror film is for it to provide the thrill of superficial fear. Whatever artistic or other merits the film may have, if this has not been achieved then the film is a failure as a product and example of its genre. To produce a successful example of this seemingly straightforward genre, conventional wisdom suggests a certain formula needs to be applied. I will explore this formula, and see if it can be applied to the two case studies mentioned.

It could be suggested that the horror film formula is the easily recognisable iconography, mis en scène and narrative, and also the non-diagetic elements of musical score and clear directorial traits that are common to all films which attempt to build suspense and derive shock. The formulaic features would be: a score which is contrapuntal and attempts to manipulate the emotions of the audience; working alongside camera movement which frames scenes with the sole purpose of creating as much prolonged suspense and fright as possible. In terms of the mis en scène, low key lighting is expected, and the iconography should feature a memorable monster or object of fright. The narrative, according to the formula, has a protagonist who survives the whole ordeal unscathed, and for whom the audience roots. At the climax, the monster is defeated, but comes back to life for one final scare. Everything should combine to create an atmosphere of unease, dread and fear.

Halloween, viewed now as one among the many truly great horror movies, appears to be rigid in its formulaic attributes, and a peerless example of the formula evident in the genre. To investigate this in more depth, this essay draws particular attention to the finale of the film where Michael Myers is stalking Laurie Strode. She appears to kill him and he lies still on the floor but, unbeknownst to her, he is not actually dead and sits back up.

This film covers many of the clichés of child horror movies. First of all there is the helpless, young, all-American valley girl who seemingly has a natural gift for very long and very loud screams. Then there's the monster chasing her. And it is dark all the time. There is the tension-building, dread-inducing orchestral score. With his camera, Carpenter is adept at visual flair as well as basic (yet primal in its simplicity) framing. In the last scene in the film, the oblivious Laurie sits on the floor, relieved it is all over, while Michael slowly rises behind her intending to gut her. She had previously defeated him in a desperate struggle – using a coat hanger, amongst other things – and he fell down, apparently dead. But of course, true to the formula, he is not actually dead.

Initially *Scream* appears to be a carbon copy of *Halloween*, but on closer examination it is apparent that it is not. On the contrary, it is a highly original piece of horror film-making. It plays on the audience's awareness of the formula and uses the viewer's relationship with the stereotypical lead character to provide surprises. *Scream* challenges the audience/character relationship, it could be argued, from the very first scene where the blonde girl – quite a well-known actress and sympathetic character – is brutally slaughtered. Although this is not original – more than thirty years earlier Hitchcock killed off his heroine in *Psycho* – it is rare, and especially as you are led to believe she will escape. She is the virginal heroine for the audience to cling to, right up until the knife slices into her breast. The narrative of *Scream* unfolds to reveal that the classically iconic monster is anything but – two obsessive high school kids were behind the suit. This is intelligent and witty storytelling, and, as happens frequently in this film, a complete dismantling of what the audience thinks they know.

For the purposes of this essay, particular attention is drawn to the finale of *Scream*, which explicitly, purposefully and knowingly subverts our expectations of the supposed established formula. The film's heroine, Sidney, turns the tables on the killer. She becomes the stalker and stalks the people behind Ghostface. She jumps out of a closet and stabs the villain. A complete role reversal has taken place, which is almost unsettling in its revolutionary deviation. Later on, the heroine lets it be known she is aware the villain will come back for one last scare, and she casually waits for him to do just that, before finishing him off for good with a bullet to the temple. 'Not in my movie' she quips, denying the monster his formulaic grand exit.

Scream invented the post-modern horror movie, which purposefully acknowledges the formula and ridicules it within the film. Even on paper this seems dangerous; the film-makers were taking a gamble. However, audiences clearly responded to Craven's unique reinvention of the formula. *Scream* became one of the most commercially successful horror movies ever made.

However, so did *Halloween*. On its initial release, it became the highest grossing independent film ever made. Therefore, it can be deduced it is not solely variation on genre which audiences respond to. *Halloween* was not reinventing the formula, even through the use of Carpenter's much noted and much imitated tactic of having a big build up, then making it look like nothing is going to happen, then providing the scare when the audience's guard is down. This tactic, while technically brilliant and arguably original, is not subverting the audience expectations; you know Michael Myers is going to jump out from the shadows, just not when. *Psycho* (1960) and *The Texas Chain Saw Massacre* (1974) had already planted the seeds of the stalk-and-slash movie, which would later sprout into the teen slasher movie, that most notorious sub-genre of horror. *Halloween* certainly set the template for the teen slasher movie, which would later be brought to trashy fruition by *Friday the 13th* (1980). But as influential as this particular brand of horror would be, even starting a sub-genre, it was still formulaic in the strictest sense. The clearest way to identify this is the narrative. *Scream* is not formulaic because it alters the narrative: the hunted (Sidney) becomes the hunter (Ghostface). On the other hand, *Halloween* keeps the narrative linear and unequivocally recognisable with great success. *Halloween* kept alive the traits of studio-era horror, such as the Dracula movies (monster rises from the dead at the end, almost all scenes take place in near total darkness) and brought them into our new, contemporary blockbuster age, tweaking them ever so slightly to inject emotional realism and audience empathy, just as *Scream* would add socially aware and psychologically relevant post-modern humour eighteen years later. Although the two films are similar, they represent the paramount fact that all genres depend upon difference and repetition equally in order to sustain the genre, and carry it forward. *Halloween*, an iconic genre paradigm, is not limited by its reputation, just as *Scream*, an instant genre paradox, is not limited by its differences. Both films thrive on their audiences' expectations: the former, by fulfilling them, the latter by subverting them. If *Halloween* fulfilled all the audience expectations and had no surprises, it would be boring; and if *Scream* subverted all the audience expectations, it would be an unrecognisable perversion. *Halloween* surprises in its 'build up' to 'all clear' to 'big shock' tactic, while *Scream* is, for much of the film, a straightforward slasher movie.

The films we watch are formulaic, yet only in as much as they are generic works of art that just happen to fall under particular categories, and only if it can be maintained that film formula is actually a facet of cinema and not just a psychological projection one makes through memory and identification.

Practical application of learning

This chapter looks at how the information on micro and macro elements, which have been discussed in the previous chapters, can be applied practically. This means using our knowledge of film language, convention and expectation to create something interesting and, as far as possible (knowing that genre films are formulaic), original. The practical work should be the embodiment of all your learning so far on narrative, genre and cinematic codes. You have the theory and the knowledge, now it is time to apply it.

Video-making, screenplay/shooting script and storyboards

Your coursework requires you to apply your knowledge of film through the production of one of three pieces of creative work:

- a practical video-making project
- a screenplay/shooting script, or
- a storyboard

The practical video-making project

With the increasing availability of DV cameras and digital editing facilities making your own 'film' may be an option that is open to you. However, this kind of project requires lots of organisation, teamwork (films are rarely made by one person), and time. The undertaking of this option needs thorough planning and preparation. It may be that you still need to produce a rough storyboard before you begin shooting or need a shooting schedule so that everyone working on the production can visualise the end result and what their role is in it. The best way to approach video-making is in small teams with clearly defined roles. For example, groups of four with one person each being responsible for:

- mise en scène (including casting, set design/dressing or location-finding and costume)
- cinematography (this will also involve lighting)
- editing (this includes titling)
- sound (this includes sound recording and sound editing, which may mean sounds which have to be added later).

Apart from the roles outlined above it is also useful to elect one member as 'director' (supplemental to their technical input): this person should assume the role of decision-maker should any creative tensions arise which need to be resolved. The director should also take control of organising the shoot.

Each person will ultimately evaluate their own contribution to the finished production.

Screenplay/shooting script

A screenplay is a story specifically written with the screen in mind.

However don't be fooled into thinking that because the screenplay does not contain images that it does not require the *visualisation* of ideas. Where a storyboard does this with images, the screenplay has to work even harder to produce this with words.

Normally a screenplay will not include camera directions or lots of detail regarding mise en scène as this is normally seen as the director's decision (you wouldn't dream of telling Spielberg where to put the camera!) However, for our purpose and for that of the exam board, try to think of your screenplay as more like a 'shooting script' that *would* include these details for the benefit of your crew. Remember, you are trying to demonstrate your technical knowledge as well as your knowledge of narrative in this piece of work.

Storyboards

The storyboard is a series of pictures showing the shots that will make up a narrative sequence. The storyboard can be hand drawn or it can be made up of digital photographs. It sounds simple but it actually requires much thought in terms of perspective (angles of shot), transitions, and movement. Also, especially if using digital photography which makes details easier to capture, aspects of lighting/mise en scène may play an important role.

The storyboard should be the next best thing to actually seeing the finished film itself. It needs to be clear in communicating ideas visually. It acts as a 'visual script' and as such should contain lots of detail including dialogue and sound effects as well as narrative information. If choosing the storyboard option then try to choose a sequence from your story idea which contains little dialogue as this will force you to concentrate on the visual communication of ideas. For example, action sequences, chases and slapstick comedy all work well in this format.

Both the storyboard and the screenplay/shooting script require a structured format that adheres to professional conventions and layout, which we will come to later in the chapter, but first we need a story!

The story idea

The story idea will demonstrate your knowledge of the macro elements of film form and will require you to focus on the concepts of narrative and genre.

It may help initially to decide which genre of film you would like to work in. Alternatively it may help to discover a storyline and adapt it for a certain genre.

Stories are all around us and if you have difficulty coming up with something you can find them in a variety of places.

key terms

Internal motivation
something *within* the main character that drives the narrative (e.g. revenge, jealousy or love).

External motivation
some external event that makes the narrative agent act and start the chain of cause and effect (see Chapter 2 on narrative). This could be anything relevant to your story but usually involves the hero's goal, e.g. to get the girl, find the treasure or win the race.

Obstacles
things or events that get in the way of the hero reaching his goal and which have to be overcome. If the man gets the girl just by asking her then there is no story!

key terms

Synopsis
a summary of the story that gives all plot events and twists including the final outcome.

analyse this

The following are all good sources of stories. By considering each you may discover something which you can adapt or tweak to make an interesting piece of cinema.
- True life events (and these do not have to be famous or dramatic; stories retold among your family or friends make unusual and personal pieces of drama, comedy, etc.).
- Historical events. You may wish to take the event and adapt it for a different or contemporary genre (for example, the gunpowder plot could be a thriller!).
- Newspapers are full of stories. Look particularly at the smaller more obscure columns for something interesting.
- Novels/books may be adapted or they may act as a stimulus from which you are inspired to write further.

Once you have a story in mind the narrative structure needs attention. Will it be straight forward (Proppian/Todorovian) in its structure (equilibrium – disruption – equilibrium)? Or are you attempting to subvert convention by not supplying a neat resolution? How are you going to engage your audience? Characters need to be carefully thought out with believable internal and external motivation and obstacles which they can overcome (or not as the case may be).

Cinematic ideas including brief summary of the story idea

This part of your work will take the form of 500 written words with 100 of these words devoted to a brief summary of the storyline of the film (synopsis). The genre and narrative style of your story will be evident from this summary.

Within this piece of work you must then explain what cinematic ideas you have for the film/sequence. This will include any references to other films which have influenced your visual ideas. For instance, you may wish to create a 'Matrix-style' look for your film, including cold, green sci-fi lighting and special CGI effects. You may have a particular setting/location that is a vital part of the visual communication, a certain editing technique that complements the themes, or a special soundtrack/aural motif that you feel is important to the mood or ambience of the sequence. Perhaps it requires the casting of certain stars that you feel are particularly aligned to the roles you have written because of performance styles you have seen previously. The cinematic ideas will give a sense of 'cohesion' to your work: a detailed explanation of the combination of technical choices within it.

FILM: MAKING MEANING (FS1)

Activity

As practice for writing the bare minimum required for a synopsis, think of a film you have recently seen and try to write down the plot summary in 100 words.

Having written your cinematic ideas/brief summary you must now decide which part of the structure of your story you intend to script or storyboard. The opening? The end? The climax? Try to avoid scenes that are largely dialogue driven as this will not give you the scope to demonstrate your range of cinematic – or visual – understanding.

Now you have the story idea and the specific scene you wish to work on you need to lay out your idea as either a script extract or a storyboard. Each must be approached professionally and therefore must be 'formatted' (laid out on the page) correctly.

Formatting

Screenplay format

A screenplay should be laid out in a certain way so that the reader can visualise the action. Again, think of this as a 'shooting script', which would include visual description and direction that not only *you* can follow but also your cast and crew. A straightforward screenplay (the type you can buy in bookshops) is the type of thing that is usually sent to actors and producers but will not contain enough technical information for our purposes (to demonstrate our micro and macro knowledge).

analyse this

Read the following web page that offers a simple but informative guide to laying out your script. Remember to apply all the points made when you lay out your screenplay.

Script layout

Why does my screenplay have to be formatted?

So it's easy to read. It may be OK to have a scruffy looking script if you are the only one who will use it, but to allow your cast and crew to make sense of it, applying a few rules of formatting makes it easier to read.

Layout

- Scripts are best typed on only one side of the paper in 12-point courier.
- Double spacing between lines allows you to read the script more easily.
- Leave good borders around the script.

Keep to the above tips and you will have a well laid out script. This can help you time your script, as now one page of screenplay will equal one minute of screen time.

Now read the sample script below and follow the guidelines.

```
EXT. BEACH — DAY
Dawn breaks, waves pounding the vast empty beach.
LS — Making his way amongst the tide line of flotsam and jetsam is a BEACHCOMBER,
clad in scruffy shorts, battered sand shoes and a threadbare shirt.
He stops, eyes something amongst the rubbish and stoops.
                         BEACHCOMBER
                           Eh?
MS — He holds up what looks to be a bottle. He turns it over in his hands, holds it
to his ear and shakes it, listening. Tentatively he tries the cork. It is stuck.
He pulls hard on the cork using the full force of his wiry frame. HURRGHHH! No luck.
Exasperated, he bites the cork between his teeth and pulls. HURGGHHHH!! POP!!
He flies back, and the cork arcs through the sky. The bottle falls to the sand.
Picking himself up he takes the bottle between his hands. Smoke begins to pour from
its neck.
                                                                   CUT TO:
```

Scene heading/Slug lines

INT. FRANKENSTEIN'S LABORATORY – NIGHT

The scene heading/slug line: Consists of either INT. (Interior, eg. in a room) or EXT. (Exterior, e.g. on the street), the location (e.g. CITY STREET. NEW YORK) followed by either DAY or NIGHT (Forget about morning/afternoon/sunset etc. as it makes no difference when it is being filmed – no one is going to shoot you for filming in the afternoon and pretending it is the morning).
Here are a few examples to give you a rough idea.

INT. MORTUARY – NIGHT

EXT. RACE TRACK – DAY

Scenes inside cars are INTeriors despite the fact that the car is outside. You may occasionally see EXT/INT or INT/EXT on a script. This occurs when the camera is in one location and the action is happening in another. For example:

INT/EXT. HOTEL LOBBY/CITY STREET – DAY

(The camera or a character is watching the action occurring outside.)

EXT/INT. CAR/APARTMENT – NIGHT

(The camera or character is sitting in a car watching something happening through an apartment's window. Hey, maybe they're on a stakeout or something!)

The actors' direction/description

The scene direction. This tells the reader what is going on. Clear, concise. Always showing rather than telling. Don't say that:

> **DAVID is suffering inner torment because of his wife's kidnapping.**

...show us!

> **DAVID runs his hands through his hair. Picks up a shot of bourbon, tastes it and winces. He throws the glass across the room, hitting the mirror which SHATTERS.**

Oh yeah! Write in the present tense. It gives events and action much more immediacy, like they are really happening, which is what you want.

Dialogue

Dialogue appears in a column down the *centre* of the page indented from the business. It's in the form:

NAME
(Direction)
Hey, this is what your character says.

The name goes in Upper Case.

The direction isn't always given. The only occasion you might put some in would be if dialogue was directed specifically at another character, '(to Alberto)' or if it has to be said in a particular style '(whispering)'.

And finally *the dialogue* itself. Try to keep it to a minimum, no long speeches here. That way there is less for your actors to remember and less for them to muck up. Good actors will always make the best of what you have written for them and can provide so much more with their intonation and body language, which you simply cannot write. I'm sure I read somewhere that only 20% of communication is speech.

Avoid exposition (that's when you character explains something in detail) – try and show rather than tell. Keep it simple.

Character names

When a character first appears, their name in the scene direction should be in CAPITALS. After that their name is in lower case.

Sound

You can put important sounds in CAPITALS, so that monsters SHRIEK and cars EXPLODE, but this is up to you. Some people like to, others don't. If you do put sounds in upper case try not to overdo it.

You see the word OVER used in scripts. This means that there is an important sound OVER the normal soundtrack, for example music (non-diegetic).

Camera directions

As this is a shooting script we can add camera and actor directions to the script. In a screenplay script you wouldn't do this – just like you wouldn't turn round to Coppola and say, 'Do a close-up here'. But as this is our show we get to play director.

There are several abbreviations to speed the writing and reading along.

C/U	Close-up
MS	Medium shot
LS	Long shot
Two-Shot	Shot of two characters in the same picture
V.O.	Voiceover
O.S.	Off screen
P.O.V.	Point of view
M.O.S.	Without sound (mute of sound). Great for when your characters are staking out some joint, watching the bad guys pull off some drug deal and they can't hear what they are saying.

Camera movements

PAN
TILT
TRACK/DOLLY
ZOOM

(See Chapter 2 for an explanation of these terms.)

FILM: MAKING MEANING (FS1)

Transitions (editing)

These are how you change from one scene to another. They always sit over to the right of your script and on the whole you will find yourself using 'CUT TO:' which is a straight change of picture from one scene to the next.

There are some other transitions available but be careful, they have different connotations to the viewer.

DISSOLVE TO: The final shot of the previous scenes fades into the first shot of the next scene. This can be used to suggest the passing of time.

FADE IN: Usually used at the start of films, with FADE OUT used to end the movie. You can also use CUT TO BLACK and CUT FROM BLACK/CUT IN. You can use these transitions together to alter the mood and pace. For example:

NICK grins at ALBERTO.

NICK
You're even uglier than I remember.

Alberto scratches his head, thinking, before pulling his fist back and hitting Nick full on in the face.

CUT TO BLACK:

FADE IN:

INT. BEDROOM – DAY.

Nick comes around, groggy at first. He gingerly feels his chin, pulls himself off the bed and over to the sink. He grimaces and spits out a few teeth.

Source: Edited from http://www.exposure.co.uk/eejit/script/#slug.
© Exposure 1996–2004.

Grade 'A' exemplar material

EXT. TOKYO SUBURBS — **SLUMS. NIGHT**

High angle (ELS) of an empty street in Tokyo suburbs at night. It's almost silent. The only sounds are those of window shutters slamming open and closed, and an unsettling breeze blowing coldly in the night. A sinister looking, slim figure wearing black emerges from the shadows. His left hand resting by his waist, his right hand firmly tucked into his right trouser pocket, and a COWBOY HAT pulled down over his forehead hiding his eyes. The figure looks very out of place in his current surroundings. He is KEICHI.

CUT TO:

Ground level (LS) of the street. Wrecked, derelict buildings and broken, flickering streetlights are all than can be seen around. A footstep is heard, and echoes throughout the street as a (CU) of the back of KEICHI'S right leg steps into the shot.

                                                           CUT TO:

Tracking (LS) of KEICHI slowly walking through the street from the front. To tracking (LS) of Keichi walking from the side, Keichi then comes to a sudden stop.

                                                           CUT TO:

To (CU) of the right side of KEICHI'S face. Keichi's eyes are hidden by the shadow from his HAT, and MUGGERS emerge from an alley hidden in shadow to Keichi's left.

                            CHIEF MUGGER
                          (Distant voice)
                  Well, well… looky here, Christmas in July?

                             (snigger)

Fast zoom to (MCU) of the muggers showing them stepping out into the light. They're ill-coloured, deformed beings who are outcasts of society. They have barbaric weapons such as MACES and SHARP KNIVES welded into their arms replacing their ordinary limbs. One of them has a blood encrusted HUMAN JAW hanging from his neck — he's the Chief Mugger. He has a smug grin on his face.

                                                           CUT TO:

(LS) from behind KEICHI as MUGGERS begin surrounding him.

                            FAT MUGGER
                    (looking Keichi up and down)
                      What you got, pretty boy?

                                                           CUT TO:

Panning shot from right to left (ECU) of KEICHI'S eyes hidden by the shadow from his hat. Keichi remains silent as the MUGGERS circle him. FAT MUGGER becomes annoyed with Keichi's silence.

                            FAT MUGGER
                            (angrily)
                      Hey pretty boy! You deaf?!

                                                           CUT TO:

(LS) of KEICHI from behind.

                            CHIEF MUGGER
                          (to FAT MUGGER)
                I don't think our guest likes you too much.

                             (snigger)

Flickering streetlights give us a brief look at the outlandish weapon Keichi keeps on his back, TESTAMENT. The bizarre, silver and black, sword type weapon is made up out of two, long, Katana blades linked at the handle by a sturdy, shimmering chain.

Chief Mugger's attention is drawn to Keichi's right hand in his trouser pocket.

                                                           CUT TO:

(CU) of KEICHI'S face. Keichi and CHIEF MUGGER begin exchanging words.

> CHIEF MUGGER
> What's in your pocket, punk?!

> KEICHI
> (quiet voice)
> You don't wanna know

CUT TO:

(MCU) of KEICHI from behind, flickering light gives the audience a slightly better view of TESTAMENT

> CHIEF MUGGER
> (patronising voice)
> Oh but I do, now show me… before I show myself.

> (snigger)

> KEICHI
> (quiet voice, a sly smirk)
> Well… if you put it that way…

(Keichi begins removing his hand from his pocket but then suddenly halts)

> But before I show you…
> (voice becomes louder and more solemn)

> Have any of you worthless scumbags got any last words?!

CUT TO:

(MLS) of CHIEF MUGGER pulling an irate face. He lets out a war cry and runs towards KEICHI waving his arc/MACE around in a threatening fashion. The Chief Mugger runs towards the camera.

CUT TO:

Brief (ECU) as KEICHI calmly lifts his COWBOY HAT just enough so that his eyes are in view, a scar is revealed over his right eye.

CUT TO:

Brief (MCU) of KEICHI from behind, he removes his right hand from his pocket and brandishes TESTAMENT. Simultaneous with this shot is a diegetic sound which resembles that of a knife being drawn quickly from its metal stand.

CUT TO:

High angle (ELS) showing KEICHI using TESTAMENT to slice each MUGGER up at lightning speed.

CUT TO:

(MLS) of KEICHI from the side, travelling just off the ground, from left to right, slicing FAT MUGGER'S stomach in slow motion. The camera pans from left to right, tracking Keichi. Fat Mugger has a dazed figure expression. Sounds of flesh being sliced, the Fat Mugger shrieking, and the wind blowing takes place simultaneously with the shot.

CUT TO:

High angle (LS) of KEICHI travelling vertically across the shot, slicing TALL MUGGER'S chest in slow motion. The camera tracks Keichi's movement across the shot, and Tall Mugger's figure expression shows he's in disbelief. The sound mimics that of the shot prior to this.

                                                                    CUT TO:

Brief (MCU) of KEICHI travelling horizontally, from right to left, slicing CHIEF MUGGER'S neck in slow motion. The camera tracks Keichi's movement, whilst showing Chief Mugger's figure expression of severe pain. The sound mimics that of the shot prior to this. The fight ends quickly

                                                                    CUT TO:

Panning from right to left (LS) of KEICHI, from the front, he is on one knee with TESTAMENT tightly gripped in his right hand. The MUGGERS stand stiff, as if paralysed, in a circle around him. Keichi's long black coat hands wide open and blows in the wind, making a rustling sound. Keichi remains still for a few seconds, puts TESTAMENT back on his back, comes to his feet, and places his right hand back in his right trouser pocket.

                                                                    CUT TO:

(CU) of the right side of KEICHI'S face, he's unmarked, he lifts his left hand, places his finger and thumb on the brink of his COWBOY HAT. Camera rapidly zooms out to an (ELS), placing the MUGGERS in view. Keichi pulls his HAT down over his forehead, obscuring his scar from view. As this happens, all the Muggers simultaneously split into pieces, creating a slicing sound as they collapse into a pool of their own blood. Keichi walks forward.

                                                                    CUT TO:

High angle (LS) behind KEICHI. The camera slowly tilts up and away from him changing the (LS) to an (ELS) as Keichi walks into the distance.

Storyboard format

Again the storyboard has to be used by many people so it has to be clear in communicating ideas. Make sure you design a template of approximately six shots per A4 page and leave enough space under each frame to indicate any other detail. Just as with the script, points to remember include:

- descriptions (mise en scène)
- camera directions
- transitions (editing) and duration of shots
- sound (dialogue and sound effects to be written underneath the image)

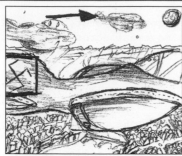

1. Shot type: **CU to LS**
Sound: **Plane engines**
Description: **Zoom out from swastika to show German planes. Tracks the planes for around 15 seconds**

2. Shot type: **MCU of speakers**
Sound: **Air raid siren**
Description: **Camera moves up from base of speakers to the top.**
Duration – 10 seconds.

3. Shot type: **Low Angle ELS**
Sound: **Air raid siren**
Description: **Tilt up to show planes, moon and top of St. Pauls Cathedral.**
Duration – 15 secs.

4. Shot type: **MLS to CU**
Sound: **Air raid siren**
Description: **Soldier shouting and moving civilians into the shelter. Cut to CU of face to show emotion. Duration – 10 secs.**

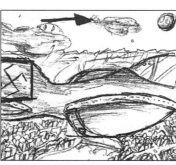

5. Shot type: **CU**
Sound: **Plane engines & foot steps**
Description: **Soldiers running.**
Duration – 5 secs.

6. Shot type: **LS to ECU**
Sound: **Gunfire and plane engines**
Description: **Above shots 5 secs, quick cuts between ECU of eyes and ECU of gun fire. Duration – 20 secs.**

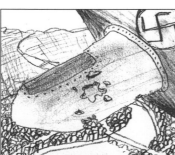

7. Shot type: **MS Tracking**
Sound: **Plane engines**
Description: **Bullets destroying plane wing. Duration – 10 secs.**

8. Shot type: **LS**
Sound: **Explosion**
Description: **CGI explosion of the plane.**
Duration – 15 secs.

Cut to
Cut to
Cut to
Cut to
Cut to
Cut to
Cut to

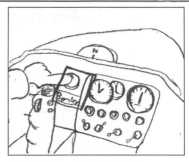

9. Shot type: MS
   Sound: Plane engines
   Description: MS of Nazi pilot in cockpit
   speaking in German, unsubtitled.
   Duration – 25 secs.

Cut to →

Pan to right →

10. Shot type: MS to CU (POV)
    Sound: Plane engines
    Description: Shot above 10 secs. Cut to
    CU of 'bomben' button being pushed.

Cut to

11. Shot type: MCU Low angle shot, tracking
    Sound: Whistling of bombs
    Description: Tracks the bomb being
    released for 10 secs.

Cut to →

12. Shot type: Birds eye ELS
    Sound: Bombs and engines
    Description: Slowly tracking the planes
    flying and dropping bombs 25 secs.

Cut to

13. Shot type: (HA) ELS
    Sound: Gun fire and engines
    Description: HA to make gunners on
    roof seem vunerable.

Zoom in to
framed soldier →

14. Shot type: CU to ECU
    Sound: Whistle of bomb
    Description: Zoom in on soldiers eye.
    During zoom in facial expression is of fear.
    10 seconds slow zoom in.

Zoom in to eye

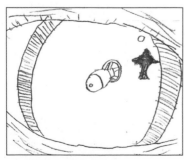

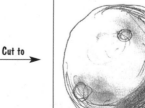

15. Shot type: ECU of Eye
    Sound: Whistle of bomb
    Description: Reflection of bomb heading
    toward the sodiers plane. Duration – 5 secs.

Cut to →

16. Shot type: LS of moon
    Sound: Silent but grass hoppernoises
    Description: Graphic match from eye to
    moon in the new scene.

FILM: MAKING MEANING (FS1)

Evaluating your work

Whichever medium of practical application you undertake (video-making, storyboard or script) always remember to evaluate your work as it progresses. This may mean showing your 'rushes' to other members of the class/group for an impartial assessment before editing begins. It may mean passing around storyboard and scripts whilst they are in the development stages to gain feedback on where you are going right and where you are going wrong. Your fellow class members or family members will quickly point out if anything is unclear or confusing and their reaction to your work will give you lots of information on what to keep and what to change. If you do find yourself making alterations, note down the reasons why as this will be useful in the final evaluation. For instance, if they laugh or gasp in the right places or are intrigued to know what happens next then your ideas are working but if they *don't* have those expected responses at the appropriate places you may need to make some adjustments. Remember film ideas and scripts go through many drafts before they are finalised.

Questions to consider when evaluating your work:

questions

1 How does the final product differ from your original idea?
2 Compare the *intended* response to your work with the *actual* response. (It may help to have others read the work or even to attempt to act it out.)
3 What elements of the work did you have to change to improve it? (Genre? Narrative? Camera direction?)
4 What effect did those changes have?
5 What are the strengths and weakness of your finished product?
6 If you were given a similar assignment what might you do differently?

5

The historical development of the Hollywood film industry

In Part 2 of this book, we will explore some deceptively simple but vital questions about the nature of the film industry. Why do we get to see the films that we do? Why does American and Hollywood film still dominate in our cinemas? How is the film industry organised and who really controls it? What place does British film have in the industry and how successful is it? To understand our contemporary film industry we also need to know something about how the industry was founded and has developed.

We shall begin by looking at how film can be viewed as an industry, at the early pioneers of film and how they tried to control the fledgling industry. We will trace how Hollywood on the West Coast of the United States began to replace companies on the East Coast where the first film-makers had worked as the most important area for the production of films. We will see how the studios, with their production bases in Hollywood gradually came to dominate both distribution and, most importantly in this era, exhibition. We will also suggest some ideas as to why they made such popular and successful films.

In doing this we will begin to examine the different parts of the industry: production, distribution and exhibition.

Thinking of film as an industry

In Part 1 we explored some of the ways in which complex and subtle meanings can be communicated in film. We learnt a technical vocabulary of mise en scène and cinematography including lighting, editing and sound that enable us to 'take apart' any sequence of a film and begin to explain how it works. We also explored how narrative and genre are used in film to surprise, reassure, amuse and engage audiences.

In doing this, and by now you're probably driving your friends and family crazy by explaining how directors achieve their effects in films, you have probably begun to see why some people see cinema as the most important art form of the last century.

In Part 2 we will look at film from an entirely different, but just as important perspective, that is, seeing films as part of an industry, which like any other is about producing products (the films themselves) that paying customers (the cinema audiences) will want to buy. Remember, unlike when we buy a meal in a restaurant, having bought a ticket to a film we can't then refuse to pay if we don't like the film. For this reason

Figure 5.1 ▶

key terms

Production
the phase in the process where the actual shooting of the film takes place.

Post-production
the phase in the process after production where the film is edited and music and effects are added.

Distribution
the process of making more copies or prints of the film, and transporting them to cinemas.

Exhibition
the showing of the films in the cinemas and getting a local audience in to watch the film.

we are actually very wary of what films we will go to see. Few things are worse than sitting through a film we don't like, although interestingly not many of us will get up and leave. Understanding films from this perspective is remarkably helpful in understanding why stars and genres, and star directors, are central to the industry.

Put very simply, and it will get much more complex later on, the film industry is divided into three stages: production (including post-production), distribution and exhibition.

The origins of the film industry

The first film producers

It is probably no surprise to you to learn that *Titanic* or *Gladiator*, or to an even greater extent, *The Lord of the Rings* made huge amounts of money. At the time of writing in June 2004, *Shrek 2* has taken just eighteen days since its release to bring in $300 million in ticket sales at the US box office alone. Although income has not always been this huge, controlling the film industry – and its potential profits – has been a struggle from the industry's beginnings.

The origins of the film industry are a matter of dispute. However, most people agree that the first film-makers were the Lumière Brothers. These manufacturers of the first rudimentary cameras made their first film in 1895. It showed workers leaving their factory. These films were shown at first as curiosities by travelling showmen who would buy the films outright. The films would last no more than a few minutes and would simply delight in the illusion of reality that they created. Early films would, for example, show a family having tea in a garden with the audience fascinated by the play of light on the leaves of the trees, or a wall being knocked down and then as the film is re-wound through the camera the wall is shown miraculously rising up again! Most famously one film showed a steam train arriving at a station platform, with the audience not entirely comfortable that it wasn't best to run screaming from the cinema before they got run down!

talking point

Such simple techniques to surprise early cinema audiences seem hardly credible today. But are there ways in which the latest effects-laden action adventure movie, like *The Matrix* series, or even the latest computer-generated animation film, such as *Shrek 2*, have basically the same appeal?

The nickelodeon

Early in the twentieth century, the demand for films became so great that high street stores were being converted to little cinemas, or, as they were commonly known as they cost five cents to get into, nickelodeons. One of these was run by the Warner Brothers – Jack, Harry, Sam and Albert – in New York. Like film-makers ever since they were never entirely sure whether their films would get an audience. When a film proved very popular they had an arrangement with the funeral parlour next door to take some of their chairs for extra seating!

Cinema has always been controversial, and with their largely poor, immigrant, and working class audiences, these new gathering places were regarded with suspicion by the authorities, and there were calls for the films to be carefully regulated and censored, especially as the films began to feature playfully sexual scenes of women undressing or couples kissing on trains.

talking point

Film, video and now DVDs are regularly blamed for society's problems. You may have heard of the tragic Jamie Bulger case in the early 1990s when two boys killed a toddler. People still closely associate the murder with the film *Child's Play 3*, although the judge at the trial specifically stated that there was no evidence that the two boys had watched the film. Why do you think this is?

Can you think of any films in recent years that have been controversial and led to calls for censorship, or closer control of the film industry?

The first film distributors

key terms

Rental
the proportion of the ticket price that the film exhibitor returns to the distributor for the right to show their film.

The buying of films outright was prohibitively expensive for these small-scale entrepreneur exhibitors and any individual film would, of course, soon be valueless as their local neighbourhood audience was constantly demanding new products. This was solved by film exchanges which bought the films from the producers and then rented them to different nickelodeons in turn. Rentals, that is the amount exhibitors of films to audiences pay to distributors, the modern day film exchangers, are still a matter of argument and hard bargaining.

Some people think that the relatively low proportion of the rental that goes back to film distributors and producers in Britain is part of the reason that our film industry is still so relatively unsuccessful in comparison with Hollywood. Back in the first decade of the last century exchanges were also regarded suspiciously and might let you pay for a film print that was so worn out it was difficult to follow the story.

The Motion Picture Patent Company

At first the films were largely the work of individual cameramen, such as Billy Bitzer, who went on to work with the most famous of early directors, D.W. Griffiths, or Edwin S. Porter, who made *The Great Train Robbery* in New Jersey on the East coast. This was a landmark film since it contained some clear narrative development.

Porter worked for the Edison Company and it was this company and the Biograph company, who made the first of what would be many attempts down the years to control the fledgling film industry. Their combined company – the Motion Picture Patent Company (MPPC), which also drew in other producers such as Melies, Selig, Essanay, Vitagraph and Pathe – tried to get anyone using their technology, whether that was a camera to make a film or a projector to show one, to pay them a fee.

The MPPC was eventually declared illegal in 1915 but by then it had had two major effects.

The first was that many foreign film-makers were frozen out of the US market. In this period before the First World War, we might be surprised to learn that the most powerful film industries internationally were European, in particular those in France, Italy and Denmark. One of the French companies was Pathe. And they, of course, are still around and were one of the winners of the lottery franchise in Britain in 1997. In 1907, 1200 films were released in the US but only a third were produced there. What a different situation from today! The MPPC's policy was essentially protectionist and allowed the film-makers at home in the US a greater proportion of their home market.

Secondly, many film-makers and film distributors, resenting the power of the MPPC, headed off to the West coast to try and evade this control, among them the Warner Brothers, Carl Laemmle, who would found Universal Studios, and Marcus Loew who would own MGM. The small town they found, which they and others decided with its almost permanent sunshine

Figure 5.2 ▶

The development of Hollywood

Carl Laemmle was the head of Universal Pictures and was typical of the pioneers who would come to dominate the industry. Like William Fox, Marcus Loew and the Warner brothers, Laemmle had got into the film business first of all through exhibition, by owning nickelodeons in a major eastern city, Chicago. By 1907 he had added a film exchange business to his group of store front theatres in defiance of the MPPC. He put producers and exhibitors together to ensure a steady supply of new films for enthusiastic audiences. Feeling the pressure from the MPPC he set up with some other independent companies a rival group, the Universal Film Manufacturing Company. A few years later he sold his theatres to raise the cash with which he could buy a ranch, 230 acres north of Hollywood, California, and concentrated his efforts in production and distribution.

questions

From the reading we have just done explain briefly what you think each of the terms below means:
▶ production
▶ distribution
▶ exhibition.

key terms

Director
the person in charge of the shooting of the film itself. He or she must understand technically what is happening, the implications this might have for the budget, and still be creative in making a film that will be enjoyable and distinctive.

Producer
the person in overall charge of the film from conception to the delivery of the final finished film to the distributor.

Let's now look at each of these fundamental terms in a bit more detail before we go on to try and understand why Hollywood was, and is, so hugely successful.

Production

Production itself falls into three stages:
● pre-production, where the director and the producer work together to get a deal with a distributor;
● the shoot, or the production itself, when the director is in charge and must get all the footage he is going to need for the final stage;
● post-production – this is the editing of the film, the addition of sound and increasingly the time when special effects will transform the filmed footage.

Making a film is a highly complex undertaking involving dozens of people if not hundreds. Just look at the credits for a mainstream movie – the crew will contain all kinds of specialist technicians. Some film critics believe its nonsense ever to talk about films as the artistic vision of one person because so many people are involved.

PRODUCERS AND AUDIENCES (FS2)

Distribution

In today's industry this is the most powerful section. The worldwide scale of the film industry today means that distribution of films is the key to their making a profit. Hollywood now makes the majority of its income from the box office outside the US and, unlike the US, these overseas markets are still expanding. What effect this may have on the content of future films is unclear, although the subtitled martial arts adventure *Crouching Tiger, Hidden Dragon* from Korean director Ang Lee may be a sign of things to come from Hollywood.

As we shall see, distribution is also key because it is the distributors who also sell the rights to films to go on to video, DVD and then satellite, cable and terrestrial television. This means that films that were flops at the box office can still go on to make money. Films that have been successful can make yet more money! The BBC is believed to have paid £7 million for the right to show *Titanic* on Christmas Day 2000.

Exhibition

A joke often goes around the offices of distribution companies, that they spend six months negotiating multimillion dollar deals to get the film made and then a year planning and creating a massive global multimedia marketing campaign that will set their film apart, and then they give it to exhibitors who open the cinema doors and sell the tickets.

However, although exhibition is not the centre of the industry as it was during the heyday of the Hollywood studio system from the late 1920s to the end of the 1950s, exhibition is still vital. Indeed some people believe it is obvious in retrospect that the reason cinema-going collapsed in the early 1970s is because the cinemas themselves had become run down and uncomfortable, not much better than the 'flea pits' of the early days of cinema.

The arrival of multiplexes in the mid-1980s in Britain with their high levels of comfort and cleanliness and their high levels of service have been a major factor in the revival of cinema-going as a popular leisure activity. Reasonable prices (compared, say, to going to a Premier league soccer match), comfortable seats, air conditioning, the latest digital surround sound systems, and sweets and drinks from the concessions stands in the foyer all make for an enjoyable experience.

Activity

Recent exam questions have focused on students' experience of their local cinemas. If you don't go to the cinema regularly you need to start! List the cinemas you've been to recently. Why did you go there and what kind of service did you think you received? The examiners value local knowledge very highly.

Hopefully you can now see how the industry will collapse if any one of these sectors is not being run properly. No wonder the biggest companies in the film industry have always tried to get as much control over all sectors as possible. The film business is highly risky. The rewards are great but a single film whose budget gets out of control can destroy a studio. This happened with the film *Heaven's Gate* in 1975. The company United Artists gave the director, Michael Cimino, a lot of independence and accepted his going over budget, betting he would have a great success as he had done previously with the Oscar-winning film *The Deer Hunter*. However, the budget ballooned and when the film flopped at the box office, United Artists was effectively destroyed as a film-making company. Ironically the film is now being re-evaluated and may yet become a classic!

talking point

Why do we go to see a film? Rack your brains and think back to the films you've seen over the last couple of years. List the reasons why you went.

key terms

Word of mouth other people telling you what a film is like and recommending it (or not!).

Your list will have contained a whole range of reasons, but likely to feature heavily is word of mouth.

Although tricky for the executives in the industry, research has shown word of mouth is the single most important reason why people go to see a film. It is also one of the best things about the industry. Nobody can tell us what to like, and no matter how much money is spent on it, or what $20 million megastar is in it, if we don't like a film we'll say so and the film will flop.

Hollywood executives have endlessly sought to get round this simple fact and ensure the holy grail of repeat purchase.

Activity

Think of as many different ways as you can in which the film industry tries to ensure we will go to see a film.

Your list will have included, stars, star directors, sequels, genres, special effects, special offers and merchandising.

PRODUCERS AND AUDIENCES (FS2)

We shall soon consider how in the 1980s and 1990s the use of the blockbuster 'event' movie attempted to combine production, promotion and merchandising, and exhibition strategy to 'bypass' word of mouth.

The Hollywood studio system, 1930–1949

However, we first need to briefly consider the period during which the major Hollywood studios had, more or less, complete control of the industry globally. That is the classic period of studio production, usually dated from 1930–1949.

To take up again the story that we began to tell in our section on the origins of the industry, in 1908 the MPPC, or the Trust, as is it was more commonly known, was still largely in control of the industry, imposing charges through their patents on anyone who wanted to use their equipment, whether this was using a projector to show a film, or a camera to make one. However, ambitious men like Carl Laemmle were already setting themselves up as alternative, independent providers of films to nickelodeon owners.

Establishing themselves far from the Trust companies' bases in California, Laemmle and others – such as Marcus Loew who went on to create MGM and Adolph Zukor who made Paramount – could see, as the Trust did not, that the key to success, with increasingly sophisticated audiences, was the creation of films with longer and more complex narratives. Long before the terms 'blockbuster' or 'event movie' were ever used these men could see they needed to market each film as unique, never to be repeated and unmissable.

These soon-to-be movie moguls were also keen to create a new respectability for the movies that would encourage middle-class audiences to see films and discourage the authorities from trying to censor their films. Largely ignoring the many cinemas in working-class districts that were often not much better than nickelodeons, or flea-pits, they created new movie palaces in the centre of the big cities. These two thousand or so cinemas that the Hollywood companies owned then had the right to show the latest Hollywood films before anyone else. By 1920 those cinemas had three-quarters of all the industry's audience receipts! With large-scale investment of over $100,000 in each film, making more prints and sending them to cinemas abroad made sense too. In this way the studios controlled the production of the films in their new studios in Hollywood, the distribution of the films around the United States and the world, and the exhibition of their films in their new movie palaces. As companies they were, in a classic phrase, vertically integrated. The dominant companies were known as the 'big five'. The names will probably be familiar to you. They were MGM, Paramount, Fox, Warner Brothers and RKO. There were also three companies who were integrated into the system but did not own cinema chains. The 'little three', as they were known, were United Artists, Columbia and Universal.

key terms

Vertical integration when a company owns all stages of the production, distribution and sale or, in the case of cinema, exhibition of its product.

Controlling the independent cinemas

These new movie moguls nonetheless feared that the large number of independent cinema owners could, by favouring non-Hollywood films, be a threat to their control of the industry. They used a few key business practices to tie these exhibitors into their product:

- **Block booking**. First, the major studios would insist independent cinema owners bought up to a year of the studios' films in advance.
- **Blind bidding**. The cinema owners were also not allowed to see any of the films before they bid for and bought them.
- **Run zone clearance system**. The major studios divided the United States up into zones that different studios would control in terms of distribution. They would decide when cinemas got the latest Hollywood films. In those days films would only be shown in a limited number of cinemas to maximise the audience for what was called the film's 'first run'. This usually lasted 4–6 weeks. To have a film for its first or second run was clearly an advantage for a cinema owner. But the independent cinema owners had to accept the right of the studios to have their films' first exhibition or 'run' in their own prestigious picture palaces. Exhibitors who readily agreed to these arrangements might then be granted second or even first 'run' status themselves by the studios.

As the studios formed an oligopoly they sold all their films together. For the exhibitors they had to choose to be in the system fully or not get any Hollywood films.

Stars and genre

It is in this context that we can see the very important function of genre and stars. Disgruntled by the obviously unfair arrangements with the studios, the independent exhibitors could be reassured that although they had not seen the films in advance, they would be gangster films or westerns or historical romances that audiences loved, and would star popular actors like James Cagney, Errol Flynn or Bette Davis. Star and genre here played a key economic role.

An assembly line production system

The studios were very carefully organised in production. As the only home entertainment was the radio, the cinema had become hugely popular and the studios needed to produce a large volume of films regularly to satisfy the demand for new film entertainment every week. The studios managed to produce around fifty films a year each, an astonishing one a week! Presumably they had a week off for Christmas and a summer holiday! In part they were able to do this because of the bright Mediterranean-type climate that southern California enjoys and also because of the wide variety of scenery that was easily accessible from Hollywood: the Pacific Ocean, the Rocky Mountains, and local farmland. However, the crucial reason for this amazing creative productivity was the organization of the studios themselves. Everyone, from the studio

analyse this   Look at the poster reproduced below. Can you identify the star and the genre easily from the poster?

chief and the stars to the cleaners, was on long-term contracts and knew exactly what was expected of them. Everyone's job was clearly defined and specialised and there was a clearly defined hierarchy so everyone knew who the boss was. Bosses, like Laemmle at Universal, or Irving Thalberg and Louis B. Mayer at MGM, planned a programme of films a year in advance. The Head Producer would allocate shooting schedules and assign art directors to design and construct sets. Directors could not be overly concerned with any one film; they might be working on several films at the same time and rarely edited their films. Some of the great directors of the era retained artistic control by filming only what was needed to tell the story. When the great western director, John Ford, handed over his footage to his editor he told him all he had to do was put the sequences in the right order and the film would be there.

Genre

Genre was of key importance too in enabling an efficiently run system. It was used as a guide for designers, make up artists and cinematographers to know what kind of 'look' they should be attempting to achieve for the film. In the same way the crew would use their knowledge of a star, like Bette Davis or Jimmy Cagney, to identify the style of film they would be making.

It also enabled the publicity and marketing departments of the studios to know what kind of artwork was needed for posters and other publicity materials.

Stars as workhorses

One group of people, however, hated the assembly line production system: the stars. In complete contrast to today where stars are in control and may make at most three or four films a year, in the studio era, they were expected to work long shifts day after day like everyone else. Stars like Errol Flynn and Bette Davis made hundreds of films for Warner Brothers. The stand-up arguments between the stars and a studio chief like Jack Warner were legendary. After one such argument Bette Davis decided to escape, and fled to England. She didn't return for several years. Jack Warner constantly frustrated Errol Flynn's desires to have more serious roles by putting him in action adventure films. Flynn said in his autobiography, *My Wicked, Wicked Ways*, that he had been happiest as an actor when he was part of a theatre company in Northampton in England because he got to play a whole range of roles!

The stars were usually on seven-year contracts. The key to the studios' control of them, however, was the suspension clause. This meant that if a star, from exhaustion or pique, refused to work, then they were 'suspended' by the studios and the days that they were suspended would simply be added on to their seven years. As Humphrey Bogart quipped about Warners, 'This studio has more suspensions than the Golden Gate Bridge'.

Unable to work legally for anyone else while suspended most stars did eventually toe the line. The studios' control of the stars began to disappear in 1945 when the star Olivia de Havilland won a case against Warner Brothers, claiming that the suspension clause was in breach of California state law. No one, star or garage attendant, could be forced to stay with one employer for longer than seven years.

A key question that would then seem to arise was how was it that the films were on average as good as they were? Many of the films are classics and their stars and directors recognised as wonderful creative artists. How could this be in such a rigid and hierarchical system? This is a fascinating question. Part of the answer seems to lie in two key concepts, what became known as the Institutional Mode of Representation, and the Classic Hollywood Narrative.

Classic Hollywood Narrative

The moguls understood that the key to making films that audiences would want to watch was a good story based around characters with clear goals and desires. The protagonist, or main character's, goals would usually be opposed to that of a villain and so conflict and drama would be created. Though characters' pursuit of their goals would enable the audience to identify with them, the characters did not need to be psychologically complex; more important was that the narrative would keep the audience interested. For this reason they insisted that all of the scenes of a film should move the story on. If you watch films from this era you will see that in every scene something happens, the plot develops.

Alfred Hitchcock, a British director, who made his greatest films in Hollywood, complained that many films in the 1960s and 1970s were not really films at all because they 'were just people talking'. Even today many Hollywood films, whether romantic comedies, thrillers, or action adventure films, still make sure every scene moves the story on and so, hopefully, keeps the audience interested.

Activity

Find a film from the studio era of the 1930s or 1940s (they are often on BBC2 or Channel 4 on weekday afternoons) and record it. Then go back and watch the first twenty minutes. List the scenes and identify the main character and their goals. Does the plot develop in each scene?

Institutional Mode of Representation

The development of the Classic Hollywood Narrative was also closely related to the Institutional Mode of Representation. This was essentially developing a style of film-making – and, in particular, editing – that would allow the audience to focus on the story. It was an attempt, if you like, to make the process of fitting the story together 'invisible'. Central to this process was the development of what became known as continuity editing. This had a few basic rules: the 180 degree rule, the match on action edit, the eyeline match and the graphic match. You will have learnt about these in more detail in the previous chapters covering FS1. What was most important was that it made the editing of the scenes 'invisible' so the audience would not be distracted from following the story. Incidentally this form of editing is so successful in doing this that it has become the 'natural' form of editing that almost all film-makers use.

Activity

Choose a scene from the studio era film you've been analysing and look at the editing. Can you identify the use of the techniques of continuity editing?

Warner Bros house style

Of the eight studios in Hollywood at this times, Warners was the seventh cheapest in terms of expenditure per film, yet the quality of their films was remarkably high. The modern-day director Martin Scorcese has partially explained this by the fact that directors made a very large number of films and so became very practised and skilled in their trade. As we have mentioned before, at their height the studios were producing about fifty films a year each. Almost one every week of the year! One of their main directors, Michael Curtiz, made over a hundred films during his time at Warners.

key terms

Verisimilitude a mise en scène that has to approximate closely enough to a real setting as to be credible, without paying too close attention to detail so that too much money is not spent on the sets!

The Warner brothers were also very skilled in thinking through how they could make their films distinctive but still keep costs down. Their solution was to adopt a style of mise en scène in many of their films which is known as **verisimilitude**. This may be a word you have come across in your English studies. As we have seen, all the basic techniques of constructing a film have as their goal to create in the mind of the audience a credible time and place.

This was another reason why it was very important to have a storyline that kept the audience guessing and involved. With sets limited in detail the studio learnt to make what it had dramatic and engaging by using light. Cinematographers became very skilled at using light and shadow to create atmosphere and emotion from a set that had perhaps already been used in a couple of other films! You might look at the scene where Jimmy Cagney is marched from his cell to the electric chair in the gangster film *Angels with Dirty Faces* made at Warner Bros in 1938. All the drama here is in the camera angles and the lighting.

Figure 5.3 ▶

Warners also knew that music was an area of film production that rewarded investment. So they employed perhaps the greatest of composers for film of the studio era, Max Steiner. Again, his deepening of the audiences' involvement in hundreds of movies meant his substantial salary was great value for money.

Warner Bros is, of course, still a major studio, and is part of the world's largest media company, Time Warner.

analyse this

Try to find a Warner Bros picture from the period. Classics like *Casablanca*, *The Maltese Falcon*, or *The Big Sleep* would be ideal. Identify how they show the imprint of Warners' studio style.

The long decline of the studio system

As we have seen, though very effective, the organisation of the industry was deeply unfair both for independent exhibitors and for film producers outside Hollywood. There was constant pressure for the government to intervene throughout the studio era. However, it was not until the Paramount decree in 1948 that the system was deemed illegal. Interestingly, it was their cinemas, the exhibition section of their vertically integrated companies, that the studios were told to sell. To this day although the studios own cinemas in Britain and elsewhere in the world, they don't in the US itself.

1946 was in one sense the studio system's greatest year. More people attended the cinema more often than they had ever done before. In the UK a third of the population went to the cinema at least once a week. And films made in that year, like *Mildred Pierce* and so many others, showed that Hollywood was still a creative powerhouse, responding in complex ways to changes in society as could be seen in the developments of new genres like *film noir*. Its decline, however, would be steep and lengthy.

There were a number of key developments that destroyed the power of the studio system. The most important, of course, was the Paramount decree which brought the system of vertical integration to an end. The studios were decreed to have too much control over the film market by owning all stages of the industry: production, distribution and exhibition. Through the court's finding against Paramount all the studios were put on notice that they would have to sell their cinemas.

Stars, for so long the keystones of the system and for that reason strictly controlled, were also using the courts to establish their independence. As we have already mentioned the Warner Brothers' star Olivia de Havilland had correctly identified that the suspension clause was the key to unpicking the studios' control of the stars through their contracts. The stars' rush to independence of the studios was also greatly increased when James Stewart appeared in a western, *Winchester '73* in 1950. Not a bad film, it is now remembered as the first occasion on which a star negotiated a percentage of the box office takings. The film was a success and other stars, like the highest-paid star of the time, Clark Gable, saw that from one film Stewart had earned almost as much as they had earned for an entire year on their studio contract. It is of course now common practice for stars to negotiate both a flat fee, and 'points' or percentages of the box office profits for any film they are involved in.

The other much broader social change was, of course, the arrival of television. Rare at the beginning of the 1950s, by the end of the decade TVs were in everyone's home, along with other means of home entertainment like the radio and the record player. Television was seen as the enemy and studio bosses came up with new technology, such as widescreen, and gimmicks, for example 3D glasses, to try and make television look dull and insipid. They even used 'sexy' stars like Marilyn

Monroe, knowing television was being carefully censored of anything that might 'corrupt' young minds. However, within a few short years the ritual of going to the cinema each week became a thing of the past and the attendance at cinemas continued to decline right through to its lowest point in the early 1970s. At this point there were echoes of the early days of cinema as the buildings themselves lacking investment were old and decaying, little better than the flea pits of the 1920s.

However, some new thinking, new talent and some happy accidents were about to lead to a renaissance for the film industry in general and Hollywood in particular.

questions Explain how stars and genres were crucial to making independent exhibitors accept the unfairness of the organisation of the industry in the studio era.

6 The development of the contemporary film industry

In this chapter we will introduce some of the main features of the modern-day organisation of the industry. We will identify who the key Hollywood companies are and make clear how they are part of huge corporations operating across the globe with very varied interests.

We will take up again our historical review of the development of the film industry from the previous chapter with Hollywood in the doldrums from the 1950s into the 1970s and show how by luck and smart business practices the industry found new ways to make money and increase returns on its major investments. We should by the end have a really clear idea of why Hollywood so effectively dominates the industry all over the world.

We will then spend some time reflecting on our own behaviour as film fans and how far we fit into the role the industry has in mind for us.

INTERNATIONAL BOX OFFICE WEEKEND SEPT 3-5

SEA INSIDE SUCCESS ON DIRECTOR'S HOME PATCH

Alejandro Amenabar's acclaimed *The Sea Inside* (*Mar Adentro*) got off to a superb international start in the director's home territory, Spain, at the weekend. The drama, which is in competition at the Venice film festival, sold nearly 450,000 tickets in the territory at the weekend for a $2.8m (€2.3m) gross that saw it claim 12th spot in the international table, the highest-placed non-US title. Warner Sogefilms distributes in Spain with Sogepaq handling international sales. Meanwhile, top-spot openings in the UK and Italy heralded the European debut of Steven Spielberg's *The Terminal*, which leapt up the chart in its second week, after a S Korean launch.

Rank	Last week	Film (origin)	3-day gross $	Screens	Cum $	Terrs
1	1	**The Village** (US)	$9,721,816	2,411	$45,218,358	23
2	2	**Garfield** (US)	$8,328,079	3,358	$77,743,856	38
3	19	**The Terminal** (US)	$6,898,562	958	$10,630,589	6
4	5	**The Chronicles of Riddick** (US)	$6,016,150	2,148	$45,671,291	23
5	*	**Van Helsing** (US)	$5,248,379	499	$161,591,106	3
6	4	**King Arthur** (US)	$5,229,387	2,982	$118,314,684	36
7	6	**Fahrenheit 9/11** (US)	$4,747,167	1,626	$75,283,199	26
8	3	**The Bourne Supremacy** (US)	$4,078,730	1,067	$33,392,153	13
9	10	**Shrek 2** (US)	$3,622,721	2,469	$439,894,889	28
10	7	**I, Robot** (US)	$3,378,850	2,559	$146,736,796	31
11	12	**Mean Girls** (US)	$2,907,105	1,009	$34,613,307	20
12	New	**The Sea Inside** (Mar Adentro) (Spain)	$2,795,480	329	$2,795,480	2
13	14	**Anacondas: Hunt For The Blood Orchid** (US)	$2,739,307	877	$7,205,097	10
14	13	**Nin X Nin Ninja Hattori-Kun** (Japan)	$2,603,472	251	$8,526,406	1
15	8	**Dodgeball: A True Underdog Story** (US)	$2,573,630	564	$10,567,004	3
16	28	**Home On The Range** (US)	$2,448,002	1,932	$32,551,612	23
17	25	**13 Going On 30** (US)	$2,404,977	1,269	$25,338,863	34
18	*	**Hellboy** (US)	$2,329,501	1,101	$21,520,841	26
19	11	**House Of Flying Daggers** (China)	$2,317,046	415	$34,320,983	4
20	20	**Alien Vs Predator** (US)	$2,068,558	852	$8,440,524	10
21	9	**Spider-Man 2** (US)	$1,857,994	1,757	$374,950,000	50
22	15	**Harry Potter And The Prisoner Of Azkaban** (US-UK)	$1,510,000	1,170	$524,750,000	36
23	21	**Stasky & Hutch** (US)	$1,303,427	327	$77,442,474	3
24	New	**A Family** (S Korea)	$1,207,625	184	$1,311,429	1
25	24	**R-Point** (S Korea)	$1,135,082	163	$7,546,197	1
26	New	**5x2** (France)	$1,130,622	235	$1,130,622	2
27	18	**Ils Se Marierent Et Eurent Beaucoup D'Enfants** (Fr)	$1,123,105	499	$4,138,106	3
28	17	**Catwoman** (US)	$1,088,000	1,500	$21,570,000	23
29	16	**(T)Raumschiff Surprise – Periode 1** (Germany)	$1,061,002	963	$72,742,005	3
30	22	**Naruto** (Japan)	$963,820	251	$10,394,639	1

*RE-ENTRY   ©SCREEN INTERNATIONAL, COMPILED BY LEONARD KLADY

Hollywood

'Hollywood' is the dominant force in today's film industry. A glance at the international box office returns for the weekend of 3–5 September 2004 makes that clear. No non-US film appears until number 12 and of the 30 top performing films, 20 are US productions and one is a US–UK co-production.

What is Hollywood? As the urban theorist, Mike Davis, has pointed out in his book on Los Angeles, *Ecology of Fear* (Picador, 1998), this is a deceptively difficult question. In fact the apparently even simpler question, where is Hollywood, is a very difficult question to answer. 'Hollywood', California, has different city and county boundaries and no film production takes place there and hasn't since the early 1930s. The core of the Hollywood district is now in fact one of the poorest areas in the United States, a hyper-violent slum, with income among the Salvadorean and Mexican immigrants who live there less than half the national average.

Two of the studios have responded to this social emergency by recreating Hollywood in Florida. Disney and Universal have rival theme parks there vying to give the authentic 'Hollywood' experience.

Of course, in another sense it is very easy for us to say what Hollywood is. It is those companies who we have just been discussing in the previous chapter who dominate global film production, distribution and exhibition.

Activity

Can you name the dominant Hollywood studios? Guess from the names that come up as you remember films starting at the cinema and you won't be far wrong.

They are Disney, Warner Brothers, Universal, Fox, Columbia and Paramount. With the exception of Disney – and Columbia, which was one of the smaller companies in the studio era – these companies should be familiar from the previous chapter and we can recollect how they controlled the global film industry in that era too. However, all of them, again with the exception of Disney, are now owned by far larger companies. A term we can use to describe these huge parent companies, which are often called conglomerates, is **transnational corporation** (TNC).

This has the advantage that it keeps us alert to the global nature of these companies and how, though they are largely US owned, their revenue, their interests, and, to some extent their ownership, is much more global than just the US.

> ### key terms
>
> **Transnational corporation**
> a global company made up of many smaller companies throughout the world in a range of different markets.

Who owns whom?

A question that then arises is who really in the end owns and controls the Hollywood studios.

Fox studios is owned by Rupert Murdoch's News International (Australian). This company is, of course, very important in the British media as News International owns *The Times*, the *Sun* and the *News of the World* newspapers, and is a major shareholder in the Sky satellite TV channel.

Universal is owned by General Electric, a US conglomerate who also own one of the major television networks, NBC.

Paramount is owned by Viacom, who also owns MTV, Nickelodeon, Blockbuster video stores, and Showcase Cinemas.

Warner Brothers is part of the world's largest media company Time Warner, about which we learn much more later in the chapter.

Disney, which includes Buena Vista, is itself a huge TNC, owning one of the largest independent film companies Miramax, as well as many toy stores, the famous Disneyland theme parks in California, Florida and Paris and television channels around the world.

Columbia Pictures is owned by the giant Japanese electronics company, Sony, suppliers of televisions, videos and other electrical goods. It is very likely that you have Sony products at home.

Less significant than it was in the studio era, but still an important player in Hollywood, is MGM. In September 2004 Sony of Japan and Comcast of the US paid US$5bn (£2.8bn) for MGM.

talking point

The films of these companies dominate cinemas all over the world. However, it is clear from our discussion above that film is just one of many products they produce and sell. Can you see any problem with this? Is a film just a product like any other, like a bottle of whisky or a DVD player?

Case Study   Time Warner

Now let's look in a bit of detail at just one of these companies, Time Warner. This is the largest media TNC in the world, and includes Warner Bros, Home Box Office, and New Line.

Time Warner Corporate Timeline

1890s
1898 – Henry Luce, son of an American missionary, is born in China

1910s
1918 – The four Warner brothers, Jack, Albert, Harry and Samuel, open their first West Coast studio

1920s
1921 – Luce and Yale classmate Briton Hadden begin working together as reporters for *The Baltimore News*
1923 – The four brothers' film distribution and production business is incorporated and called Warner Brothers Pictures Inc.
1923 – Luce and Hadden use the $86,000 they raised to release *Time* magazine. Hadden becomes editor while Luce serves as business manager
1927 – Warner Brothers Film Production releases the first 'talkie', Al Jolson's *The Jazz Singer*
1928 – First *Time* Man-of-the-Year features Charles Lindbergh
1929 – Hadden dies of a streptococcus infection. Luce takes over as *Time* editor

1930s
1930 – *Fortune* magazine is launched by Luce as part of Time Inc.
1931 – *March of Time* radio programme first airs
1934 – Luce launches *Architectural Forum*
1935 – *March of Time* runs its first newsreel
1936 – *Life* magazine is launched
1937 – Detective Comics (DC) is created
1938 – Ted Turner born in Cincinnati

1940s
1940 – Bugs Bunny appears for the first time in a Warner Brothers' short *A Wild Hare*
1942 – *March of Time* becomes straight news programme
1944 – Leon Schlesinger sells his cartoon studio (Looney Tunes) to Warner
1947 – Jack Warner testifies before House Committee on Un-American Activities
1948 – Warner Brothers sells film library to MGM. The Supreme Court's anti-trust Paramount Decree forces movie studios to divest themselves from owning cinemas

Continued

1950s

1950 – Elektra Records is founded by a college student, Jac Holzman

1952 – *House and Home* magazine launched. Time makes first investment in television industry by purchasing KOB-TV Albuquerque

1954 – *Sports Illustrated* is launched

1958 – Warner Bros. Records is founded. Label is later called WEA (Warner/Elektra/Atlantic)

1960s

1960 – Brown University expels Ted Turner

1961 – Time-Life Inc. is formed to be Time Inc.'s book division

1963 – Ted Turner's father Ed commits suicide because of financial difficulties. Ted takes over family's billboard business

1963 – Animation division at Warner closed. Frank Sinatra sells his Reprise record label to Warner Brothers

1967 – Henry Luce dies in Phoenix, Arizona

1967 – Seven Arts Ltd buys Warner Brothers for $84 million. Company becomes known as Warner-Seven-Arts. Warner-Seven-Arts purchases Atlantic Records

1967 – New Line Cinema formed

1967 – Kinney National Company, a funeral parlour conglomerate purchases D.C. Comics and All-American Comics. Kinney also buys Ashley Famous talent agency

1968 – Time-Life Inc. acquires Little, Brown and Company

1969 – Kinney National Company acquires Warner-Seven-Arts and in 1972 renames the company Warner Communications Inc.

1970s

1970 – Holzman sells his Elektra Records to Warner Communications

1970 – Turner purchases Atlanta UHF television station, WJRJ, renaming it WTCG (Turner Communications Group)

1972 – Time Inc. buys Home Box Office (HBO) from Charles Dolan. HBO transmits first programming to 365 subscribers in Wilkes-Barre, Pennsylvania. *Money* magazine launched

1974 – *People* magazine launched

1976 – Ted Turner purchases Major League Baseball's Atlanta Braves. Turner Broadcasting's WTCG becomes cable television's first Superstation as it is beamed via satellite to cable homes across the country

1976 – Video game pioneer Nolan Bushnell sells Atari to Warner Communications for $28 million

1977 – Turner Communications Group purchases the National Basketball Association's Atlanta Hawks. Turner wins yachting's Americas Cup

1978 – Warner Communications acquires cable operator American Television & Communications (ATC)

1979 – Turner Communications Group becomes Turner Broadcasting System, Inc. WTCG is renamed WTBS

1980s

1980 – The first 24-hour, all-news network, CNN, is launched with 1.7 million subscribers

1982 – Turner Broadcasting launches CNN Headline News and thwarts a takeover attempt by Westinghouse

1984 – Warner Communications sells most of its stake in Atari off to Jack Tramiel, deposed president of Commodore Computers

1986 – Time acquires Scott Foresman & Company book publishing unit

1986 – Turner Broadcasting buys MGM library of movies and television shows

1987 – Warner acquires Chappell Music

1988 – TNT cable network launched

1989 – Time Warner Inc. is formed after Time merges with Warner Communications

1989 – Publishing houses Scott Foresman and Little, Brown sold off to Harper Row

1990s

1990 – *Entertainment Weekly* is launched

1991 – The internet bulletin-board system Quantum Computer Services changes name to America Online. Steve Case is one of the company's founders

1991 – The Tribune Company receives a 9 per cent stake in AOL after making a $5 million investment in the company

1992 – Gerald Levin takes control of Time Warner after death of Steven J. Ross. New York 1 News launched

Continued

1992 – America Online becomes a publicly traded company
1992 – Turner Broadcasting launches Cartoon Network
1993 – Turner Broadcasting System merges with Castle Rock and New Line
1994 – AOL reaches 1 million subscribers
1994 – Turner Classic Movies is launched
1994 – Warner/Chappell Music becomes the world's largest music publisher after it acquires CPP/Belwin
1994 – *In Style* magazine is launched
1994 – Edgar Bronfman Jr.'s Seagram company acquires a 14.5 per cent stake in Time Warner
1995 – AOL launches services in Europe. AOL purchases WebCrawler
1995 – Time Warner acquires Houston Industries
1995 – WB network broadcast network is launched
1996 – Telecommunications Act of 1996. Time Warner acquires Turner Broadcasting System
1997 – Time Warner sells *American Lawyer* magazine to investment bankers Wasserstein Perella
1997 – AOL acquires CompuServe and ICQ
1998 – AOL acquires Netscape
1999 – AOL acquires Spinner, Winamp, SHOUTcast and DMS
1999 – Turner acquires a National Hockey League expansion franchise. The Atlanta Thrashers begin play in 1999

2000 – Present
2000 – AOL acquires MapQuest
2000 – Time Warner makes deal with Tribune Company for Times Mirror magazines that include *Golf*, *Ski*, *Skiing*, *Field & Stream*, and *Yachting*
2000 – AOL and Time Warner announce their $183 billion merger. The largest corporate merger in history is finalised in January of 2001. The world's largest media and entertainment company changes name to AOL Time Warner
2001 – AOL Time Warner acquires the United Kingdom's top magazine publisher, IPC Media, from Cinven for $1.67 billion.
2002 – AOL Time Warner buys out AT&T's stake in Time Warner Entertainment. AOL-Time Warner then creates its own cable operation while AT&T merged with Comcast
2003 – Steve Case steps down as AOL Time Warner chairman. Dick Parsons replaces Case. AOL Time Warner reports $54.24 billion quarterly loss. Company changes name back to Time Warner
2004 – Time Warner sells the Atlanta Hawks, Atlanta Thrashers, and Philips Arena to a local investment group
2004 – The Time Warner Center opens
2004 – Time Warner finalises deal to sell the WEA CD and DVD manufacturing division to Cinram International. The company agrees to sell Warner Music Group (including its record labels Warner Brothers, Atlantic, Elektra and music publishing division Warner Chappell) to private investor group led by Edgar Bronfman, Jr.

Look through the time line that is taken from the Columbia Journalism Review. It gives an outline of the historical development of the company. See if you can identify from it the company's range of interests.

Having identified the range of interests, compare it with this list that we have drawn up:

- 24 magazines including *Time, People* and *Sports Illustrated*.
- The second largest book publishing business in the world including Time Life Books
- Warner Music Group
- Warner Bros. film studio, which also produces many television programmes
- Majority interest in WB, a US television network, reaching 25 per cent of US television households

Continued

- New Line film production company
- Cinema chain owner with over 1000 screens outside the US
- Fifty per cent of DC comics including *Superman*, *Batman*, and others
- HBO, the largest pay cable channel in the world
- Cinemax pay cable channel
- Six Flags theme park chain
- Warner Bros movie world theme park in Germany
- Over 150 Warner Bros shops
- A library of over 6,000 films, 25,000 television programmes, books, music, and thousands of comics and cartoons
- The news channel CNN, The Cartoon Network, TBS and TNT
- 50 per cent stake in Comedy Central channel
- Also owns the Atlanta Braves professional sports teams

. . . and many others besides.

We now need to introduce a crucial term for understanding how the film industry operates alongside its sister companies, and plays a key role in linking them together. The term is synergy. This is a crucial term for understanding the modern media and the role of the film industry within it.

If we take the example of *Spider-Man*, we can see how the film would have been reviewed and advertised in the company's magazines, for example *Time*, as well as on their television channels, like WB network. It would have been heavily promoted in the company's own Warner Village cinemas globally. They would also have issued the soundtrack on their Warner Bros label and the book of the making of the film in their own publishing company. *Spider-Man* would also become an attraction at the theme park in Germany. The video and DVD of the film, along with other Spider-Man merchandise, would be on sale in the 150 Warner Bros shops. So a synergy is created across the transnational corporation minimising costs and maximising income with the movie launch as the flagship around which many other products can be sold.

We will look at this in a lot more detail in relation to *Charlie's Angels: Full Throttle* in Chapter 7.

key terms

Synergy
the way in which a single product, such as a film, can be used across a whole range of the company's interests to generate profit.

Activity

Find out about the range of companies that fall under one of the TNCs we have been looking at: General Electric, Viacom, Disney, Sony or News International. This can quite easily be done by going to the company's website and choosing the corporate link.

The birth of the New Hollywood

We will now take up again our story of the development of the contemporary film industry.

The arrival of television in the early 1950s and the Paramount decree of 1948 forcing the studios to sell their cinema chains had led to a slow decline in the popularity of the cinema in the 1950s, 1960s and into the early 1970s.

Note, however, as we have just been discussing above, how the studios have become vertically integrated again, outside of the US, with Warners owning over a thousand screens worldwide.

talking point

Some of the key figures in the rebirth of Hollywood in the 1970s were film directors. You will undoubtedly have heard of at least two of them, George Lucas and Steven Spielberg; the other, Francis Ford Coppola, you may not have heard of. Discuss what very famous films you associate with these directors.

analyse this

To appreciate the radical transformation of the whole industry that these directors ushered in, we only have to remember the main features of the studio era – block booking, blind bidding and the run zone clearance system.

Can you remember what these key terms mean? If you can't, go back and check them in the last chapter.

At the end of the 1960s Hollywood and the major studios were, as we have seen, in disarray. Unsuccessful in their attempts to compete with television, the studios had little overall strategy to improve their situation and cinema audiences were still declining. By the late 1950s over half of their film projects were given out to independent production companies. By the mid-1960s they had begun to co-operate with and merge with television companies. However, they still had no clear idea how to keep cinema popular and arrest its long-term decline.

The Godfather **and a new form of cinema exhibition**

Crucially, although television had clearly replaced the cinema as people's staple entertainment, films were still released into cinemas in much the same way that they had been in the studio era; that is, using the run zone clearance system.

The kind of mass exhibition that is so successful today was discovered quite by accident in 1972. Francis Ford Coppola was working on his most famous film, *The Godfather* (see pages 19–20, 40, 79). He had gone well over his production budget. Reports filtering back to the studio bosses, Paramount, were also that the shooting and then the editing were not going well. The studios feared they had a 'turkey' on their hands that would flop terribly in the cinemas and leave them with lots of bad publicity. At the test screenings the exhibitors were unhappy at the film's length, just short of three hours. This would mean no possibility of two showings in an evening, reducing their profits. The studio executives at Paramount, who had funded the film, insisted that they should open the film more widely than usual, abandoning the first run system, to compensate for the length of the picture. This was a tactic that was occasionally used by the studios at this time in the hope of bringing in a larger amount of income through the box office in the first few days before word of mouth from audiences might 'kill' the film.

The film opened in New York on five screens and nationally in 316 cinemas with staggered starting times. With its mould-breaking cinematography by Gordon Willis and extraordinary performances by Marlon Brando and Al Pacino, audiences loved it.

By mid-April the film was bringing in $1 million a day. It had become the highest-grossing film of all time by mid-September. The ability of this form of mass releasing of a film to generate huge profits in a very short period had been clearly demonstrated. The run zone clearance system might have generated income from cinemas over a longer period but never in such huge amounts. Studio executives as we shall see were soon to discover other ways to extend the 'life cycle' of their films.

The film had pointed the way to the future for the film industry in terms of exhibition. And the logic of this release pattern would ultimately lead to the mass or 'saturation' release pattern that is made possible by our modern type of cinema, the multiplex.

Activity

Look at the listings page reproduced here. Count up the number of screenings that are now available of the same major film releases on any individual day.

Would it be true to say that there are many more screens than there is choice of films to see?

Are multiplexes really about providing choice?

Continued

Jaws, television and how a film can become an 'event'

A second key element in the birth of what has become known as 'New Hollywood' was the realisation that other media, and television in particular, did not need to be seen as the enemy, but could be used to create publicity for a film and a sense that you *must* see this film. The first 'event' movie, in this sense, although it wasn't called that at the time, was Steven Spielberg's 'breakthrough' film, *Jaws*.

In 1973 two producers at Universal studios, Richard Zanuck and David Brown, paid $175,000 for the rights to film Peter Benchley's novel *Jaws*. Steven Spielberg, at this time, couldn't get his idea for a film about visiting aliens off the ground. This would later become *Close Encounters of the Third Kind*. He read a rough draft of the *Jaws* script and asked if he could do it. Like *The Godfather* before it and *Star Wars* after it, it became a story of conflict with studio bosses, and during filming, apparent impending disaster.

The studio, Universal, that was financing the film initially tried to put Charlton Heston into a starring role but Spielberg resisted this as he said, 'I wanted somewhat anonymous actors to be in it so you would believe this was happening to you and me. Stars bring in a lot of memories with them and those memories can sometimes, especially in the first ten minutes of a movie, corrupt the story.'

The central role was refused three times by Richard Dreyfuss, but eventually, he says, 'I went with the fish movie. We started the film without a script, without a cast, and without a shark'.

The film's projected budget was $3.5 million. The mechanical sharks wouldn't work properly. One of the three sank. The original 55-day schedule became 159 days and the final budget overran by over $7 million. Known by the crew as 'Flaws' the disastrous shoot was becoming notorious all over Hollywood. As the producer, David Brown, put it, 'Everywhere we went, people treated us with sympathy, like we had some kind of illness.'

When it came to editing, the shots of the shark looked silly. So Spielberg carefully crafted the film to emphasise the tension and fear of the characters and it worked. The preview screenings indicated that despite all the setbacks they might well have a hit.

However, it was in the marketing strategy and in the key role that was played in this by television that *Jaws* showed the way forward for the film industry.

Remember that at this point television was still regarded as the enemy of the film industry, draining their audiences and their profits. However, Columbia had recently begun to experiment with television advertising of their films. First of all they did this locally with a film called *The Golden Voyage of Sinbad* and then nationally with a prison picture called *Breakout*. In both cases the audiences and revenue increased dramatically.

For *Jaws* Universal decided to spend over $700,000 on half-minute advertisements in prime time television shows. A 'buzz' was created around the film so that people felt they had to go to see it.

Taking their lead from *The Godfather's* exhibition success Universal released *Jaws* at over 400 theatres. With Michael Balhaus's extraordinary handheld camerawork, John Williams' hyper-tense soundtrack, and Spielberg's and Verna Field's masterful editing the film was a huge hit with audiences. Again, like *The Godfather*, the film became the biggest grossing film of all time bringing in $129 million. The film's budget of $10 million, and overrun of $7 million, did not seem so important now. It held this record for two years until the arrival of the third of the great triumvirate of films that revolutionised the film industry, *Star Wars*. The shark had transformed Hollywood.

Figure 6.1 ▶

Source: The quotations above from Steven Spielberg, Richard Dreyfuss and David Brown are taken from *Easy Riders, Raging Bulls: How the Sex, Drugs and Rock 'n' Roll Generation Saved Hollywood* by Peter Biskind (Bloomsbury, 1998).

Stars Wars, **special effects and merchandising**

Although Universal had skilfully used *Jaws* to promote merchandising tie-ins, like t-shirts, soundtrack albums and the 'Jaws Log' a book about the making of the film, it was really *Star Wars* that showed how merchandising could be an even greater money spinner than the film itself.

Based on spectacular profits from the film and the selling of ancillary rights, *Star Wars*, with its prominent special effects, was a blockbuster as we now understand the term. And indeed the formula continues to work with the series now in its second trilogy, the most recent release being *Epsiode II Attack of the Clones*.

Like Coppola and Spielberg, from the beginning of his career the *Star Wars* director George Lucas found himself at odds with the studios. Working under his mentor, Francis Ford Coppola, at his independent company, Zoetrope, his first – experimental – film, *Electron Labyrinth: THX-1138:4EB* had unsympathetic characters but was innovative and exciting in its use of sound and setting. Warner Brothers, the film's distributors, hated it, demanded their money back and effectively closed Zoetrope down.

Chastened by this experience, Lucas was determined that his next film, *American Graffiti*, which was released in 1973, would show the studios he could write sympathetic characters and make a straightforwardly popular movie. What he discovered was that he understood audiences much better than the studio executives did. Filmed in just 28 days for only $780,000, test audiences loved the film, but studio executives didn't and threatened to send the film straight to television without giving it a showing in cinemas. Coppola offered to buy his friend's film from them, and at this the executives relented, agreeing to a theatrical release but with little promotion, and further humiliating Lucas by cutting four and a half minutes. It became a huge hit through word of mouth and grossed more than $100 million.

Negotiating the deal for Star Wars

It was within this context of conflict with studio executives that Lucas attempted to get his idea for *Star Wars* financed. Even though *American Graffiti* had been so profitable Lucas's ideas were rejected by three studio chiefs before an executive at Twentieth Century Fox, Alan Ladd Jr, agreed to support the idea with a budget set at $3.5 million. Lucas knew this would not be enough but was afraid of frightening Ladd off by a more reliable estimate of the cost. He agreed with Fox studios that he would be paid $15,000 to develop a script, $50,000 to write it and $100,000 to direct the film. As the profits from *American Graffiti* racked up Lucas felt confident enough to renegotiate his deal for *Star Wars*. He was offered a big increase in his flat fees for direction to $500,000 but waived this to get included a clause that he should retain the ownership of the soundtrack, the sequel rights and, most importantly, the right to license merchandising from the film. The studio agreed, not considering this clause important!

Star Wars and merchandising

As I'm sure you know from your own childhoods *Star Wars* dolls and games and toys can be found in any toy shop in the country. Lucas had always conceived *Star Wars* as a mythology, a whole universe of characters, events and stories that could expand and grow over time, just like the comic books that he read as a child, or the Saturday morning cinema serials such as *Flash Gordon* that he had watched. The films would be central to the 'universe' but would not exhaust it. The characters could also appear in novels, comic books, on CDs, or latterly, of course, in computer games. A visit to the online official *Star Wars* shop shows hundreds of products for sale, video games, action figures, Lego, mugs, magnets, lunch boxes, cards, collectible figures, masks, watches, helmets, even limited-edition hand-painted art work. The breadth of this merchandising does not, however, mean Lucas does not monitor closely what is produced. When the book publishers Bantam wanted to do the background story of Yoda, Lucas refused as he felt this might detract from the mystery surrounding the character. Income from *Star Wars* merchandising is estimated in billions of dollars. On May 19, 2005 *Revenge of the Sith* opened at theatres all around the world to record box-office grosses. Lucasfilm executives have predicted 'Episode

III' will generate $1.5 billion in merchandise sales vs. $1.2 billion for 'Episode II' and $2 billion for 'Episode I.'

Lucas's retaining of the rights to sequels and re-releases has also proved financially astute. In 1977 *Star Wars* opened on 43 screens and grossed $1.6 million. The digital re-release in 1997 opened on 2100 screens and grossed $35.9 million.

Lucas's personal wealth is estimated to be around $2 billion. No distribution company would ever make the mistake of giving up merchandising rights again! Companies indeed now partially judge whether to fund a film or not on the basis of how much merchandising revenue it might generate. Spielberg's *Jurassic Park* generated several hundred licensing agreements for merchandising.

talking point

Do some research among your friends and your parents to find out if they have ever had any *Star Wars* merchandising. The examiners are keen on your personal experience and behaviour as a film fan.

Lucas and special effects

Lucas has used his fortune, among many other things, to pay for the most technically advanced special effects studio in the world, 'Industrial Light and Magic', whose first project was the first *Star Wars* movie. For many critics the priority that *Stars Wars* gave to dramatic visual spectacle over complex character and narrative has given rise to two decades of blockbusters whose basic reason for existing is their new, even more dramatic special effects. Industrial Light and Magic has, indeed, been directly involved in many recent blockbusters being employed to create special effects for many of these films such as *Master and Commander, The Day after Tomorrow, Van Helsing*, and *Terminator 3*.

talking point

Can films be ruined by too great an emphasis on special effects?
Can you think of any examples?
Have you ever come across films, perhaps on video or DVD, that didn't really use special effects but were still very effective?

Summary

Having reviewed the role of *The Godfather, Jaws* and *Star Wars* in establishing key elements of the contemporary industry, such as saturation release patterns for the exhibition of blockbusters; extensive marketing through a 'blitz' in many media including television; merchandising and special effects we are almost at the point of switching our attention to our own behaviour as film consumers, but first let's remind ourselves that film today means more than just the cinema.

The contemporary film industry and ancillary rights

The revolution in business practices in the film industry that began in the 1970s has been driven since the development of videocassette recorders in the 1980s by new technology. Film-makers and distributors now know that there are many more means of 'exhibiting' films today than just the cinema.

Remembering that the total average cost, including marketing, for making a Hollywood movie has now gone beyond $100 million, for the first time we can see that today distribution is as much, if not more, concerned with making profit from the selling of films to be shown on

- video and DVD, both sale and rental
- subscription satellite and cable channels
- terrestrial network television channels
- and syndicated television

as it is with cinemas.

Network television in the US is made up of the four national broadcasters – ABC, CBS, NBC and FOX TV. Syndication is the selling of the rights to the hundreds of city- and state-wide television stations that exist across the US. This latter can generate very large revenue. The Hollywood studios will look to cover their costs for making a film in sales at the US box office; after that all other sales are essentially additional profit, or 'clear blue sky', as it is sometimes referred to. For some smaller producers cinema exhibition's primary purpose is to generate interest so profit can be made from higher charges for these ancillary rights.

Activity

Represent this sequence of distribution via different media as a flow chart, beginning with cinema exhibition and making the distinction between rental and outright purchase of DVD and video.

In a later unit we shall look in detail at the exhibition strategy for a blockbuster or event movie and for a smaller independent film.

analyse this

In the week of writing, at the end of September 2004, we can see Hollywood's saturation release pattern and mass marketing campaigns dominating in both the US and Britain.

Use the tables and the comments from *The Guardian*'s film critic to discuss to what extent the week's results reinforce the ideas about Hollywood's power that we've been considering

Collateral starts at the top. It did the same in the US, but lasted for only one week. The movie, which stars Tom Cruise, has had a chequered history, with Russell Crowe considered for the lead role later offered to Edward Norton and Colin Farrell, and Adam Sandler and Robert de Niro – well, he's proved he can play taxi drivers – touted for Jamie Foxx's part. Frank Darabont wrote an early version of the script and Steven Spielberg, Martin Scorsese and Spike Lee all had the opportunity to direct before Michael Mann came on board. **Trauma**, with Colin Firth, is the only other new film to make a mark, but starts at a disappointing no 13, while **Garfield**, back at 10, has lasted longest.

Jude Law gets the title role in **Sky Captain and the World of Tomorrow**, a writer-director debut for Kerry Conran, which also features Gwyneth Paltrow and Angelina Jolie, financed, allegedly, on the back of Conran's six-minute short. **Mr 3000**, at 2, has nothing to do with OutKast's Andre 3000, but is about an old baseball player who comes out of retirement in a bid to reach 3,000 hits. It stars Bernie Mac and sounds like a straight-to-video release here. At 4 is **Wimbledon**, the latest in a long line of dithery-Brit-bloke-meets-sparky-American-gal rom-coms. Sadly, it takes the big screen to give a bloke a chance of winning our own tournament – game, set and mismatch.

Top 10 UK films

	Last week		Weeks	Screens Sep 17 – 19	Gross Sep 17 – 19	Total gross
1	(–)	**Collateral** Dir: Michael Mann	new	450	£2.23m	£2.23m
2	(1)	**Open Water** Dir: Chris Kentis	2	382	£878,421	£3.40m
3	(2)	**The Terminal** Dir: Steven Spielberg	3	422	£774,331	£4.69m
4	(3)	**Dodgeball: A True Underdog Story** Dir: Rawson Marshall Thurber	4	322	£770,168	£7.86m
5	(4)	**Hellboy** Dir: Guillermo del Toro	3	326	£345,439	£2.72m
6	(5)	**Anchorman** Dir: Adam McKay	2	288	£331,928	£1.17m
7	(6)	**The Bourne Supremacy** Dir: Paul Greengrass	6	228	£275,318	£11.10m
8	(7)	**The Village** Dir: M Night Shyamalan	5	252	£258,398	£9.98m
9	(10)	**A Cinderella Story** Dir: Mark Rosman	5	274	£207,384	£3.34m
10	(14)	**Garfield** Dir: Peter Hewitt	8	368	£191,274	£8.96m

Top 10 US films						
	Last week		Weeks	Screens Sep 17 – 19	Gross Sep 17 – 19	Total gross
1	(–)	**Sky Captain and the World of Tomorrow** Dir: Kerry Conran	new	3,170	$15.58m	$15.58m
2	(–)	**Mr 3000** Dir: Charles Stone III	new	2,736	$8.67m	$8.67m
3	(–)	**Resident Evil: Apocalypse** Dir: Alexander Witt	2	3,284	$8.65m	$37.03m
4	(–)	**Wimbledon** Dir: Richard Loncraine	new	2,034	$7.11m	$7.11m
5	(2)	**Cellular** Dir: David R Ellis	2	2,749	$6.79m	$19.70m
6	(3)	**Without a Paddle** Dir: Steven Brill	5	2,610	$3.63m	$50.32m
7	(4)	**Hero** Dir: Zhang Yimou	4	1,926	$2.83m	$46.09m
8	(10)	**Napoleon Dynamite** Dir: Jared Hess	15	1,024	$2.28m	$33.34m
9	(8)	**Collateral** Dir: Michael Mann	7	1,605	$2.26m	$95.97m
10	(5)	**The Princess Diaries 2: Royal Engagement** Dir: Garry Marshall	6	1,902	$1.94m	$91.89m

The modern cinema audience: a self-portrait

How do you fit into all of this and the industry's plans?

Having looked at how films, and the film industry, have become very skilled at getting us to know about and see their films, we also need to reflect upon how we individually fit into the audience.

questions

Try to answer the following questions.

The cinema

Are you a keen cinema-goer, going at least once a month?
Are you a regular/average cinema-goer, going three or four times a year?
Do you go, but infrequently, once or twice a year?
Do you never go?

DVD/Video

Do you watch films first by renting or buying the DVD/video?
Will you buy films you've particularly enjoyed on DVD/video?
Do you have a collection of DVD/videos?

Would you buy special editions or directors' cuts editions on DVD/video?

How many DVDs/videos will you buy/rent in a week?

Film on television

Do you have specialist film channels at home, like Film Four, or Sky Box Office?

Will you just watch films when they have their terrestrial premieres on BBC or ITV?

How many films a week do you watch on television?

Merchandising

Have you ever bought any spin-offs from a film, like a soundtrack album, or toys?

Do you have any film or star posters?

Film magazines/newspapers

Do you read any film magazines, like *Total Film*, *Premiere*, or *Sight and Sound?*

Have you ever bought a magazine/newspaper to read about a specific film star or film?

Internet

Have you ever visited official websites or fansites for any films or stars that you like?

Have you ever contributed to a fan's website?

Activity

Choose an event movie forthcoming in the next few months. New movies usually have websites up even before they have finished shooting. Identify all the different ways the visitor to the website is being invited to be involved in the film and its spin-offs.

We shall look at what it means to be a film fan in Chapter 10 when we look in some detail at stars.

Further resources

The story of how Hollywood discovered a new way of both exhibiting and making money from films is a fascinating story, at least at first, of chance and experiment. The full story can be found in Peter Biskind's award-winning book *Easy Riders, Raging Bulls: How the Sex, Drugs and Rock 'n' Roll Generation Saved Hollywood* (Bloomsbury, 1998). Don't believe everything you read in it though. Steven Spielberg said there wasn't one word of truth about him in it! You might also try Steve Neale and Murray Smith's *Contemporary Hollywood Cinema* (Routledge, 1998).

Film production

In this chapter we will look at the different stages of a film's production and explain who the key people are in getting a film made. We will identify the elements that a film must contain to be attractive to film financiers. To do this we will look in some detail at the film *Charlie's Angels: Full Throttle*. We will also look at film production in Britain, sources of finance for British film, and we will study a low-budget British film production company, Vertigo Films.

Pre-production, production and post-production

The production stage of making a film has three distinct parts, as you will probably recall from Chapter 5. The first of these is pre-production, when the idea for the film is developed and the cast and crew found and financing put in place. Production is the actual shooting of the film. Post-production is the editing of the footage, the addition of sound as required, including any original music, and the addition of special and computer-generated effects.

Let's look at pre-production first.

Difficulties in getting a film made

First of all we need to get a sense of how difficult it is actually to get a film made and released.

If you've produced a good script or play or novel that might successfully be made into a film, then the first step is to get a film company or producer interested. If you achieve this then a company may buy, or option, as it is often called, the right to make the script into a film. This may be lucrative but does not mean the film will get made. Film companies option many more scripts than they ever make. Once it is optioned it can take as long as seven years before it is sold to someone else who might actually make the film. The largest source of funding in Britain, the Film Council, who allocate government funding, have a specific fund to support film development. *Screen International*, a film industry magazine, has recently revealed that the conversion ratio, that is the number of scripts supported by development funding that make it into production, is very low. In fact 73 per cent of the companies that had received single project development funding since the fund was set up had failed to make a single film (cited in *Sight and Sound*, September 2004, p. 4).

Once your film has been made, however, you will be disappointed to hear it is more likely than not that it won't be released. Companies produce more films than they, or a distributor, think worthy of the additional costs of prints, advertising and promotion. Most likely the film will join the many other thousands of films that simply remain on the shelves.

The making of any film, however, begins with the story.

The story

In considering the economics and business aspects of the industry it is easy to forget that the single most important element to the success of a film is a good story. Judging by the number of truly terrible films made out there, people in the industry forget this too.

On the other hand, in 1999 the major Hollywood studio Sony, owners of Columbia Pictures, showed how highly they valued writers and the need for good stories by putting 31 A-list Hollywood writers on a special deal whereby they were committed to writing at least one script offered to them by Sony over four years. They were allowed to refuse up to four proposed projects. In return the writer would get two per cent of the film's box office gross receipts after the studio had got back their costs. The writer of the first *Spider-Man* movie, David Koepp, is believed to have made over $19 million out of this deal. Perhaps Sony were not that happy with the writer making that large an amount of money though, as none of the four writers who have written *Spider-Man 2* are on that deal.

talking point

Good stories can come from all kinds of different sources. Have you, your family or friends had any experiences that you have thought would make a good film? Why? Have you read any books that you thought would make a good film? Again what qualities did the story have that you thought would make it a good film?

Don't forget that there is a creative element to your first AS unit so you will need to come up with at least one good story before the end of the course.

Writers, then, are the creative heart of a film – without them a decent film will not be made. However, they are not the most important person involved in actually getting a film made. That role goes to the producer.

The producer

Film producers operate in different ways but essentially they have the responsibility of overseeing the progress of a film from script through to the handing over of the completed film to the distribution company within the budget they have raised to pay for the film's production. They hire the cast and the crew. They organise the financing and they will liaise with the distribution company over the dates for the marketing, promotion and eventual release of the film. In broad terms the director will be in charge on location, or in the studio but the producer is in overall charge of the whole production. It is easy to see how crucial the relationship is between the director and the producer.

The producer needs to have a number of qualities. They must be astute in business terms, have a sound understanding of basic legal arrangements and responsibilities and have enough sensitivity to encourage and support the creative people, the writers, directors and actors on whom the success of the film depends.

Blockbusters of course may also have other producers responsible for specific aspects of the production such as marketing or special effects. *Spider-Man 2*, for example, has two producers, one co-producer, and three executive producers.

Working with the director and/or the scriptwriter, the producer will put together a **film package** to try to get financial backing for the project.

To get a 'star' name attached to a project will make a huge difference in getting a film financed. Quentin Tarantino, a first-time director, was struggling to get backing for his *Reservoir Dogs* script until the established Hollywood actor, Harvey Keitel, read the script and took on the role of executive producer. The talent list will include the lead actor and actress, the director, the writer, and perhaps the cinematographer/ director of photography. The full script may or may not be included in the film package.

The treatment

A brief treatment for *Gladiator* may well have run something like this.

> 'This is a story of the heroic Roman General, Maximus. Having secured a final victory for his emperor, Augustus, in Germania, he yearns only to be freed by him so he might return to his farm in Spain. His dying emperor, however, imposes one last duty on him, to save the Empire from his son, Commodus, and see the Empire declared a Republic again. After Augustus's death, however, he is betrayed by his comrade Quintus and he cannot prevent either Commodus assuming the throne or his own family being slaughtered and, despairing, he is captured and is sold into slavery. Only by succeeding as a gladiator can he return to Rome and have the opportunity for revenge.
>
> Ridley Scott, acclaimed director of *Alien*, will direct, and the lead will be played by Russell Crowe (*LA Confidential*), a male screen idol in the traditional heroic mode. Screen legends Richard Harris (*Harry Potter*) and Oliver Reed will also be seen in the film. Young star Joaquin Phoenix will play the villain Commodus . . .'

PRODUCERS AND AUDIENCES (FS2)

Activity

Try to write a similar (brief) treatment for a film you have seen and enjoyed recently. Identify what would have been the main and most appealing elements of the plot and of the casting for any possible financiers.

Reducing the risk

We must not forget, however, what we have already learnt about the modern film industry and how hard the major studios work to reduce the risk in film-making. We remember from our reading in Chapter 5 that Hollywood has taken a huge leap forward in eliminating risk by the much greater number of distribution windows and opportunities for merchandising that can generate additional income beyond the theatrical exhibition of the film itself.

When someone has an idea for a film for a major Hollywood studio, they and the producer will convert it into a package made up of individual elements that will appeal to a wide audience, but they will also want to create confidence in the studio executives that their film presents lots of opportunities to generate profit using the *synergy* that a major distribution company within a transnational corporation has. We will now look at an example.

Case Study   **Sony Corporation's** Charlie's Angels: Full Throttle

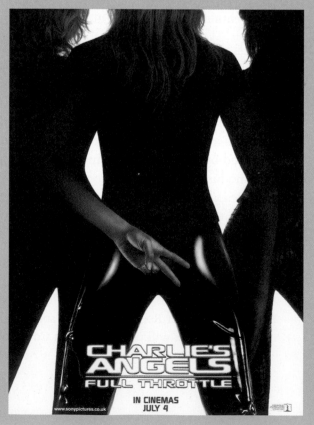

Continued

A fine example of such a modern day major studio package was *Charlie's Angels: Full Throttle* made in 2003. There were many reasons why the studio, Columbia-Tristar, part of the Sony Corporation, felt that the risk of investing the $120 million that it cost to make the film would be worth it.

1   Like many other successful films of recent years it was *a sequel* to the highly successful first *Charlie's Angels* film released in November 2000 which grossed, that is, brought in in ticket sales at the box office, $125 million in the US alone.

talking point

How many other examples can you think of, of successful films that have become what are sometimes called franchises, spawning one or more sequels?

2   It was also based on characters that had previously been successful in *another media form*, specifically, the *Charlie's Angels* television series of the 1970s. This was useful as a means of attracting the older, middle-aged, generation, who would remember the original series and wonder how this new dramatisation would differ. They were also catered for in the return to the screen of the 41-year-old former A league star, Demi Moore, as a former Angel gone bad.

talking point

Hollywood today is highly derivative, finding its storylines and characters in books or comics or television series, or remaking older films. How many other examples of these types of films can you think of?

3   *The film's director*, McG, had made his reputation as a music video producer and director and his highly energetic dynamic filming and editing style would successfully appeal to the core 16–24-year-old target audience for the film.
4   *The films' stars*:
   - Cameron Diaz, repeatedly voted one of the sexiest women on the planet in various 'lads' magazines, but also having some reputation as a comic actress after her role in the hit film directed by the Farrelly brothers, *Something about Mary*.
   - Lucy Liu, a fast-rising star, formerly in the television series *Ally McBeal*, again attractive to young men and women and appealing to Asian and Far Eastern audiences.
   - Drew Barrymore, a former teen star, her on-screen role in *Charlie's Angels*, ironically, reflected her feisty off-screen image, including having overcome adolescent drug addiction. Through

▶

Continued

her Flower Production company she was also an Executive Producer on the film which may in part have contributed to a more *female-friendly* approach to the overall feel of the film. For example, though there is lots of highly choreographed violence, there are no guns used in the film. It was her company, incidentally, that produced the cult hit film *Donnie Darko*.

talking point

Lucy Liu described the film in the following way:

'I think the movie touches upon the idea that women can be feminine and also be capable and strong, not only physically but mentally, and I think that balance is clear'.

Source: Interview with Lucy Liu, actress, talking about her role in the *Charlie's Angels* sequel, *Charlie's Angels: Full Throttle*, Todd Gilchrist, www.filmstew.com

The character of Ripley, played by Sigourney Weaver in the *Alien* movies is often seen as having been the first really physically powerful, aggressive, violent female character in modern film history. There have been many examples since, such as Trinity in *The Matrix* or Lara Croft in *Tomb Raider*. Do you agree and is this a good thing? For girls and for boys?

- Bernie Mac, the new Bosley, replacing Bill Murray, and with a previously successful career in his own show on television, was used to appeal to the black audience, an important element in cinema-going in the US who visit the cinema significantly more often than the white audience.

5 *The film's writers*. The writer of the successful original film, John August, was joined by Cormac and Marianne Wibberley who had created the *I Spy* series.

6 *The soundtrack album*. The presence of McG and the highly prominent use of music in the film made the release of a soundtrack album a highly marketable proposition. The film contains almost 40 soundtrack songs. There was a special cameo appearance in the film by Pink, and her video was included as one of the additional features on the DVD.

7 *The DVD*, which also included a soundtrack marketing jukebox. The soundtrack featured Sony artists such as David Bowie. Different versions of the film were also released on DVD with an uncut version attempting to appeal to the older generation and a more male audience.

Sony could also use the film to promote the products of other parts of their business. This is often known as *product placement*. So, for example, in the film the Angels were shown using the new T616 Mobile phone produced by Sony Ericsson and this was used as part of the launch of the phone into that market.

Continued

The success of the film

In the event, when the film opened it brought in $38 million in just three days in the US, showing on a massive 3,049 sites; a fine example of a saturation exhibition release pattern. By its 24th day of release it had passed the $100 million mark, showing on 6,140 screens in 56 territories. A true blockbuster!

Remember, though, that in general terms a film has to make *two and a half times* its cost at the box office before it goes into profit. Costing $120 million, *Charlie's Angels: Full Throttle* would need to take $300 million before going into profit. Given the opening figures above, Columbia would be confident of achieving this. They would also be confident of extensive profits from merchandising and the selling of the film in other formats.

Activity

The film package simulation

Imagine you are the head of a film production company and wish to approach Sony for funding. Look at the list of Sony's interests in the USA:

Sony Pictures Entertainment comprising

- Columbia Tristar
- Columbia Pictures, producers of big-budget films like *Charlie's Angels* and *Spider-Man 2*
- Sony Pictures Classic, distributor of European and American independent films like Pedro Almodovar's *All about my Mother*
- Screen Gems, producers and distributors of medium budget films

Digital Studios Division

- Sony Pictures Studios
- Columbia Tristar Home Entertainment (DVD/Video distributor)
- Sony Pictures Television Group
- Sony Pictures Digital Entertainment
- Game Show Network (interactive television)
- Movelink

Sony Music Entertainment comprising

- Own labels such as Columbia and Epic
- Artists including Aerosmith, Destiny's Child

Sony Computer Entertainment

- Produces Playstations and products for Playstation

Sony Electronics

- Products including televisions, video players, videos, DVDs and computer disks

Devise your own film package, a detailed proposal, but not more than one side of A4 in which you put together a basic plot outline, with stars, director, genre, target audience (remembering that the core cinema-going audience is 18–24 year olds) and opportunities to generate merchandising and other spin-offs. Explain why you think each element would effectively target its audience and why it should generate a lot of profit for Sony.

Film production in the UK

Let's now look in a bit more detail at British film production.

As we have just seen, the films that dominate in our cinemas are hugely expensive and complex projects. As you might expect, although the specific arrangements for financing a film are very varied it is very unusual for films in Britain to have just one source of finance. Most British films are collaborations between several sources of film financing. They can include government support through the Film Council, a distributor, a broadcaster such as the BBC, and an **equity investor**.

The distributor will have the right to release the film in the cinema and on video/DVD in certain countries or, as they are sometimes called, territories. The broadcaster will obviously have the right to broadcast the film on television in their own country. These financing deals can become extremely complicated and it is for this reason that film festivals, such as Venice, or Berlin are so busy. It is an ideal opportunity to get deals organised.

British film production can really be seen at three levels. First, there are the big Hollywood co-productions, typified by the Bond movies and Working Title, who although they work very autonomously are ultimately owned by the Hollywood major, Universal. This can make it very difficult to identify a film as definitively British or not.

key terms

Equity investor a person or company who puts money into the film and then recovers their investment when the film is released plus a share of the profits.

talking point

The Beach made in 2000 was based on a book by a British author, Alex Garland, with a British director, Danny Boyle; but had an American cast, led by Leonardo DiCaprio, and an American distributor, and was filmed in Thailand. Is it a 'British' film?

Secondly there are then large independent companies that produce or distribute, such as Pathe, Redbus, and Alliance. Even these large independents will seek to co-finance films with other sources of finance such as the Film Council, or the BBC.

Finally there are the many small-scale, often short, productions that people finance from their own pockets or from those of their parents and friends. The biggest independent film festival in Britain is 'Raindance', which takes place in October. Of the thousands of films they receive to be considered for screening in the festival, over 80 per cent have been paid for in this way. Only five per cent have received any financial support from people within the industry.

The Raindance website is a mine of useful information for the aspiring film-maker. The following guide to sources of film finance is adapted from there.

Sources of film finance

Inside the British Film Industry

1 UK Government Money: Film Council, Scottish Screen, etc. distribute government money. It is oversubscribed and they will not fund more than 50 per cent of the film.
2 Euro Government money: Most is distributed by a European Union quango called MEDIA +. Visit their website and see which one of their twenty-odd programmes relate to you.
3 UK film companies: BBC Films and FilmFour Lab are both film companies which happen to be owned by television companies and have money available for feature film and short film projects. Again they rarely fund more than 20 per cent of the film.
4 Pre-sales: a commitment by a distribution company, like Metro-Tartan, to purchase the distribution rights for the film for a certain country (territory) before the film is completed, or before the film is started based on the strength of the story or the elements attached in the package (i.e. cast, director).
5 Gap finance: certain companies fill the gap between sales and production budgets. This requires pre-sales agreements and reliable sales estimates. They barely fund more than 20 per cent of the film.
6 Sale and leasing back of the film and pre-production financing is provided by several UK finance houses. Essentially the film is sold to an investment fund and then leased back by the producer. The producer's lease payments are equal to, or greater than, the interest on the money provided, and potential sales revenue is also factored into the equation. There is a net cash benefit to the producer, and the investors save or defer income tax payments along with potential profit participation in the film, depending on how their deals are structured. They rarely fund more than 30 per cent of the film.
7 Banks: depending on the credit-worthiness of the producer or strength of the pre-sales.

Outside the British Film Industry

1 Hollywood will engage in co-productions with companies in other countries putting up a percentage of the budget in exchange for certain distribution rights.
2 Stars: certain actors, such as Tom Cruise, fund movies using their own production companies.

3 Locality funds: many countries, regions and cities throughout the world have funds in place to encourage film-making and international co-production in their locality. The Republic of Ireland, with favourable tax laws for 'creative' projects has been very successful in attracting producers to the country. *Braveheart* and *Saving Private Ryan* were both filmed in the south-east of Ireland. Swedish Regional film fund, Film i Vast, based in the small town of Trollhattan, has seen the area become one of the major centres for film-making in Europe. Film i Vast can potentially provide up to one-third of a film's budget.

4 Television companies: often the production of a movie for television is cheaper than acquiring a movie from a movie company.

5 Independent producers: a producer who has just had a hit movie may be willing to invest in your project. They may also be willing to assist you in securing the balance of the financing in exchange for a further fee, or increased equity in the project.

6 Angels: Sometimes 'angels', essentially people with money to spend who like your idea, may finance a film, even up to considerable budgets.

7 DIY: Private investment from friends and family forms the easiest, quickest and by far the most common way to finance your movie.

Source: www.raindance.co.uk and *Raindance Producers' Lab Lo-To-No Budget Filmmaking*, Elliot Grove (Focal Press, 2004)

New technology: new opportunities for independent production?

Independent production has, of course, been greatly enhanced, and the power of the transnational media corporations has been challenged by developments in new technology.

In terms of production, new technology essentially means the use of digital cameras for shooting and editing films. Amazing special effects are enabled by this technology and this area of computer-generated imagery is being colonised by the Hollywood majors, and especially George Lucas's Industrial Light and Magic. We can easily see how this approach favours the big-budget event movies that are so central to Hollywood's current approach.

For independent producers it is rather the accessibility and cheapness of the equipment that represents a great new opportunity. Responses have varied from that of the Dogme group, who developed a whole alternative philosophy of filmmaking out of the new technology in the 1990s, to that of established directors like Michael Winterbottom who made his award-winning refugee 'road movie' *Out of this World* on DV, and the work of many first-time filmmakers who have revitalised in particular the short film form. The UK Film Council has sought to support digital short films since August 2001. They set aside £1.5 million to produce one hundred films a year.

Case Study

Vertigo Films

Vertigo Films was founded in 2001 by James Richardson and Allan Niblo. These film producers had enjoyed some success with the club world hit *Human Traffic* in 1999 and believed there was a gap in the market for intelligent, contemporary low-budget movies that could still be appealing commercially. A crucial element in keeping their budgets low, below $2 million, is that the films are shot on High Definition Digital Video. As Richardson himself says,

'We are making films for an eighth of what other people call low budget.'

Source: Screen International, 10 September 2004.

Vertigo's complex financing of their film, *The Football Factory*, is a good example of the issues discussed above. They secured backing from a range of investors, among them Rockstar Games, the games publisher behind the Grand Theft Auto games series. However, they also maintained an element of self-financing in that the cast and crew were paid a relatively low amount upfront but would receive further payments if and when the film became successful.

Although the film had modest box office receipts in the UK, only $1 million, the film will go into profit next year because of 28 international sales deals and income from 120,000 copies of the film for sale on DVD.

Their next film, *It's all Gone Pete Tong*, was released in the Spring of 2005. The film was distributed by Redbus on 200 prints in the UK.

Film distribution

As we have seen in our discussions in the previous chapter, before any film can go into production it has to be very carefully thought through in terms of the most important stage of the industry: distribution. This is the most important, lucrative and powerful part of the contemporary film industry and, measured by income from ticket sales, Britain is the largest market in Europe. In this chapter we will summarise the main parts of the distributors' job and look at some recent examples of films that amply demonstrate the key role the distributors play. We will also consider how distributors estimate their marketing budgets at the different levels of certification, the distinction of above-the-line and below-the-line costs, and we will examine a successful distribution and marketing campaign. Finally, we will again look at the situation here in Britain.

Distribution worldwide and in the UK

The global filmed entertainment industry currently has annual revenues of approximately $60 billion with annual growth of 6 per cent forecast until 2007. The UK, where cinema box office takings exceed $1.2 billion, is the third biggest market in the world behind the US/Canada and Japan.

The distributors' job is complex and diverse but essentially it is to identify and interest as large an audience as they can in their film, and to motivate them sufficiently to go out and see the film. They will work out with the film's producer or the parent studio the best strategy to get the audience in and then to sustain interest in the film, so that subsequent launches of the film onto video or DVD will also be successful.

The role of the distributor

First of all, let's consider in a bit of detail what a distributor actually does. It varies with individual companies of course but generally, they:

1 Buy the film or agree to finance or part-finance a film before it goes into production.
2 Negotiate the number of film copies or prints to be made and arrange their production in time for release into different countries or territories.
3 Negotiate when the prints will be released for exhibition with the owners of the cinemas in the different territories.
4 Arrange the transportation of the prints to the various territories globally.

5 Provide trailers and publicity material for the people showing the film – the exhibitors.

6 Provide advertising and publicity material to promote the film in various media.

7 Arrange promotional material to tie in with the film.

8 Dub or subtitle foreign language films being screened in the UK.

The distributors will need to have good working relationships with the film's production company, with the exhibitors and a host of external suppliers, such as publicists, designers and advertising agencies.

They also need to 'sell' the film not just to the public but also to their marketing partners, the exhibitors and the media.

This all amounts to very diverse tasks so a distribution company breaks down into the following departments:

- Film sales – booking films into cinemas.
- Print department – making copies of the films for the cinema.
- Marketing – responsible for launching the film.

Estimating the budget

As we have seen, no film, even an event movie with an all-star cast, is guaranteed to be a success at the box office, yet it is the distributor's job to ensure that no movie that should have been a great success and generated lots of profit fails to do so because not enough money was spent on promoting the film. That, rather than promoting a film unsuccessfully, is the worst thing a distributor can do. They must always believe in their product.

Working out exactly how much to spend on distributing a movie in Britain is always a careful calculation. They will consider the following factors.

key terms

Marketability is the ease with which the film will generate interest because of its stars or its director.

Playability is the degree to which a film will continue to attract an audience because audiences like it and it gets good 'word of mouth'.

1 The cast and crew of the film, especially the presence of 'bankable' stars. This will often be the decisive element in whether the film has marketability, that is, whether or not it can easily generate interest on the part of the public.

2 Certification and target audience. We will discuss this further below.

3 Audience research, both from the US and in the UK. Test screenings and opening weekends will suggest whether, even if the film does not have 'marketability', it has playability.

4 Number of film prints to be generated.

5 Timing of the US release and release into other worldwide territories, remembering the importance of the holiday period and other films being released at the same time.

6 Estimated rentals. A rental is the amount of money given to the distributor from the sale of each ticket.

Once a marketing campaign has begun the distributors will use market research to assess how successful it is being in ensuring people have heard about the film. This feedback may lead to changes in the marketing campaigns. Although they will want to get to as broad an audience as possible they must above all make sure they get to the target audience and that they are motivated to see the film.

Certification

Every film that is released in the UK must be viewed by the British Board of Film Classification (BBFC). This will determine the age range of the potential audience.

The classification categories are as follows:

U   **Suitable for all ages.**
PG   **Parental Guidance.**
12A   **No-one younger than 12 may see a '12A' film in a cinema unless accompanied by an adult.**
15   **Not suitable for those under 15 years.**
18   **Not suitable for those under 18 years.**

The 12A certificate was created in June 2002 when local authorities were inundated with complaints from children and parents that they couldn't get in to see *Spider-Man*. There had previously been complaints about under 12s being excluded from *Titanic* and the most recent Bond films. The authorities in areas like North Norfolk, Tameside in Manchester, and Solihull ignored the BBFC's certification of 12 and let the children into their cinemas. An embarrassed BBFC introduced the 12A category.

talking point

What in general is likely to be the view of studio executives as regards certification? What certificates would be most valuable? Are there circumstances in which an 18 certificate would be desirable?

Activity

Visit the BBFC's website and identify how the Board justifies its role in 'classifying' films. Do you think they would be being more honest if they called themselves censors, as this is the most important part of their role?

Marketing a film

A marketing campaign is divided into three areas:

1 Advertising
2 Publicity
3 Promotions.

It is also divided into above-the-line and below-the-line costs.

Above-the-line costs are mainly for advertising. The distributor will buy advertising space on billboards or in the press, and will buy 'spots' on radio or television. These costs are usually clear and the audience reached easily identifiable.

Below-the-line costs are those that are used to generate publicity but without any absolute guarantee what, if any, coverage in the press or on television will be gained. Flying a star in from Hollywood for the premiere of a film in London would be one way of generating publicity. For the premiere of *I Robot* at a cinema in Leicester Square in London in August 2004, Will Smith spent two hours speaking to the crowd and the media before the film, doing his best to ensure the launch was successful. The distributor cannot guarantee, of course, that all publicity will necessarily be positive. However, they will try to shape the media response. Audiences at the launch of the 'turkey' (a film everyone can agree was really terrible) *Battlefield Earth* in Leicester Square in 2000 were not allowed to leave the cinema early though many people wanted to! But if it is successful much greater coverage can be obtained than could ever be paid for. No amount of money can buy coverage of your film on the front page of the *Daily Mirror* or the *News of the World*, but a glitzy premiere can put it there.

Promotions are also part of the below-the-line costs. They are usually developed with other companies, such as toy manufacturers or food outlets, like McDonalds, to promote the film and the other company's products.

Activity

Refer back to the film package you put together in Chapter 7 on production. Try to work out what kind of publicity and promotions strategy you would put together for your film.

Let's now look at a very successful campaign put together by the distributors of an Oscar winning film for a release in the UK.

Case Study   The English Patient

The multi-Oscar-winning *The English Patient* began as a novel written by Michael Ondaatje, published in 1994. With its complex narrative and serious themes it did not immediately seem like a good choice of novel to film. When it was filmed with its main star being Ralph Fiennes, it did not seem like a possible box office smash. However, as the film gained recognition and Oscar nominations in the United States, the film's distributors, BuenaVista International, part of Disney, designed a marketing campaign that they hoped would move the film from art house to a mainstream hit in the multiplexes. They wanted the film to 'cross over' from a niche target audience to a mainstream audience.

The film was released in the US on 15 November 1996, but BVI decided to delay its release in the UK for five months. This, they hoped,

Continued

would allow interest in the film to slowly build through magazine and newspaper coverage of reaction in the States. It also allowed the distributors to study the information gained on the audience for the film.

BVI decided to release the film to tie in with the Oscar nominations period in February and March of 1997. This they did, releasing the film on 14 March 1997.

BVI's publicity campaign developed over five months, highlighting the British content of the film, and initially targeting the readers of *The Guardian* and *The Independent*.

The main campaign, however, was based on the film's twelve Oscar nominations, emphasising the size of this achievement. A full third of the budget for the campaign was held over until after the award ceremony itself when *The English Patient* won nine Oscars. The day after the ceremony, newspaper advertising carried the good news. Although there was a promotional tie-in with Jaeger clothes, the only other merchandising was a new edition of the novel and of Herodotus, the Classical poet whose work is featured in the film.

The poster campaign

Crucial to the success of the 'cross-over' from readers of *The Guardian* and *The Independent* to that of *The Sun/Daily Mirror* was the poster. Initial posters had an emphasis on the narrative enigma of the patient who has lost his memory; however, by the time of the Oscars a much more straightforwardly romantic image was used, designed to appeal to a mainstream audience. As soon as the awards were announced the posters were changed overnight creating the sense of a film that was a cinematic masterpiece and as such an 'event' that could not be missed.

This strategy was a great success. Unlike the majority of films which achieve their maximum box office returns in the first week, and then

Continued see their audiences fall off quickly, *The English Patient* actually increased its receipts in the second week and maintained this into its third week. In the sixth week, immediately after the film won more awards at the British Association for Film and Television Awards (BAFTA), receipts rose steeply again.

In the first eight weeks of its UK release the film took over £11 million and over a 26-week period in the US took more than £47 million. A very successful marketing campaign and 'cross-over'.

analyse this

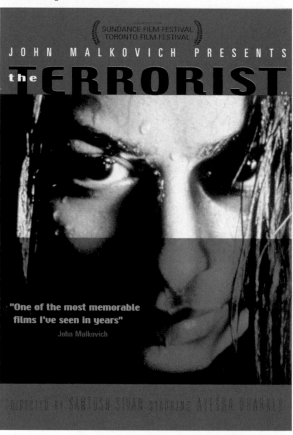

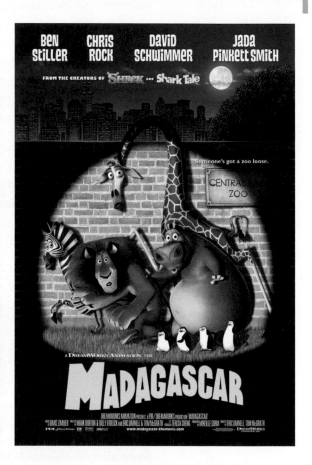

Film posters have formed the basis of the examination questions set for FS2. Take a look at the materials reproduced here – posters for *The Terrorist* and *Madagascar*. The set question was:

'What are some of the different ways that those responsible for the marketing of films use advertisements of this kind (in magazines or on billboards) with the aim of creating audiences for their products?'

Have a go at answering the question yourself before you look at the analysis that follows.

Analysis

The two posters clearly contrast strongly. They are aimed at two distinct audiences.

The poster for *The Terrorist* is aimed at an **arthouse audience** who enjoy films made outside of the Hollywood mainstream. It attempts to give itself a certain prestige within that world by including at the top of the poster reference to the film having been part of the Sundance and Toronto (independent) film festivals. An appeal is clearly being made to the fans of John Malkovich, a well-established actor noted for his choice of unusual roles and his highly sardonic star image. This image was strongly reinforced by the surprise cult hit, directed by Spike Jonze, *Being John Malkovich*. His arch, ironically amused style is suggested on the poster by the mocking use of his 'recommendation' of the film that he has himself produced. The image that dominates the poster is intense suggesting, along with the title, a tense, dramatic film but it is clearly not an action adventure movie and the absence of a clear genre identity would make it more attractive to an arthouse audience. The film also makes a clear appeal to very particular geographically based audiences in London and specifics the particular cinemas where the film will be shown, such as the well-known arthouse cinema, the Ritzy in Brixton. One could speculate that this is the first stage of a platform release and if the box office take is good then the film might be opened up on more screens nationally.

In contrast to the *The Terrorist*, the poster for *Madagascar* appeals to a mainstream and inclusive audience. It immediately enables the audience to identify the film as animation and comedy. The central animal 'characters' are caught in a spotlight outside their zoo. That they have escaped is made clear by the Central Park zoo sign, and the tag line, 'Someone's got a zoo loose', a play on the idea of someone being crazy because they have a 'screw' loose. A narrative enigma is thus created accessible to children and adults. How have the animals escaped and what will happen now? The animals are reassuringly anthropomorphised (given human characteristics) with big rounded eyes and upright postures making them appealing and sympathetic.

The star names who 'voice' characters are given prominence in a way typical of mainstream film promotion. All have a background in comedy. Chris Rock is best known as a comedian and David Schwimmer was in the television comedy *Friends*. Ben Stiller and Jada Pinkett Smith are both best known for acting in film comedies. Audience expectations are further refined by the reference to previous hit animations for Dreamworks, *Shrek* and *Shark Tale*. Finally the skyscrapers 'place' the film in New York, a city, leaving us to imagine the comic possibilities of wild animals loose in such a setting.

Activity

Find two film posters (there are lots of examples in any film magazine, like *Premiere* or *Totalfilm*) and answer the questions below. Any one of the elements below may be prioritised over the others on a poster.

- The *title* of the film often dominates for obvious reasons, but look at the kind of font or typeface that is being used and the kind of colours for the lettering. Do they communicate anything as well?
- Does the poster suggest a *genre?* As we know, this is a key way in which the industry targets its audience. How clear is the genre in the poster and which specific elements 'clue' us in to the genre?
- Is the *star* (or stars) featured heavily? Are they a key selling point for the film?
- Does the poster contain a suggested storyline, sometimes known as a *narrative image*, that draws out our interest in the film? Sometimes the poster will tease us with questions creating a mystery, or *enigma*. This may come in the form of a *tagline*, such as 'Just when you thought it was safe to go back in the water . . .'
- Sometimes the *director's* name will be used to sell the film, especially if they have had big box office successes already. 'From the maker of . . .'
- Comment taken from *reviews*, or star ratings may also be included if they add to the film's prestige.
- Website addresses will also be included especially with big budget movies which will draw you into all the accompanying merchandise.

The computer games industry

A key development for distributors considering whether a film proposal, or completed film, is worth the huge costs of marketing and promoting has been the growth of the computer games industry. There are a number of reasons for this but the most important one is the most obvious, as anyone knows who buys computer games. They are very expensive, costing £20 to as much as £40, representing a much greater profit on each individual sale than a cinema ticket. Developing a game is only likely to cost £3–4 million, a fraction of the cost of a mainstream Hollywood production, and in the US sales of computer games in 2001 reached over two hundred million. In 2000 the video games industry had greater income from sales than cinema. In the UK the games industry grossed more than cinema, video sales and video rental combined! (Huw J. Williams, *The Guardian*, 19 December 2002).

As you might expect, Hollywood has not been slow to exploit this market. *Spider-Man*, *Star Wars*, the Bond series are all to be found among many others in the shops as computer games. The game derived from *Harry Potter and the Philosopher's Stone* sold over ten million copies. The President of George Lucas's computer game generating company, Lucas Arts, describes how in the process of making a new *Stars Wars* film the requirements of the game are in the director's mind.

'When George is putting a script together he works with us to see what sequences will make good games.'

Source: Huw J. Williams, *The Guardian*, 19 December 2002.

Clearly not all types of movie lend themselves easily to adaptation as a game. It is action adventure movies that tend to work best. Another reason, perhaps, why this genre continues to dominate at the box office. However, games are becoming more sophisticated in their characterisation and storylines. Some game spin-offs such as 'Wolverine's Revenge' was released to coincide with the release of the second *X Men* movie but contained an original storyline that was not seen in the film.

It is also the case, of course, that some highly successful games are made into films. The best example, perhaps, is *Tomb Raider* made into a film starring Angelina Jolie as Lara Croft.

Figure 8.1 ▶

Activity

Buy, or borrow, one of the many gaming magazines that are available in newsagents. See how many of the games that are featured have their origins in films.

We will now turn out attention to the situation in Britain.

The British film industry and distribution

In this section we will explore how British film companies attempt to find a way of surviving in this highly competitive global industry. We will look at some film financing deals in some detail and at how distribution is organised overall in the UK.

British film finds itself in a strange dilemma. Unlike the French or Spanish film industries to whom the US market is essentially closed by the language barrier, British film would seem to have a natural advantage. The profits to be made by success in the US are also very tempting. Indeed individual

PRODUCERS AND AUDIENCES (FS2)

British films, such as *Four Weddings and a Funeral*, have been hugely successful. On the other hand, there is no guarantee of success in the US and many films, for example *Lock, Stock and Two Smoking Barrels*, failed to find an audience. Ironically, however, this very success has seemed to imply state support for film is unnecessary in Britain, whereas it is taken for granted in France. As we shall see, the most ambitious attempt yet to create a thriving and globally competitive film industry in Britain through government support, the lottery funding initiative, has been widely regarded as a failure and a new system has been put in place through a new Film Council.

Distribution in the UK essentially falls into three sections:

- The majors. Most powerful are of course the Hollywood majors: Fox, Universal, Buena Vista International (Disney), Columbia Tristar, UIP (the international distribution arm for Paramount and Universal) and Warner Bros. It is these companies' films that dominate the multiplexes especially during holiday periods with event movies such as *Shrek 2*, or *Spider-Man 2*.
- Large independents. There are then large independent companies that produce as well as distribute, such as Pathe, Redbus, Alliance/Momentum and Entertainment.
- Small independents. Finally there are small companies like Metro-Tartan, Metrodome, and UGC who release arthouse movies or foreign language films. The profit margins for these companies can be very slim indeed and it can be very difficult for these small independents to secure access to screens especially in multiplexes. The rentals, that is the percentage of the box office gross that the exhibitors give back to the distributors, is in Britain also lower than almost anywhere else in the world.

These companies need to consider and be resourceful in how and when they release their films. UGC, for example, tend to deliberately time their releases to coincide with the big Hollywood blockbusters in the summer in the hope of finding the 'arthouse' audience who are desperate for something different. So, for example, on the same weekend as *Shrek 2* opened they released a Russian film *The Return* on 17 screens, getting a healthy box office return of $4,780 from each screen. The following week's receipts only dropped by 11 per cent. Similarly when *Spider-Man 2* was opening on thousands of screens all over Britain, UGC opened *The Story of the Weeping Camel* on 19 carefully chosen arthouse screens, bringing in on average for each screen over the first weekend $5,200. Again the box office for the following week only dropped 16 per cent on the basis of good word of mouth.

Let's now look at the costs that a small independent like UGC are faced with.

Distribution costs

A small independent can expect a cost of up to £60,000 to distribute a film. The costs will include:

1 £800–£1,000 for each print of the film made.
2 Up to £1,000 to the British Board of Film Classification to certify the film.

3 Production of cinema trailer.

4 Print and advertising campaign.

Any profit they make is dependent on the deals they can negotiate for DVD, video, cable, satellite, and terrestrial television rights.

Source: Adapted from *Screen International*, 30 July 2004.

Activity

Think of a book or play that you think might make a good film. What package would you put together to attract the support first of a backer in Britain – Film Four Lab for example, the Film Council or the BBC – and then the interest of a major US distributor?

Film funding and the National Lottery: a failed experiment

In 1997 the British Government announced that National Lottery funding would be available for British film production. Three companies were successful in their bids and they were to receive over £90 million over a five-year period. The intention was to create effectively 'mini studios', so the winning groups were to have expertise in production and distribution. Each film was to be only part financed by the lottery.

The winning consortia were:

- Pathe Productions, who committed themselves to 35 films with £35 million from the lottery.
- The Film Consortium to make 39 films with £30.25 million.
- DNA Film Ltd to make 16 films with £29 million.

Having studied AS Film Studies so far we are sure you are immediately struck by how, although the overall budget seemed quite large, individual films would receive relatively small amounts. And the crucial question, 'who will pay for advertising, promotion and distribution?' also arises. We can contrast the marketing budget for the highly successful British film *The Crying Game* which, in the US alone, was $14 million.

Very few successful films were made and fewer still that were popular, and the system was abandoned in 2002. The reasons for its failure have not been agreed but range from poor amounts of money available for promotion and marketing and the inability to get into the multiplexes, to a lack of decent scripts.

Although the situation for financing British films in some ways became easier with the introduction of lottery funding, it was still the case that most people would see many of the films made for the first time on television. Take, for example, a film made in 1999 by Pathe Productions with lottery funding called *Ratcatcher*. This film was shown to great critical acclaim, was selected to be shown at the prestigious Cannes film festival, and won the best new director's award for Lynne Ramsey at the Edinburgh Film Festival. However, it sank without trace at the box office, getting only a limited distribution and, again, got its biggest audience when it was eventually shown on the BBC, who also part financed the film.

The Film Council

Government support for film has now been transferred to the Film Council. They will allocate much smaller sums than the lottery had available. They have three funds: a Premiere Production fund with an annual budget of £8 million to invest in films to appeal to a broad commercial audience; a New Cinema fund of £5 million annually to support short films and low-budget films, acting as a laboratory for new styles and ideas; and a Development Fund of £4 million per year aimed at supporting films through their development. Addressing one of the issues that had been at the heart of the failure of lottery-funded films, they also have a Distribution fund to support the promotion and advertising of films.

Its Chief Executive Officer, John Woodward, has made clear that they wish to support commercial, popular films.

> 'We certainly won't support small art films with a tough, social subject matter or European foreign-language films which won't find a distributor in Britain.'
>
> *Source*: Interview with Agnes Poirier, *The Guardian*, 25 August 2002.

As we shall see, some of the most distinctively creative, and successful films produced in Britain have been films by directors like Mike Leigh and Ken Loach who, very deliberately, make films with a 'tough, social subject matter' and which are yet successful and find an audience. We will be looking at Ken Loach's *Sweet Sixteen* as our Close Study film in a later chapter.

The Film Council have already enjoyed some success in backing Robert Altman's *Gosford Park*, a critical and commercial success. The film in some respects was part of a very strong British tradition of historical costume drama within which might also be included films like Emma Thompson's Oscar-winning adaptation of Jane Austen's novel *Sense and Sensibility*.

The Film Council and digital film-making

On the other hand the Film Council has also funded highly experimental and innovative film-making like director Michael Winterbottom's *In this World* (Fig. 8.2). The Film Council believe that the use of digital technology should be encouraged as a means of reducing costs while maintaining quality. This was part of their reason for supporting Winterbottom's plans to explore the experiences of Afghan refugees coming into Britain from camps in Pakistan. Filmed on location along the route to Britain it was shot using handheld digital cameras and using a minimal crew. The film's budget was only $1,900,000. The film took the Golden Bear award for Best Film at the Berlin Film Festival. Released by the Sundance Channel's Film Series the film was also shown in Loew's Theatres in ten American cities.

talking point

What should the aims of the new Film Council be? Should British film be just about making a profit, or about helping us to understand our own society better? What kind of films should they make? Costume dramas? Literary adaptations that are likely to do well in the US? Hard-hitting social realist drama about the realities of life in Britain? Or innovative experimental work, like *In this World?* Do you agree with John Woodward?

The demise of FilmFour

After the demise of the lottery funding system, the summer of 2002 also saw the winding down of the nearest thing Britain had to its own successful mini studio, producing films but also distributing them, FilmFour. Separated out from Channel 4 in 1997, the new company had been launched a few months after the lottery franchises were awarded and with the same degree of optimism. However, without a hit since *East is East* in 1999, with flops such as *Charlotte Grey* which cost over £12 million to make but brought in only £1.3 million at the UK box office, and with declining television advertising revenue for the parent company, Channel 4, FilmFour's budget was cut to £10m. By that time, FilmFour had invested in over 300 movies.

Channel 4 had pumped into the British film industry up to £40 million a year. When the channel was launched at the height of Mrs Thatcher's premiership in 1982 it had a clear and exciting remit to serve minorities and provide media access to the otherwise marginalised in society. The Channel 4 films that developed at this time were social realist, serious reflections on society by directors like Mike Leigh and Ken Loach. In the 1990s they successfully invested in *Four Weddings and a Funeral* and funded fully the youth-oriented hits from the director Danny Boyle, *Shallow Grave* and *Trainspotting*. The latter was hugely successful: costing only £1.7 million to make, it grossed twenty times that worldwide. They were responsible also for funding one of the key films of the 1980s, Stephen Frears' directed story of a gay Pakistani entrepreneur, *My Beautiful Launderette*. One could clearly see in such a film, built around an ethnic and sexual minority, the guiding principles of the Channel's remit. The same was true of the Neil Jordan directed film *The Crying Game*, about a love relationship between a gay transvestite and a straight Irish republican terrorist. Their final success was *East is East*, set very specifically, and with a tender, comic intimacy, in a racially mixed working-class community in the 1970s.

It is arguable that these small-scale distinctive films, arising from their specific English (or Scottish) locales were successful internationally by not trying too hard to appeal internationally. Appealing directly to British, or arthouse audiences, these films successfully 'crossed over' into the mainstream. Skilful marketing and promotion also played its part in making the films a success. This was particularly the case with *Trainspotting* and *The Crying Game*.

When a new chief executive, Paul Webster, took over in 1999 he announced an alliance with Warner Bros to try to make films that would be unashamedly commercial and compete with Hollywood. *Charlotte Gray* was one of the first films in this experiment as was *Death to Smoochy*, a dark comedy starring Danny DeVito, which also flopped. The final nail in the coffin was *The Birthday Girl*: poorly promoted, it failed at the box office despite featuring Nicole Kidman, one of the world's biggest stars, in the summer of 2002.

A difficulty here was perhaps that the kinds of production budgets being used, figures of £6–7 million, while large by the standards of British cinema, are small by comparison with that of Hollywood studios whose average budget is $40–50 million and who will regularly spend $10–15 million on advertising and promoting their films. We might recall that a crucial moment in giving confidence to FilmFour in its early days was the huge success of *Four Weddings and a Funeral*, yet the key moment in ensuring that film's success was the investment by Polygram of millions of dollars in promoting and marketing a film that had only cost £4 million to make.

Getting it right: Working Title

One British company above all, however, has demonstrated how to appeal to audiences successfully. Working Title have brought us *Four Weddings and a Funeral, Elizabeth, Notting Hill, Bean, Bridget Jones's Diary, About a Boy* and *Captain Corelli's Mandolin*. Their small-budget production arm, WT2, which works with budgets under $5 million, also produced *Billy Elliot*. They have also been the producers behind the work of the critically acclaimed directors, Tim Robbins (*Bob Roberts, Dead Man Walking*), and the Coen Brothers (*O Brother, Where Art Thou?, Fargo, The Hudsucker Proxy* and many others).

The company is run by Eric Fellner and Tim Bevan. They both started out producing pop videos in the 1980s. Bevan founded Working Title with Sarah Radclyffe in 1984. Radclyffe left in 1990 and has gone on to produce such films as *Ratcatcher*, which we discussed earlier. The company's first film, *My Beautiful Launderette*, was directed by Stephen

Frears, and was a tremendously important film in representing modern multicultural British society.

Fellner was meanwhile producing small-budget cult movies, such as *Sid and Nancy*, and *Straight to Hell*, directed by Alex Cox. Fellner proved himself very adept at getting money even for such small-scale films with little broad box office appeal. Cox tells a story about Fellner during the shooting of *Straight to Hell*:

> 'We were supposed to be making the film in three weeks and it looked as if we would run out of time and wouldn't have enough money to go into a fourth week, and so Eric got on a plane and went to Los Angeles, and came back with a suitcase full of money to finish the film . . . I've never seen that before there actually was a suitcase full of money . . .'
>
> *Source*: Mark Morris, *The Guardian*, 19 December 2002.

Fellner joined the company in 1992.

The Tall Guy

Many critics believe that the formula that has made Working Title such a success was first used by Bevan in his 1989 film *The Tall Guy*.

The film was clearly a genre film, a romantic comedy. As we have seen genre, along with stars have always been crucial elements in Hollywood's marketing strategies. Genre understanding helps everyone on set know what they are involved in and helps audiences know what they are going to get! It was scripted by Richard Curtis, probably best known at this time for his work with Ben Elton on the television series *Blackadder*. The stars of the film were American, Jeff Goldblum; 'posh' British actress, Emma Thompson, and comic actor, Rowan Atkinson.

Many of the same elements were of course present for what they call their 'break out' commercial success, *Four Weddings and A Funeral*, written by Richard Curtis, starring an American, Andie McDowell, and a 'posh' Brit Hugh Grant, as well as Rowan Atkinson. Interestingly it is genre, however, that Bevan emphasises:

> 'For me the most important thing about *Four Weddings* was that I learnt you could make a different sort of movie, you could make a genre movie in England that could reach an audience. A romantic comedy is a genre movie, it's not a frock movie, or a streets of London movie . . . '
>
> *Source*: *Empire*, June 2001.

Activity

Think about Working Title's recent hits, *Wimbledon, Captain Corelli's Mandolin, Bridget Jones: The Edge of Reason* and *About a Boy*. How far can 'the formula' be applied? With the release of *Bridget Jones: The Edge of Reason* the company announced that it would be the last of their 'rom com' style of movies. Were they right to abandon the formula?

The Hollywood connection: Universal

Undoubtedly Working Title have achieved remarkable success. *Four Weddings* took $250 million at the box office, *Bean*, $230 million from a $20 million budget, and *Notting Hill*, $350 million. However, it is not often remarked upon that the company is now closely allied to the Hollywood studio, Universal. In a £389 million deal Universal granted complete freedom to Bevan and Fellner to produce films budgeted up to £15 million. Above this, however, Universal's agreement must first be obtained. *Captain Corelli's Mandolin* was Working Title's biggest budget yet at $45 million. This is still only around the average cost of a Hollywood movie.

talking point

Many of your friends and family will be familiar with Working Title's films. Conduct some research that tests out how far 'the formula' described above accounts for their appreciation of the film, or are there other reasons why they like or dislike the films?

New technology and distribution

As we saw in the last chapter, new digital technology has allowed small-scale film companies like Vertigo Films to find a successful niche in the film marketplace. These new digital film-makers have also been able to use the new technology of the internet as a means of distributing and exhibiting their work. Websites such as Britshorts, Ifilm, atomfilms and the short films site hosted by Channel 4, have allowed new films by unknown film-makers to reach a wide audience.

 **Activity**

Visit these sites, and make notes on the films you like:

atomfilms.shockwave.com/af/home
www.britshorts.com
www.ifilm.com
www.channel4.com/film/shortsandclips

The net is a form of distribution that the studios will find it increasingly difficult to control. To look at an obvious parallel we need only think of the music industry. The music companies, who are, of course, largely part of the same TNCs that own the Hollywood studios, succeeded in closing down the most famous music file-sharing website, Napster, only for many similar websites, like Kazaa, to spring up and take its place.

The nightmare scenario for the studios is that broadband technology that is now being made available in the US and Britain will allow films to be pirated across the net. And indeed as was the case with *Spider-Man* this is already happening. The studios have responded by releasing their films simultaneously in as many territories as possible, making the pirated films less attractive.

Film exhibition

In this chapter we will study how audiences for film have developed in our contemporary era and suggest some ways of exploring audience's attitudes. We will then consider the different types of cinema that exist in Britain and how they meet the needs of different audiences. Finally, we will also look at the difficulties in getting films made outside of Hollywood and how independent film-makers are constantly looking for ways of getting films to audiences.

Film isn't just the cinema anymore

We, perhaps, need to make explicit at this point something which we take for granted in practice but could usefully maybe think about a bit more – what it is to be a spectator of film and how our experience of film, unlike that of audiences even in the 1950s and 1960s, is now dominated by other media than the cinema. Modern technology has transformed our relationship with film.

Let's consider our experience of film in these different media.

The cinema and spectatorship

In one way this is the most sociable way of seeing a film. The average group size for attending a multiplex is three. Very few people go to see a film on their own. If they do they are probably older than the core audience of 16–24 year olds and are going to an arthouse cinema. Regardless, there is a sense of a shared experience in the cinema itself. 'Going to the cinema' is still much more of an event, requiring much more planning and effort than simply watching the telly. The cost is considerably higher as well of course. The trailers and advertisements that precede the film make the experience feel more like the normal daily flow of commercial television and radio, dominated as it is by advertising, but then as the film itself begins very few of us will not have some sense of excitement. The scale of the screen, the darkness, the clarity of the sound, and the sense of a communal experience all create this pleasurable tension.

The film itself may then of course turn out to be a disappointment but we can see how the context perhaps encourages the studios to make 'event' movies: blockbusters full of amazing special effects, that will capitalise on the particular sense of drama that the cinema experience creates. In a way, very similar to the earliest filmgoers, we are looking to be amazed by the spectacle before us. There are some films, as people regularly tell each other, that you have to see at the cinema. And in relation to this form of film consumption more than others, 'word of mouth' is still the most important reason why other people may choose to go and see the film. Although usually silent when watching the film the experience only feels complete when you've had the opportunity to discuss it afterwards and pass your experience on to other people.

As we shall see elsewhere in this chapter the use of films as the basis for video/computer games also reinforces this tendency for films at the cinema to be dominated by the action adventure blockbuster.

Video

Nowadays the poor relation of DVD and the cinema itself, video, was at its most interesting in the early 1980s when it showed what a huge demand there was for home movie entertainment. Per head of population more video players were bought in the UK than in any other country (although quite a few people got stuck with the betamax format – ask your parents . . .) and video rental stores set up on every high street. The fact that videos did not at first come under the control of the censors, the British Board of Film Classification, also meant there was a huge trade in horror videos that could not get certification for exhibition in the cinema. Videos were brought under the control of the BBFC with the passing of the Video Recordings Act of 1984.

DVD

Increasingly, however, the dominant form of watching movies at home is DVD and this involves a very different kind of relation to the viewing experience, a very different kind of spectatorship from that of visiting the cinema.

Digital versatile discs (DVDs) are, of course, part of the ongoing wave of new digital-based technology that is slowly integrating all our communication technologies. They can be played on the home PC, on a DVD player hooked up to the television or integrated into a games console, like Playstation. In terms of enabling people to become reflective critics of the films they enjoy and to increase their understanding of film, the DVD represents a breakthrough. In the 1980s people, most famously Quentin Tarantino who worked in a video store, could build up collections of videos, 'possessing' and re-playing films in an entirely new way. DVDs with their much greater available space for information, now often come with 'bonus' material, a lot of which, like 'the outtakes' are purely for entertainment, but some of which, like directors' commentaries, can be very revealing and educational. Trying to 'open up' a market for home rental or purchase of DVDs and videos for students of film has been particularly enhanced by the vogue for re-issuing famous films in the 'directors' cut', such as Ridley Scott's re-edited version of his notoriously confusing sci-fi detective film *Blade Runner*. Another example might be the re-release of the cult hit *Donnie Darko* in a director's cut in 2004, although most people think the original version is a more successful film!

DVDs can also be marketed on the basis of their being linked to a sporting event, such as the film, *Mean Machine*, starring the ex-footballer Vinnie Jones, released into video and DVD stores just at the end of the 2002 soccer World Cup.

Releases of major titles, such as the Harry Potter films, onto video and DVD can be marketed as major events themselves – 'your first opportunity to own . . .'. In the autumn of 2004 the original *Star Wars* trilogy was once again re-released, this time 'for the first time on DVD'. Film magazines, such as *Total Film* or *Premiere* also carry reviews of films released onto DVD with ratings for the film itself and for the bonus material that accompanies it.

Activity

Review your own collection of films. How many do you have on video or DVD? Look at, and make some notes on, the bonus material that may be on your DVDs. The examiners always value highly personal experience.

The internet

Part of the same digital revolution that has brought DVDs, the internet has also enabled the 'streaming' of films onto home PCs. This facility has been used legitimately to create a vibrant online community of short film producers, who produce their films using DVD cameras and then 'upload' their products on to sites like 'atomfilms'. There has also been the illegal 'streaming' of feature films like *Spider-Man* across the net that has led the studios to try to release films simultaneously in as many territories as possible to minimise the impact of this piracy.

The internet has also, of course, made possible online communities of film fans and critics who can discuss the latest films.

Activity

Take a group of your friends or class mates and try to find out the following. Remember, though, that Film Studies students might give you very unreliable information as they have a different relationship to film than 'normal' people.

Videos/DVDs

1 Do they have a television in their room? How many televisions are there in their household for how many people?
2 Do they watch films on video or DVD? How many films do they watch a week? Do they watch them on their own? With family? Or with friends? Is it done at a regular time each week? Are any other types of activities, such as eating together, planned around the screening of the film?

Continued

3 If watching a film on DVD do they look at the bonus material? Why? Just for fun? Or to learn more about the stars or the directors? Do they have a collection of DVDs or videos? Is it just haphazard or are they collecting particular types/genres of films, or the films of particular stars or directors?

4 When watching the film do you stop it for any reason? What difference does this make to your opinion of the film? Do you discuss it as it goes along? Does it get watched again by others or by the same people if it was enjoyed?

The internet

5 Do they ever download films from the net? (Reassure them you won't tell anyone!) Do they do this with friends and then watch and discuss the film together?

6 Do they ever visit any specialist short film and animation sites, such as 'atomfilms'?

7 Do they visit or contribute to film websites, fansites, or film gossip sites, like 'ain't it cool news'?

Home editing

Finally, the arrival of relatively cheap editing equipment may mean we can recreate the film, editing it ourselves to create a different ending, give increased screen time to our favourite star, or change the overall atmosphere of the film. According to a recent examination paper (WJEC film studies examination paper, 15 January 2003), an independent film-maker and fan of the famously cold director Stanley Kubrick, appalled at what he regarded as the sentimental treatment given to his film *AI* by Steven Spielberg after Kubrick's untimely death during the making of the film, re-edited the film at home, using the DVD and an editing programme on his PC, and is making it available to other devotees as *AI – The Kubrick edit*.

The development of the modern cinema audience

As we have seen, no matter how sophisticated the distribution and marketing strategy the film industry can never be absolutely sure of securing an audience. The event movie strategy began to seem vulnerable in the 1990s with the success of small budget movies like *The Blair Witch Project* and the box office failure of blockbusters like *Godzilla*. However, the use of literary sources and the sequels they enable, such as *The Lord of the Rings* and the *Harry Potter* books have effectively created massive marketing franchises with the films as the central marketing tool.

Overall the film industry remains in good shape because there has been a long-term growth in cinema audiences in the US and in Britain.

How has the industry achieved this?

The peak of cinema attendance was 1946. In the US there was an average weekly attendance of 95 million. In the UK average weekly attendance was also at its peak in this year at 31.5 million. Audiences declined because by the end of the 1950s in the US and in the UK it had been replaced as the main source of entertainment by television. Television was at the heart of a more home-based suburban lifestyle away from the town centres and their increasingly neglected cinemas. Despite the industry's attempts to re-present films as spectacles that television could not compete with through such technology as Cinemascope and even gimmicks like 3D glasses audiences continued to decline. Responding to the uniform blandness of television and its strict avoidance of any sexual content in its programming the studios promoted such clearly sexy stars as Jayne Mansfield and, most famously, Marilyn Monroe. Their most successful innovation, however, was one that moved with the grain of the social trends of the time and that was the creation of the drive-in. By 1954 there were over 3,800 drive-ins in the US, mainly located out of town and allowing families to reproduce the nuclear family arrangement of the suburbs in their cars at the cinema.

None of these measures arrested the long-term decline in attendance though. This accelerated in the mid-1970s as many cinemas began to physically deteriorate through lack of investment. In the UK by the mid-1980s weekly attendance was not much more than a million.

Audience research

As we know, the situation is very different today compared to the mid-1970s. *Shrek 2* has just become the biggest grossing movie of all time, with the biggest single box office take on any single day of over $44 million! The year 2000 was a significant date for exhibitors in Britain with cinema attendance returning to the levels seen in 1974, the year when the long, steady dropping off of postwar cinema attendance abruptly came to an end and went into a rapid decline.

We are aware of many of the reasons for this turnaround because of the studies we have already made in distribution and production. However, the exam board is very keen on students exploring what is happening in their own locality.

Before we set you a specific research project to undertake it is worthwhile knowing a little about research techniques.

Forms of research

There are basically two forms of research.

Quantitative

This is information based on relatively simple facts and figures that can be clearly recorded and analysed. For film studies, it might be questions such as:
- How often do you go to see a film?
- Who is your favourite star?
- Which cinema do you most often attend?

- If you had a choice of a British film and a Hollywood film which would you go and see?

The advantages of these types of questions is that they are quick for the person questioned to answer, and the information is relatively straightforward to interpret.

To maximise efficiency, the questions used are often 'closed'; that is they can only be answered with yes or no response; e.g. 'Would you go to see a film purely because your favourite star is in it?'

Qualitative

As you might expect, this type of research is less concerned with numbers than with people's feelings and attitudes. As such, what you find out can be very thought provoking. On the other hand, the information is less reliable in that it needs to be interpreted. You encourage people to talk or write at length by using 'open' questions; that is, ones that cannot be answered with a simple yes or no response: e.g. 'Why do you go to that particular cinema rather than that other one?'; 'Why do you think people like multiplexes?'

Research methods

Again, it is worthwhile choosing carefully the method you are going to use to talk to cinema audiences.

Questionnaires

This is the best bet for quantitative research. No more than a dozen questions is advisable though. Multiple choice answers with tick boxes make them even more efficient to use. Samples generally need to be a minimum of 15–20 people, to be able to see any common elements in people's responses.

Interviews

These are useful for gaining more in-depth information, and best used with someone who has a very specific area of expertise to share, for example, the manager of a multiplex. When wishing to explore the public's attitudes the formality of an interview can be daunting, therefore it is better to use open/guided discussion groups.

Open/guided discussion

Bringing together a group of people, four or five, whose views you want to explore, giving them some stimulus material, say, some film posters, or a multiplex programme for a week, and then recording their views on video or audio tape, can be a very effective means of qualitative research. You may have a few very broad, open questions that will bring the group back to your topic area if the discussion 'drifts' too much.

Participant observation

This is a method of research in which you become a part of the group whose values and attitudes you wish to explore. In practice, for Film

also programme 'Bollywood' films and arthouse movies. The leisure complex that houses this megaplex is alongside the vast interchange of motorways across and under the M6 known as 'spaghetti junction'. This maximises the accessibility of the cinema to people across the West Midlands. Reflecting this, the car park has spaces for 2,700 cars. The development has been successful in hitting its target of attracting a million and a half people to the development in the last year.

A more typical example of a multiplex might be the ten-screen Odeon on the outskirts of Tunbridge Wells and a minute's drive off the A21 between London and the south coast. Alongside the cinema there is a restaurant, a bowling alley and a health club. The exhibitors have, of course, been criticised for developing green field sites and thereby damaging the environment. In their defence they say they are also interested in redevelopment of brown field sites, redeveloping derelict land as they did with the FilmWorks multiplex in Greenwich in south-east London, or the conversion of old inner-city cinemas into multi-screen cinemas.

Multiplexes 'sell' themselves on the basis of being safe family-orientated environments but this should not distract us from the fact that their key audience is the most frequent cinema-goers, that is 16–24 year olds, over 50 per cent of whom visit the cinema at least once a month.

Multiscreens

Multiscreens housing three or four screens are usually converted from a single large screen and located in town and city centres. With the multiscreen, owners are acutely conscious that just as high standards of projection, sound and general service are expected here as in the multiplexes. These cinemas attempt to target a younger audience than the more family-orientated multiplexes. They decide on their screening times on their understanding that many of the audience will want to complete the night out by discussing the film in the pub or the restaurant afterwards.

Arthouse cinemas

Independent or arthouse cinemas, have one, two or three screens and specialise in showing unusual or independently produced films. These cinemas may or may not be owned by the large exhibition companies but they will be independent in the sense that they will try to create loyalty in their audience, many of whom will be far more passionate about film than the average multiplex viewer, and on average, older too. They will do this by inviting directors, producers, or actors to come and talk about their work, or by having special screenings of rarely seen 'classic' films. Examples of these are the Cornerhouse in Manchester, the Phoenix in Oxford, or the Ritzy in Brixton.

Community cinemas

There are also a few community-owned cinemas. Like the independents above they invite in speakers, but operating with volunteers and low overheads they can charge much less than the average cinema. An example would be the Plaza Community Cinema in Liverpool.

Activity

Look at the front and back pages of the leaflet for the Plaza Community cinema reproduced here. From the information there, imagining the Plaza were under threat of closure what reasons could you give for the importance of it remaining open?

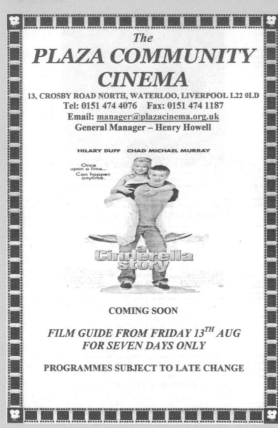

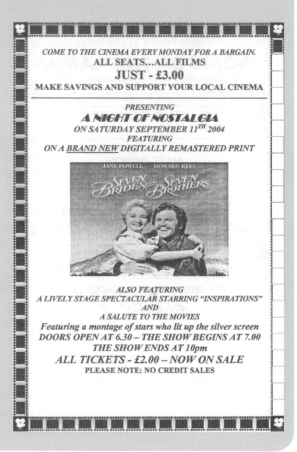

Film clubs

Dotted around the country there are also cinema clubs and societies. Some of these are linked to the British Film Institute, but some are just run by enthusiasts for film. An example might be the Film Society in Cranbrook, a village in the rural Weald of Kent which shows ten films through the winter months: one every three or four weeks. Established over 25 years ago and operating as a society under the rules of the British Film Institute, it now has well over 300 members. Selma Pickup, the Membership Secretary, sees the society's job as providing an alternative to the films shown at the multiplex, and catering for a range of tastes by presenting a variety of genres but still trying to show some of the best of contemporary cinema from across the world, especially those films that win awards at Film Festivals, such as Berlin or Cannes, which the multiplexes still wouldn't show. Prior to each film the society also screens student films from the film departments of universities and colleges in Kent, awarding a prize for the best of these at the end of the season.

Activity

Find out where your nearest film club is. Use the BFI website to help you find it. Join it. You will find the people there a mine of information and enthusiasm for film.

In what ways might you argue that film societies contribute more to creating a society that really values and understands film than the Hollywood dominated multiplexes do?

For different films, made with different-sized budgets, distributors will use different types of exhibition strategies to try to get the audience into the cinema.

The first of these suitable for big-budget Hollywood films is the saturation release pattern.

Saturation release pattern: the blockbuster

Case Study

Shrek 2

At the time of writing *Shrek 2* has just come out in cinemas all over the world. Produced by the company part owned by Steven Spielberg, DreamWorks, it is looking to eclipse *Spider-Man* as the biggest grossing film of all time. *Spider-Man 2*, however, will follow hot on its heels later in the summer. Inflation means that blockbusters from different periods are not directly comparable but nonetheless the box office receipts for *Shrek 2* are very impressive and show a clear marketing strategy.

Shrek 2 opened in the US, unusually, on a Wednesday, 19 May 2004. There were a couple of reasons for this. One was to get on to as many screens as possible prior to the opening of the film they feared might

Continued

pose a danger to their popularity, *Harry Potter and the Prisoner of Azkaban* which was due to open on 4 June. They opened on the highest ever number of screens in the US – 4,163. This was also to lessen the effects of video and web piracy, pre-empting the desirability of illegal copies by making the film as widely available as possible. DreamWorks also hoped by opening on a Wednesday to generate good 'word of mouth' for a film they believed in and that would ratchet up the box office by the weekend.

In this intention they succeeded spectacularly. *Shrek 2*'s opening Friday to Sunday, 21–23 May, generated $104 million in box office receipts, second only to *Spider-Man*'s $115 million opening weekend in 2002. The box office receipts for the Saturday were the biggest-ever single one-day take at $44.8 million. *Shrek 2* accounted for 65 per cent of the total weekend box office of $160 million. The film took just 18 days to reach $300 million beating *Spider-Man* which had taken 22 days to reach that threshold. The scale of success might be judged also by comparison with the relatively successful, *Finding Nemo*, produced by Disney, which took 51 days to reach that figure.

(Don't forget though that a film needs to take, as we've mentioned before, two-and-a-half times its budget at the box office before it goes into profit.)

Case Study

Harry Potter and the Prisoner of Azkaban

With a British cast and a British writer, and perhaps sensing the inevitability of *Shrek 2*'s dominance in the US market, *The Prisoner of Azkaban* had its world premiere in London and opened in a massive 535 locations on 31 May 2004, a Bank Holiday Monday. The film took $9.2 million, the biggest ever single-day opening in the UK market. The

Continued

following weekend, again in an attempt to pre-empt web and video piracy, it opened in 47 markets around the world and on 10,000 prints. The global marketing campaign was expected to cost in the region of $80 million. The key element of the strategy was to build the adult audience around the core children's audience. This was to be done through television advertising spots targeted at teenagers and adults, and an adult-orientated trailer to be shown before adult films such as *Troy* and *Van Helsing*.

On its opening weekend in the US showing on 3,855 screens the film grossed $92.6 million. The global receipts are likely, like its two prequels, to be in the region of $600 million.

Blockbusters are high risk

The sheer size of the amounts of money being discussed above should be sufficient to indicate that blockbusters are high-risk investments. A film is unlikely to recover at the box office from a poor opening weekend.

With DreamWorks taking much of the credit for advancing the art of animation in films like *Shrek*, the major Hollywood studio that is currently suffering most is the traditional home of animation in Hollywood, Disney. *Pearl Harbour*, made by Disney in 2001, pushed the cost of making a blockbuster beyond the $100 million mark and in an attempt to ensure a big opening weekend, Disney paid £2.7 million for a premiere aboard the USS Stennis aircraft carrier in Hawaii. Slated by the critics it only eventually managed to recoup its costs.

This year their pony express adventure film, *Hidalgo*, which cost over $70 million, with a marketing budget of over $20 million, has yet to cover its costs. Worse still, the Jackie Chan vehicle, *Around the World in 80 Days*, costing £61.1 million, and with marketing costs of £16.6 million has taken just £7.2 million in the US in its opening week. As Thomas Staggs, Disney's chief financial officer said,

'We found there is no direct correlation between spending more and making more in terms of our returns'.

Source: The Daily Telegraph, 26 June 2004.

A platform release pattern

Case Study   Topsy Turvy

This film, produced with the support of lottery funding, adopted a platform release pattern in the US. This distribution strategy, as the name makes clear, tests out the demand for a film by releasing a film in a limited way and then 'stepping up' the number of prints released if the demand appears to justify it. Clearly non-commercial, *Topsy Turvy* opened on just two screens on Boxing Day 1999, but then, when word of mouth had become effective, it spread wider onto more screens. In

Continued Britain the British director Mike Leigh was determined to try to get the film into the multiplexes. This wasn't easy for Pathe, the Distribution Company, as the exhibitors immediately identified the film as arthouse. However, it did eventually manage a release on 78 screens, a much higher number than is usual for an arthouse film in Britain. Although it did not do great business on its opening weekend, it got audiences at key cinemas over a long period, bringing in over £1 million in the UK.

Case Study Fahrenheit 9/11

A more recent film using a platform release pattern is Michael Moore's documentary film, *Fahrenheit 9/11*, which won the prestigious Palme D'Or at the Cannes Film Festival. The film is essentially an attack on the American President George Bush, and it was originally refused a distribution deal by Disney, the parent company of Miramax, the financiers of the film. Miramax's bosses decided to buy the film back and organise their own distribution. Without the huge resources of a Hollywood studio behind them a platform release pattern made sense and was the tactic adopted in different territories. In France the distributors, Mars Distribution, a subsidiary of Studio Canal, initially released the film on 220 prints, which brought in $3.7 million in five days. Encouraged by this they increased the number of prints available by 150 the next weekend. In the UK Optimum Releasing opened on 131 screens with receipts over three days of $2.4 million and then opened the film in an additional 50 venues the following week and a further 50 the week after that.

Source: *Variety*, 13 July 2004.

Undertaking your own research

As we have mentioned before, the examiners regard visiting local, and different types of cinemas, as part of what they can expect students to do. So the following questions are designed to get your research started, they are not exhaustive. Remember the research techniques discussed above and use them.

Exhibition in your area

First of all identify how many cinemas there are within a 20-minute drive of your area.

- Are they multiplexes, multi-screen, or single-screen cinemas?
- How many screens make up the cinemas?
- Who owns the cinemas? Compare this with what you already know about cinema ownership in the UK.

analyse this Check your local listings.

● What range of films are being shown?
● Is the same film being shown many times over?
● How many smaller-budget films are there being shown?
● How many of the films being shown are British?

A local multiplex

Choose a local cinema, preferably but not necessarily, a multiplex, and try to find out as much about it as you can. Try to talk to the manager, or consult the company's website.

● When was it built?
● Why was it built where it was built?
● How successful has it been?
● Are attendances rising or falling?
● What franchises/concessions stands are there within the cinema?
● What kind of prices are they charging?

Get a programme of future features.

● Is it dominated by Hollywood product, or even by the films of the studio that own the cinema!
● Is it appealing to the expected range of audiences? Young people and thirty-somethings?
● Does the cinema have any special screenings of arthouse films, or classic films, or special sessions for children, or older people?
● What facilities are available for disabled people, for the hard-of-hearing or deaf people?
● Do wheelchair users get to sit anywhere other than on the front row with a stiff neck?

New developments in marketing and promoting films

In this section we are going to consider some of the most recent developments in the production and marketing of films and the impact they may have on the future development of the industry. We will also look in some detail at the use of the Web as a tool of exhibition and promotion.

Even when films are released, as we have seen with critically successful British films like *Ratcatcher*, or Ken Loach's *The Navigators* it can be difficult to get the films widely distributed. American independent film-makers like Todd Solondz (*Happiness, Welcome to the Dollhouse*), or Paul Thomas Anderson (*Boogie Nights, Magnolia, Punch Drunk Love*) are some of the most exciting directors around but they too are struggling to find a way into the multiplexes in the US.

New forms of exhibition

The film critic of the *Chicago Sun Times*, Roger Ebert, lists the following innovations to get around what he calls 'the multiplex gridlock' in the early years of the new millennium.

The shooting gallery

This is the taking of a package of non-mainstream films for short runs in a range of American cities twice a year. The films are shown as a series in Loew's cinemas. This avoids the considerable costs of marketing and promoting each film individually. The run can be a launch pad for a more extended commercial release, as it was for the Mike Hodges directed film *Croupier*.

Integrate with cable television

Ebert writes: 'Another idea has been to integrate the production of "indie" films with the cable channels that will eventually show them.' So British director Michael Winterbottom's *In this World* was part financed by the Sundance Film channel, and after a theatrical run at Loew's cinemas in ten American cities it would have its first television airing on that channel. Although apparently new in the US, this integration of television and film is very familiar to us in Britain, as we have seen through the work of FilmFour and Channel 4.

Digital projection

Ebert goes on:

> 'The word digital brings up another possibility: digital projection which has been mooted as a cheaper alternative to celluloid. If films were supplied on cheap high-definition discs, the same title could play simultaneously in 50 cities with a national publicity campaign . . . I could see how this would help the indies sneak around the multiplex gridlock.'
>
> *Source*: Roger Ebert, 'This is a golden age for movies. So why are the cinemas showing such rubbish?', *The Guardian*, 15 May 2001.

This is a solution which is attractive too to the British government and the Film Council, who believe that the possibility of cheap reproduction of films on digital video will help to limit the huge distributors' costs that British companies find so hard to fund. The latest report from the Department for Culture, Media and Sport published in 2002 has called for the speeding up of the conversion of screens for digital use or the building of new screens and the establishing of a dedicated digital film festival.

Another option to get around the 'multiplex gridlock' that is already being widely used is the World Wide Web.

The Web – as a form of exhibition

With all of this in mind it is easy to see that far from merely being another marketing tool many film-makers believe the web may provide in the long term the best means of ensuring films get distributed and seen. There are now at least fifteen websites specialising in showing short films. Atomfilms and Ifilm are two of the better known ones. Many of them work on the basis of a chart: the higher the number of 'hits' your film receives the longer it will be kept on the website. In this way films can demonstrate their success with audiences. This was the case with the short *Atomic Tabasco*, which demonstrated its popularity on the Atomfilms site and could then generate financing to be made into a 'proper' film. As we have seen, however, the best thing about these sites is that they mean a film does actually get seen.

Activity

These sites are easy to get to and fun to explore. If you haven't already done so spend some time at home or at school looking at some of these films. Note down their details – which site, director, theme – and what you thought of the film. Remember this is the kind of research the examiners value and want to see.

The Web – as a marketing tool

Ever since *The Blair Witch Project*, an extremely low-budget horror picture, promoted itself on the web and went on to gross over $200 million, more or less every film has its own website. These will contain cast and production details, biographies, release dates and details, possibly online chats with crew members, and very likely the opportunity to buy the soundtrack album and other merchandise.

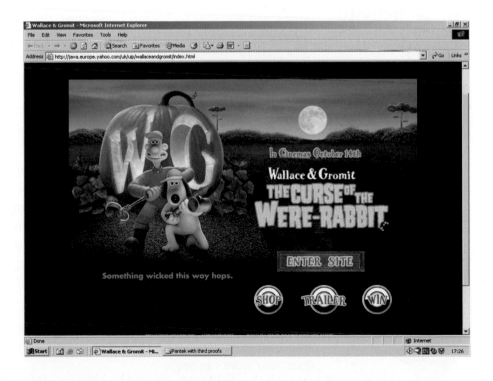

Figure 9.1 ▶

Websites have a number of advantages for marketing and promotion.

The following are generally held to be the main advantages.

1 They can be put in place even before a film goes into production, as is the case with the latest *Star Wars* episode, and they can still be around to promote DVD and video releases long after the film has disappeared from cinemas.
2 They are also much cheaper than traditional print or billboard advertising.
3 They enable a much greater degree of interaction with the target audience. Teenagers and young people are the main users of the internet and, of course, the main audience at the multiplex.

As mentioned in the first chapter, Michael Moore's Palme D'Or winning documentary *Fahrenheit 9/11* was initially prevented from having a cinema release in the US when Disney, the parent company, blocked their subsidiary, Miramax, from releasing the film. However, the Miramax bosses Harvey and Bob Weinstein bought the film back from Disney so they could release it themselves. The website they provided to allow advance bookings and to locate cinemas received 20 million hits per day in its first couple of weeks (*Guardian Unlimited*, 11 June 2004).

Activity Visit some websites for forthcoming films. List the range of information that is given, the merchandise that is for sale, and the elements of interaction with the visitors to the site, e.g. votes for best poster, etc.

The Web – gossip sites

The Web is also a place, of course, where people can discuss films and try to find out about films outside of the control of the studios. Sites such as ComingAttractions.com and Darkhorizons.com are in many ways an extension of that most important form of film 'promotion', word of mouth. As such, some people suspect the studios of trying to supply, or 'plant', stories about films that will be interesting but not damaging to a film's prospects at the box office.

Activity Visit some film gossip or discussion sites. Note down your impressions. Again this is the kind of independent research the examiner wants to see.

Stars are perhaps the single most powerful group of people in the film industry today. We will review the history and development of the star system including the very different status and role that was played by stars in the era of the studio system. We will look at the crucial economic power they wield in the industry and how we can 'take apart' the concept of a 'star'. Finally we will look at the fans' relationship to the stars they admire.

To begin thinking about this area of study do some preliminary research.

Activity

Conduct a questionnaire among your friends and schoolmates to identify their favourite stars. Try to find out why they choose particular stars, and if they would buy a magazine, or see a film, purely because that star was in it.

The history of the star system

The origins of the star system were in the early battle for the control of the industry that we looked at in Chapter 5 between the Motion Pictures Patent Company and those independent producers who would go on to found Hollywood. As we remember, Carl Laemmle was a central figure at this time, breaking with the MPCC, setting up his own Independent Moving Picture Company and later going on to found Universal pictures. He had noticed how audiences gave names to the anonymous actors in the films they enjoyed and looked out for those actors reappearing. He took one of these actors, Florence Lawrence (see fig. 10.1), who worked mainly in films made by the production company Biograph, and who was known to audiences as the Biograph girl. He hired her and planted a newspaper story that she had been killed in a car accident. When she made her next well-publicised appearance in St Louis, crowds of fans came to see her, obviously relieved that the story was not true. The story illustrated to Laemmle that stars could be made in the cinema, just as they could in the theatre or the world of sports.

The incident also showed how a key difference between a star and an actor is that information and stories about stars appear or 'circulate' in secondary sources, like newspapers and magazines, and that this can be very advantageous in creating interest in films. Stars would become

Figure 10.1 ▲

known for their lives outside of their screen roles, they would be willing to incorporate their 'private' life to some extent into their public persona. Laemmle and other producers found promotion of some actors into public figures, or stars, increased their appeal at the box office.

Stars in the studio era

By the early 1920s and the establishment of the classic studio era the box office worth of stars was fully understood by the studio bosses.

Contracted to a studio for seven years and subject to extensions to that contract if they failed to make a film when required by studio bosses, stars like James Cagney and Bette Davis at Warner Bros were in constant battle with the studios to try to get a greater range of roles.

In his autobiography *My Wicked, Wicked Ways*, Errol Flynn, the great swashbuckling action hero, claimed he had been most fulfilled as an actor playing bit parts in a theatre in Northampton because at least he got to play a variety of roles! But as we have seen, stars, and stars in particular genres, like James Cagney in gangster pictures, or Ingrid Bergman in romantic pictures, were absolutely central to making the studios' unfair exhibition practices just about palatable to independent exhibitors. Stars were expected to work long hours and stars like Bette Davis starred in over a hundred pictures for Warner Brothers. Key to controlling the stars was the suspension clause. If the star refused to work, the time they spent refusing to come on set was simply added to their seven-year contract. It was this clause that was deemed illegal by the courts in California when the star Olivia de Havilland challenged the studio bosses. When she won it created a much more equal relationship between the star and the studio.

The other key moment in the stars' realisation of their power was when the agent Lou Wasserman negotiated a proportion of the box office profits of a film for his client, the star James Stewart, for a western, *Winchester '73*. The film was a success and Stewart's pay for this one film was almost as much as the yearly salary paid by MGM to the biggest star of the day, Clark Gable. It is now common practice for stars to have a percentage, sometimes called 'points' of the box office takings of a film.

talking point

Stars obviously have much greater freedom now than then but this is also a freedom to fail. Some critics argue that stars like Brad Pitt and Keanu Reeves would never have been allowed to make some of the poor choice of movies that they have made if studio bosses were still in charge.

Do you agree? Have you always been pleased with the kind of roles your favourite stars have chosen to play?

The importance of stars to the industry

There is no real mystery about why stars are so important.

The recognition factor

The British director John Boorman (*Deliverance, Point Blank*) explains the crucial role the star now plays.

> 'Because films go out to hundreds of cinemas at the same time, they need very expensive advertising. This means the audience needs the recognition factor of a simple story and a star they can identify with. Films now have to succeed on that all important first weekend and, because they can open a picture in that way, this has given a handful of stars enormous power. They choose the projects: they are the people in charge.'
>
> *Source*: Tom Dewe Mathews, 'They're not just rich and famous. They're in charge', *The Guardian*, 19 November 1999.

The biggest box office star in the world is Tom Cruise. Having him in your film will add millions to your box office receipts in the US just on your opening weekend! Looked at that way, his usual fee in excess of $30 million per film still seems like a bargain! Around $30 million is the fee for the top male stars such as Keanu Reeves, or Tom Hanks.

The highest-paid female star is Julia Roberts who charges around $25 million per film. Bear in mind the average American movie, including marketing now costs around $100 million.

Skimping on paying for top Hollywood talent can be dangerous though. Disney tried to save money by substituting director John Lee Hancock, and star Dennis Quaid, for Oscar winners Ron Howard and Russell Crowe for their re-make of the western, *The Alamo*. The film still cost in excess of $100 million but had in the US opening weekend receipts of just $9 million.

talking point

With the opening weekend being of such crucial importance to the success of a movie, only a few tried and trusted stars are guaranteed to 'open' a movie well. Not everyone agrees on who they are though! Who would you say are the most reliably appealing stars in box office terms today?

PRODUCERS AND AUDIENCES (FS2)

181

A star's contract

Given the importance of their role here are some of the demands that may have to be satisfied in a top star's contract.

- *Script*. Will need the star's approval; they will also retain the right to make changes once the film has gone into production.
- *Director*. Needs star's approval.
- *Cast*. Stars often decide who they will act opposite.
- *Publicity*. Stars control what images of them may be used.
- *Schedule*. Stars decide when shooting will begin and end.
- *Nudity*. Contracts will also specify which parts of the star's body can be used other than hands, head and feet.
- *Final cut*. With other than the top directors, stars may also have the right to re-edit the final version of the film to suit themselves.

Stars are also not afraid to exercise these rights. Mel Gibson insisted on the removal of first-time director Brian Helgeland off his thriller *Payback*. Goldie Hawn insisted on the final cut over director Jonathon Demme on *Swing Shift*. Cher did the same with Paul Mazursky on *Faithful*.

The American director Mary Agnes Donoghue explains that a star's wages are often the determining factor in the form a film will take:

'The minute you're directing a movie in which someone is being paid $20 million you're not in charge.'

talking point Given what we have learnt about the roles of director and producer, what are the dangers the power of the star poses for the industry and for audiences?

Defining a star

The preceding discussion, however, assumes we know what a star is, and we do more or less.

talking point The American comedian Rich Hall has this to say about the plots of Tom Cruise films, and his star persona. Can you name the films?

'he's a cocktail waiter, quite a good cocktail waiter, then one day he has a crisis of confidence, he meets a beautiful woman, falls in love and becomes an excellent cocktail waiter . . .'

'he's a fighter pilot, quite a good fighter pilot, then one day he has a crisis of confidence, he meets a beautiful woman, falls in love and becomes an excellent fighter pilot . . .'

'he's a pool player, quite a good pool player, then one day he has a crisis of confidence, he meets a beautiful woman, falls in love and becomes an excellent pool player . . .'

'he's a sports agent, quite a good sports agent, then one day he has a crisis of confidence, he meets a beautiful woman, falls in love, and becomes an excellent sports agent . . .'

Source: Media Studies seminar, Queen Margaret, University College, Edinburgh.

Hall's point is a good one but what we mean by a star is perhaps more complicated and can be examined in more detail.

We know from our discussion of the origins of the star system that a star is defined as an actor whose image and character enters into secondary sources of circulation, such as newspapers, magazines, television and radio appearances. An obvious danger exists here for the stars and the studios. How do they control what is said about their stars in all these secondary sources? The joke above by Rich Hall is an example of an ironic, mocking treatment of a star in secondary circulation in this book. More serious though is malicious gossip, scandal, and intrusion into the private lives of the stars which is a constant danger. We should not underestimate the extent to which the actors' agencies, and the studios' Public Relations agencies (PR) will try to control the content of these secondary sources. Questions in television or radio interviews will have to be submitted in advance and certain lines of questioning will be specifically forbidden. Perhaps the best-known interviewer on British television, Michael Parkinson, has recently complained that he can get some of the biggest Hollywood stars on his show but then he's not allowed to ask them anything interesting. Questions have to focus on the latest film they are promoting!

From 1915 to around 1955, what we know as the studio era, the control of the image of the star was the responsibility of the publicity departments of the studio to which the star was contracted. The stars had a greater or lesser involvement in satisfying the audience's curiosity about them. Joan Crawford apparently answered personally all of the thousands of letters she received from fans.

talking point

We might recall at this point how the studios maintained their control over independent exhibitors in the studio era. Can you remember how stars and genres played a crucial role in that?

Today, it is the star's own agencies and publicists who will seek to build up and control the star's image. The cost of these agencies will be built into the budget for any film the star is working on.

These agencies, such as the Creative Artists Agency who act for Sean Connery, Will Smith, Pierce Brosnan, Tom Hanks, Tom Cruise, Nicholas

Cage, and Brad Pitt, are some of the most important players in the film industry. The stars will also have personal publicists such as the company BWR who handle any requests from the media for interviews with Brad Pitt, Leonardo DiCaprio or Adam Sandler, among others.

Activity

Collect together as many magazines, tabloid and broadsheet newspapers as you can over a week and try to identify which of the film-based or star-based stories are really just advertising the latest product, and which maybe are ones revealing scandalous or embarrassing information that Hollywood's PR agencies might be concerned about?

Stars are, like genres, fundamentally about giving the audience some more of what they liked before. However, the star's role needs to vary a bit so that the novelty, or appeal, of the star does not wear off. When we go to see a Jim Carrey film we can be pretty confident of what we are going to get, but we are also looking forward to seeing how in this film he is going to be slightly different.

Let's now look at one star in some detail.

Christine Gledhill argues that a star can be thought of as having four distinct elements:

1 The real person.
2 The characters/roles they play.
3 The persona – a combination of the first two.
4 The image that then circulates in secondary media.

Source: Christine Gledhill (ed.), *Stardom: Industry of Desire* (Routledge, 1991).

Brad Pitt: The components of a star

Real person

Although tremendously handsome and successful we are also aware of Pitt as an 'ordinary person' striving to find satisfaction in his work and in his personal life. Much of the coverage of Pitt focuses on his attempts to gain credibility as an actor in such films as *Se7en, Kalifornia*, or *Seven Years in Tibet*; his attempts to establish successful relationships, especially with the successful actress, Gwyneth Paltrow, *Friends* star, Jennifer Aniston, or Angelina Jolie; his being really an 'ordinary' guy, as much of the publicity for his time on the set of British director Guy Ritchie's *Snatch* suggested, as did his self-confessed love of the cult English singer, Nick Drake. His attempt to maintain his authenticity as an actor led to his, reputedly, supporting David Fincher's determination to retain the desperately bleak ending of *Se7en* in the face of pressure from the studio to insist on a happier ending.

The roles

The key roles that have shaped audience's perceptions of him have been his supporting role in *Thelma and Louise* and his leads in Robert

Redford's *A River Runs Through It* and *Legends of the Fall*. In these he played young men of languid beauty and charm, at ease with themselves and, especially in the latter roles, with the natural beauty of the American landscapes surrounding them. This gentler side of his screen persona was also the basis of his role as the rather passive Louis in *Interview with a Vampire*.

At times he has seemed keen to play against type, concerned that he might be thought to be no more than a 'pretty' actor, most notably in *Kalifornia*, where he plays a serial killer, but also in his willingness to support the dark vision of director David Fincher in *Se7en* and *Fight Club*, roles in which his 'pretty boy' looks were considerably knocked about.

By the time of *Troy*, playing the legendary warrior Achilles, Pitt was attempting to 'harden' his image, in a mainstream 'event' movie in particular by becoming more muscular in appearance.

Persona

The persona is a blending of role and the real person, and although still dominated by his physical beauty it contains a certain earnestness and seriousness in his choice of 'difficult' roles such as those in *Se7en* and *Seven Years in Tibet*, and that of an IRA man in *The Devil's Own*, that suggests some discomfort with how he is perceived. This accords with his decision to turn down the role of Neo in *The Matrix*. The role revitalised Keanu Reeves's career. In his choice of the role of Achilles in *Troy*, however, he took on the straightforward role of a matinee idol action-hero.

Image

Image is the set of values that that particular star has been thought to embody or personify, chiming in some way with the mood of the times. In this sense Pitt became a star almost overnight with *Thelma and Louise* when his charisma and sexual charm seemed to embody a new mood in which men would need to work harder to attract and keep women and women could be open and explicit about their sexual fantasies. As we have seen, he has often seemed to be uncomfortable with this fantasy element of his image yet he can also reinforce it as he did with the extended photo shoots of himself in *W* fashion magazine, that included shots of him semi-naked. These shots were part of the publicity drive that accompanied *Fight Club*, a film where, perhaps, his depiction of a man driven by what he saw as a creeping feminising of modern culture angrily rejected the 'new man' and re-stated a simple brute masculinity. The controversy surrounding the film suggested this development of his image chimed with the mood of the times.

talking point | Arguably Pitt's later roles have not quite caught the public mood as well as his early appearances with the exception perhaps of *Fight Club*. He was not generally considered a success as Achilles in *Troy*, described by reviewers as lacking charisma as a male hero, in comparison to, say, Russell Crowe in *Gladiator*. However, since *Troy* he has reappeared at the top of 'Sexiest Male in the World' lists in women's magazines. Does his image still fit well with the times?

Activity

Now choose a star of your own, perhaps one you really like, and try to identify the different parts of their status as a star, the real person, the roles, the persona, and the image.

Stars and their fans

As we have seen, part of the central appeal of a star is that they can somehow connect with their audience in a way that ordinary actors can't. The studios and stars' agents always seek to control the information that is given out about stars and so control people's perception of them.

Ironically, however, fans' very devotion to stars leads them to create material celebrating the star which is outside of the studios' control.

What does it mean to be a film fan?

You may, or may not, from the 'self-portrait' questions in Chapter 6 have identified yourself as an enthusiastic film fan. However, what we should be able to agree on is that the contemporary film industry has succeeded in making its products, films, spin-offs and stars, a staple part of our media, or cultural, diet. Hollywood is very hard to avoid. However, we can remember from our previous discussions of spectatorship that we each have our individual preferences for viewing films, on DVD or in the cinema, and of relating to Hollywood's films, genres and stars. We can 'negotiate' our relation to film through the friends we go to the cinema with, the film magazines and reviews we may read, and, increasingly, through discussion and news groups that are available on the internet. As a student of film your relationship to film is, of course, also shaped by your studies and the preferences of your teachers. As a film teacher and fan myself, I am influenced by the critics, and, in particular, the weekly choices as film of the week by the long-established film critic of *The Observer* newspaper, Philip French. If he recommends a film, I'm going to try to see it! Hopefully you are reading magazines like *Empire* and *Sight and Sound* to get enthusiastic about films and develop your personal taste in movies.

Let's try to explore this in a bit more detail by looking at a film fan website, the 'Keira Forever Fanboard', dedicated to the young English star, Keira Knightley, who starred in *Bend it like Beckham* and who has just starred in her first major Hollywood role as Guinevere in *King Arthur*. The discussion forum is moderated by Sarika, Smint, Emma,

Melinda and Bella and is divided into ten discussion groups. The 'Just Keira' discussion group has had over 150 topics and 500 posts, while the forum as a whole has had 909 topics and 25,741 posts and has 463 members as of 21 July 2004.

Let's look at some of the posts – the first line of each entry gives the topic being discussed.

Just Keira/ re: One day with Keira – 7.19am

Started by Marianita/Post by MarkOB

I think I would start by asking her exactly what she wanted to do.

And then do that!

Just Keira/ re: Songs that remind you of Keira – 7.29am

Started by the Black Rider/ Post by MarkOB

This is quite interesting actually. There was a song I listened to quite a lot around Christmastime when I became a fan of Keira's. It's by Katie Melua and it's called 'The Closest Thing to Crazy'.

Just Keira/Re: Keira and the Office – 7.33am

Started by the Black Rider/Post by MarkOB

I'm sure she's said something about being a fan of The Office before – However I'm still laughing to myself about the thought of Ricky Gervais in 'Love Actually'!

Keira News/Re: KK doesn't mind taking off her clothes? – 7.40am

Started by Cristiano/Post by MarkOB

on May 30 2004 6:01pm Cristiano wrote:

A Brazilian website published a note today that she would do nude scenes because she is proud of her 'genetic heritage'.

Oxico says: Probably with the intention of having all producers in Hollywood willing to hire her, Keira told reporters: 'I'm not saying I'll take my clothes off in first opportunity, but I think that sometimes it's necessary'.

Keira's Movies/Re: King Arthur thoughts – 8:05 am

Started by Sarika/Post by Kelley Z

I guess we just thought differently because I thought they did a great job with the movie!

Source: Keira Forever Fanboard website

What kind of pleasures are the contributors getting out of visiting and contributing to this website? Clearly there is a purely social aspect to it. They all share a common attraction to Keira and that then gives them a basis for social contact. Kiera, like all stars, is also clearly a fantasy figure, desirable and accessible through her movies and through such discussion groups which create an illusion of being close to her, and which indulge such fantasies as 'a day with Keira'. Although this may seem silly, these may be very young contributors who are finding ways to be comfortable with a lot of the exciting but disturbing feelings that adolescence brings about the opposite sex. The fanboard is a 'safe' place to express and explore these feelings.

The fanboard is also a place of refining and sharing critical judgements. These can be fairly straightforward like disagreeing over the quality of her latest film as Kelley Z does, but they can also be quite sophisticated and sceptical, as in Oxico's 'reading' of Keira's reported willingness to do nude scenes as an attempt to get producers to offer her more roles. The fanboard is also part of that broader ongoing 'conversation' about popular culture that the studios work so hard to be a part of, so, for example, liking Keira is made more memorable by liking a particular song at the same time as Mark OB does with a Katie Melua song, or Keira's glamorous, romantic status is made clearer by a humorous comparison with Ricky Gervais of the television series *The Office*.

Activity

Find a fanboard for a star you particularly like and analyse some of the contributions.

Topic study: the swinging sixties

This chapter deals specifically with British film and attempts to analyse it from a cultural perspective (as opposed to the institutional perspective covered earlier), and draw out the messages and values with regard to representations of social reality. Representations covered will focus largely on class and gender together with the idea that British cinema offers something distinct but multi-faceted in terms of national identity. The social and historical context that underpins the topic study will be explored in an attempt to locate the film's impact and a comparative analysis of film within the same topic area will highlight similarities and differences in terms of messages and values.

The topic covered in this section is 'the swinging sixties'.

British cinema

Before we look at any topic areas it is important to explore and define for ourselves the notion of British cinema as distinct from other cinemas from around the world, particularly (as it dominates the global film market) cinema from the USA.

To understand 'British cinema' we must first explore definitions and ideas around the notion of what it is to be British. This forms our 'national identity' – how do we perceive ourselves as a nation and how do others perceive us? Each country has its own national identity, which is conveyed through its history, arts, music, press, popular culture, etc. Cinema forms part of this and we learn a lot about other countries and their people from watching the cinema of that country; perhaps this is why we know so much about the USA. For example, we may know the states which make up North America, may understand their colloquialisms (even use some of them), know who is head of their government and so on but can we be so accurate when it comes to the same points regarding France, Italy, Germany or Spain? Of course, mass media and the control of multinational corporations, including the organisations you looked at in the chapters in Part 2, 'Producers and Audiences', have much to do with this but cinema is important as a means of conveying cultural information. If we learn so much about other countries from their cinema what do other countries learn from British cinema?

talking point

How do you think the British are perceived by other nations?

How do you think the British perceive themselves?

What aspects of 'national identity' are raised through your discussion?

How difficult is it to define 'Britishness' and why?

Britishness and British cinema

The difficulty with determining the national identity of Britain comes from the fact that being British is so many different things to so many different people.

There are:

● regional differences like dialects and accents

● cultural and religious differences

● racial differences – a range of ethnic backgrounds

● class differences, ranging from underclass and working class to upper class and aristocracy

but all have equal claim to the term 'British'.

The concept of Britishness is multi-faceted (having many different parts) and although we can list stereotypical qualities of Britishness (reserved, stiff upper lip, etc.) how many of those qualities can we really say apply to ourselves and the people we meet from day to day and how many of them are 'mythical' qualities constructed with only one section of society in mind?

It is because Britain is a multi-faceted nation that British cinema has a diverse range of films each conveying a different aspect of British life.

Activity

Look at the list of British films and assess them in terms of genre and the representation of Britishness that they convey. If you are unfamiliar with any, look them up on IMBD (Internet Movie Data Base) and read their synopses.

● *Gosford Park* (Robert Altman, 2001)

● *Trainspotting* (Danny Boyle, 1996)

● *Bride and Prejudice* (Gurinder Chadha, 2004)

● *Football Factory* (Nick Love, 2004)

● *Iris* (Richard Eyre, 2001)

● *The English Patient* (Anthony Minghella, 1996)

● *Lock, Stock and Two Smoking Barrels* (Guy Ritchie, 1998)

● *Brassed Off* (Mark Herman, 1996)

● *Sex Lives of the Potato Men* (Andy Humphries, 2004).

Being aware of the many different representations of Britishness helps in the study of British cinema as it enables us to be critical of 'blanket' statements that presume that all British people are the same.

However, there is one overriding theme in British cinema, which seems to raise its head time and time again despite the time period or the genre, and that is the issue of class. It appears that British cinema cannot disentangle itself from the country's complex class system and it could be this that makes British cinema so distinctive.

The topic that we will now explore will address the representation of class as being at the core of its interest and success. It is worth noting that although we are concentrating here on the 'swinging sixties', other topic areas of study like comedy, the war and its aftermath or passions and repressions all have social class as a key component of their distinctiveness in terms of British national identity.

British cinema: the swinging sixties

This decade was a time of great change and has been portrayed many times not only in films actually from the period but also in modern films. Your knowledge of the 1960s, if you did not live through them, will be informed by a combination of formal history, popular culture, the press and family/personal stories.

talking point What do you know about the 1960s? Discuss and describe what you understand life in 1960s Britain to have been like.

1960s social and historical context

If the Austin Powers' films are how you imagine the 1960s to have been it could be that you are languishing under a common misconception that life at that time was one great succession of parties, sex, money, groovy clothes and trendy haircuts! This 'mythical' view of the 1960s that informs so much of the nostalgia that we witness has become so entrenched in popular culture and is such a pleasant vision of the past that some of the realities of the decade have gone unchecked in recent times and this section will attempt to deal with this later. However, like all myths the 'swinging sixties' phenomena must have some basis in truth and so our first task is to explore exactly how the label of 'swinging Britain' (or perhaps more accurately 'swinging London') came about. To do this we need to look at the era's social and historical context.

The 1960s were certainly a time of great upheaval. The war had ended in 1945 and the babies that had been born during and at the end of it had now grown into teenagers and young adults. There was a feeling of wanting to break with the past, which represented the 'old' pre-war Britain with its outdated traditions. The new generation wanted to forge new lives with new values and were very forward-looking in their attitude. From this emerged what would become known as the 'generation gap', a gulf of misunderstanding between the young and their parents, and would be the basis of the perceived 'rebellion' or 'revolution' that are both held to be common features of the era. The break with the past came as young people began to reject the values of their elders and 'youth culture' became the 'hip' phenomenon that would make the decade 'swing'.

The rebuilding of the country after the war led to a buoyant economy, full employment and a drive to modernise the nation through innovation and new technology. The space race was on (man first reached the moon in 1969) and advances in communications, especially television, radios and telephones were rapid, all of which were eagerly taken up by the young generation. The Prime Minister Harold Wilson made speeches about this and how the youth could play their part:

> 'This is the time for a breakthrough to an exciting and wonderful period in our history, in which all can and must take part. Our young men and women, especially, have in their hands the power to change the world. We want the youth of Britain to storm the new frontiers of knowledge . . .'
>
> *Source*: Harold Wilson, 1964 Election Campaign speech.

Young people had a new confidence and since the 1950s the 'teenager' had gained a reputation (much of it through cinema) as a symbol of anti-authoritarian values and as being consumer-driven owing to the disposable income (ready cash) that they now had.

Advertisers and the media, including film-makers, focused on this new market-force and produced products aimed directly at the kinds of things young people were interested in. The social and political agenda was also, to a large extent, being driven by this new liberal, or as some would say, 'permissive' (anything goes) generation.

This new 'power' of young people led to social, political and cultural changes that facilitated the freedoms they had come to demand, for example, the freedom to experiment with:

- music
- fashion
- art
- drugs
- sex

and freedom from the typical restraints of

- class
- gender
- race.

This 'freedom', which often underpins the notion of the 'swinging' sixties, can only really be understood by assessing the social and moral restraints that they were kicking against.

analyse this

Take a look at some of the key moments of the 1960s in an attempt to absorb the context of the period. Take each point and discuss it in relation to 'freedom' of all kinds: political, social and moral freedom, and freedom of creative expression. If you are unsure of any of the events, research them on the internet or ask your tutor to explain.

1960   *Lady Chatterley's Lover* trial; ban lifted on what had been seen as an 'obscene publication'.
        Contraceptive pill introduced meaning women had more control over reproduction.

1961   Mass arrests of supporters of CND (Campaign for Nuclear Disarmament).
        The Beatles release first record, 'Love Me Do'.
        Immigration Act restricts immigration from Commonwealth (after the war when the country needed rebuilding and there was full employment, immigrants from Britain's colonies were actively invited/recruited to come to Britain for work).

1963   Harold Wilson (leader of Labour) makes a speech about the possibilities of new technology.
        John Profumo (government minister) resigns over sex scandal with a prostitute.
        Mary Whitehouse launches a campaign to 'clean up' (remove sex from) television.

1964   *A Hard Day's Night* is released at the cinema.

1965   Radio Caroline (first pirate radio station) begins broadcasting.

1966   Death of Winston Churchill.
        Capital punishment suspended.
        Race Relations Act passed.

1967   England wins the World Cup.
        Labour wins general election.
        Male homosexuality legalised.
        Abortion Act passed making abortion legal.

1968   Demonstrations against Vietnam War.
        Decimalisation (money converted into modern pounds and pence).

1969   British army moves into Belfast.
        Colour television starts.
        Capital punishment abolished.
        Divorce reform act make divorce less complicated.

From the list above it becomes obvious that Britain was changing rapidly and its stereotypical national identity (which prevailed in British films of the 1940/50s) – of being white, middle class and 'reserved' – was being challenged. There was a need for equality in society on many levels including class, gender and race. The perception was that everyone had 'pulled together' during the war and the new generation did not want a return to the deep class and gender divisions that had existed previously. The working class were now becoming more affluent; women who had taken part in the war effort had found a new independence, which they wanted to sustain; and in the rebuilding of the country immigrants from Britain's colonies had settled into life in Britain. All of this meant that the social fabric of Britain was evolving and British film-makers were keen to express this in their work.

key terms

Sexual revolution a term that encompasses many changes in the sexual attitudes and freedom of young people including the introduction of the pill (liberated female sexuality); divorce laws; and the legalisation of homosexuality and abortion

In theory at least, all these social changes led to new freedoms, but it was especially those relating to the **sexual revolution** that gave the impression that the country was 'swinging'.

A 'New Wave' of British film-makers who were themselves young and had come up through the ranks of television were keen to express new ideas in new ways and began making cinema that was innovative and challenging.

Films which were produced around this time contributed to the experimental atmosphere and the general feeling of lively, creative expression. Some film-makers captured the essence of the 'swinging sixties' while others, like the social realists, were keen to explore the underside, or realities, of life in the decade as it was lived for ordinary people. As we have mentioned previously, we must not fall into the trap of thinking that what may have been a swinging time for some was a swinging time for all.

One such film that epitomises the 'swinging' aspect of the 1960s was Richard Lester's, *A Hard Day's Night* (1964).

The 'swinging sixties' genre: A Hard Day's Night

If there is one film that captures the 'myth' of the 1960s perfectly it is *A Hard Day's Night*. It is a film that typifies the youthful, irreverent and playful attitude that supposedly prevailed at the time, personified in the star image of The Beatles. The Beatles were at the height of their fame when the film was made and have since become synonymous with the decade. The film is a vehicle for an album of the same name, which in itself was ground breaking and heralded a new way of marketing products at the young. As a prototype for the first 'video' (and a way of bringing a pop concert to people who could not attend in person) its influence is still with us today. It is a film that was regarded as innovative not just in content but also in style.

The themes of this classic swinging sixties genre revolve around the youth of the day (personified by The Beatles) and their lifestyles. Hence music and fashion are dominant and are symbols of their independence.

Music and fashion

Because the 1960s were a time of innovation in design, music and fashion, certain kinds of cinema acted as a 'shop window' for these new styles. *A Hard Day's Night* is certainly thin on plot but is very heavy on style (both cinematic and fashion) and an audience at that time would have been watching to see what John, Paul, Ringo and George were wearing, as much as for what they were singing and saying. Their suits and haircuts are featured prominently (they rarely seem to be out of their 'stage clothes') with both these things being given scenes, or at least lines, of their own.

Press conference scene:

Interviewer to Ringo: What do you call that haircut?
Ringo: Arthur.
Interviewer: What do you call that collar?
Ringo: A collar.

analyse this

Take a look at the 'press conference' scene not only for its content but also for its style. The Beatles are playing 'themselves' in the film and the way in which the film is shot and cut, along with the questioning, lends the scene an air of spontaneity and a fake documentary style. This realist style which was used to even greater effect in the social realist/kitchen sink films of the time (*A Taste of Honey*, Richardson, 1961; *A Kind of Loving*, Schlesinger, 1962; *Up the Junction*, Collinson, 1968) leads the audience to fuse reality and fiction which works perfectly in a film of this type where the audience want to feel they are getting close to the 'real' Beatles. Similarly in the concert/rehearsal scene at the end of the film, the event is presented as 'live', using obscured camera frames and angles which again present a documentary feel and allow the audience to feel that this is truly unfolding in front of them and they are getting a glimpse of something they would not normally be party to, when in fact the film was carefully scripted. Use of handheld cameras and jump-cuts were a direct influence from French New Wave and the 1960s opened up a whole new era of freedom of expression.

key terms

Social realism
This genre, common in the 1960s, employed a cinematic style that attempted to construct an authentic 'realism' on screen through various narrative techniques and cinematic code use. One technique was to cast non-actors to play dramatic parts. This, coupled with handheld camera, authentic mise en scène and lack of editing, created a documentary 'look' that complemented the real life issues that the films were concerned with.

Freedom as a theme AND a style of film-making: A Hard Day's Night and If....

When analysing this period it is easy to make the mistake of looking only at the content of the films for their messages and values (macro analysis) but there is much to be found, in terms of ideas and themes, in the style of film-making that some 1960s directors adopted (micro). All the ideas mentioned in this chapter regarding the freedom and rebellion of the swinging sixties, class structure and escape, can be found in the film *If....* (Anderson,1968). The class element of the film takes on a slightly different perspective and looks at the hierarchical and restrictive structure of the public school, with the rebellious theme exemplified in the 'crusaders'' need to break free. But what is also striking is the visual style of the film which in some ways can be compared with *A Hard Day's Night*. *A Hard Day's Night* was heralded for its new, trendy style of filmmaking, a style which is now established in the world of the pop video – jump-cuts, handheld camera, sped-up shots, etc – and it led to the 'kaleidoscopic' films of the late sixties which experimented with new camera angles and special effects. Similarly, *If....* experimented with a new visual look, and like *A Hard Day's Night* incorporated a surreal element into the film-making. Whereas *A Hard Day's Night* had The Beatles running alongside a moving train carriage, *If....* also played with the fictional boundaries of the film, blurring so-called reality with dreamlike/surreal sequences, for example the scene where the Reverend appears from a drawer. The film also switches film stock from colour to black and white and vice versa and even though Anderson admits this is merely because he ran out of stock, the fact that he felt brave enough to be able to do this and challenge his audience demonstrates the radical nature of film-making at this time. The effect is disorientating and yet exciting and both films use the 'newness' of their visual style to complement the theme of freedom, both socially and artistically. Equally, both films are concerned with a new generation pushing away the old order and making way for a 'revolution' of some kind.

Activity

Look at the film *If ....* and identify scenes which represent freedom of style as well as social freedoms.

Rebellion

In the 'advertising agency' scene in *A Hard Day's Night* where George is asked to promote a shirt, the 'power' of youth is conveyed. The message in both the advertising and the press conference scenes is that the youth are 'cool' and somewhat mischievous and rebellious. Young people are often misunderstood but are in control when it comes to fashion and music. Others may want to control them (market them) but they are determined to remain free and independent. This same theme is conveyed throughout the film, as their manager who takes on the 'parental' role has no authority over them.

Activity

List and describe the scenes where the band acts in a rebellious or anti-authoritarian way.
What effect do you think this behaviour would have had on the audience at the time?
How does this behaviour endear the band to us?

One of the key ways in which The Beatles are 'sold' to us and which the audience can identify with is in the representation of their apparent 'ordinariness' despite their fame.

The cult of celebrity, which was emerging in the sixties, and which is apparent everywhere today, celebrated the idea that everyone, no matter what their class, had equal opportunities. This meant that even if you were from a working class background you could 'bypass' the class system if you had fame and/or wealth: a so-called 'classless' society that The Beatles personified in this film and with their star image generally. It was cool to be working class with a regional accent was the rather utopian and romantic notion that provided the theme in many films of the 'swinging' genre.

Class representations in A Hard Day's Night

The 1960s brought a drive for equality on all fronts and not least of these was the need to bring down class divisions. British films of the 1960s, as mentioned, often depicted the working class as 'heroes', a turnaround from the pre-war films, which were dominated by middle-class sensibilities and representations.

Activity

Look at the scene with the city gent on the train and analyse how it represents the difference between the generations and the classes. Don't just consider the dialogue, also look at the details of the mise en scène and describe how they create meaning. What are the messages and values regarding class that are conveyed in the scene?

There are many other references to the working-class background of the stars throughout the film:

- The bottle of 'HP' sauce placed in the hotel mise en scène in the fan-letter writing scene.
- The accents that prevail throughout with the friendly Northern tones of the Liverpudlians contrasting sharply with the middle-class Southern accents of the 'media types' (floor manager/advertising executive etc.).
- The casino scene sees The Beatles about to be turned away for being uncouth and lower class until they are recognised and then of course they are waved through.
- When Ringo leaves the band he finds life as an 'ordinary person' much more satisfying and finds common ground with the working-class boy who has a similarly strong working-class accent and envies his independence.

The themes of escape and freedom run through the film.

Ultimately, in the final scene, The Beatles board a helicopter and fly away for yet more excitement. Throughout the film, the message urges you to escape the confines of class and killjoy authority, be free to do what you want to do, wear the clothes you want and listen to the music you like, dance, scream and shout, enjoy life and don't let anyone spoil your fun – it's the swinging sixties!

analyse this

Look at the scene where the band runs out onto the playing field. Consider its function in the narrative. What is it meant to signify? Study the cinematography and editing and how it enhances the theme of the new and modern. What is the joy of watching this scene for the audience?

But was life in the 1960s really that simple? The portrayal of The Beatles in this film was, at the time, in keeping with their 'clean-cut' image. They are seen smoking and making cheeky innuendos and, in the train carriage, John Lennon sniffs from a Coca-cola bottle in a sly reference to drug-taking, but generally the 'swinging' element is all in the independent attitude of the film and its characters. The portrayal of the sexual revolution is limited to the sight of girls who are free to follow them in a predatory fashion and scream with delight at their every move. They are gazed at by these girls with a 'look' that has previously been reserved for men looking at women: as sex objects (see the singing scene in the 'cage' on the train); but beyond that there is little overt reference to sexual freedom.

In other films from this decade, however, the theme of independence and freedom was tied in directly with the sexual revolution. The changes in attitudes towards sex brought liberation but also consequences, which means we must look a little closer at the notion (myth) that everyone was 'swinging' in the sixties. Also, those class boundaries, which seem so easily overcome in *A Hard Day's Night*, remain as rigid as ever if we explore the decade further. So how does the portrayal of 1960s' life in *A Hard Day's Night* compare with other films from the decade?

Alfie: the swinging sixties – with consequences

The sixties are often portrayed as a time of great fun with no consequences. The portrayal of characters like James Bond (very popular at the time; the first Bond film, *Dr No* was released in 1960) shows a man who is able to drink vodka-martinis without getting drunk, order food without paying, fight without getting bruised and sleep with hundreds of women without getting any of them pregnant! A nice escapist idea, but as far removed from reality as you could get – another embodiment of the myth of the 'swinging' sixties.

Other films attempted to add some reality to the portrayal of life in the sixties and one such British film was *Alfie*. (Interestingly, Lewis Gilbert who directed *Alfie* also directed *You Only Live Twice*.)

Alfie was made in 1966, a couple of years after *A Hard Day's Night*, and they are similar in some ways but at the same time different in their overall messages and values with the latter conveying the consequences as well as the fun of the swinging sixties.

Alfie: Music, fashion and independence

Alfie shares the same preoccupations with music, fashion and independence as the Beatles and, as with *A Hard Day's Night*, this reflected the interests and attitudes of the young people that would form the majority of the audience at the time.

The musical soundtrack to the film by Sonny Rollins and the title track by Burt Bacharach were popular in their own right, won independent awards and sold millions of copies on the film's release. This is similar to the way that the album of *A Hard Day's Night* was promoted through Lester's film; the pop culture of music and film share the same young audience.

Fashion also features heavily in *Alfie*, as it does in *A Hard Day's Night*. Just like the Beatles, Michael Caine is represented as the fashionable role model for trendy youth with his impeccable taste in suits and shirts. His suits/shirts are something that he is very proud of and we see women in his life constantly washing them or dry cleaning them or, much to Alfie's dismay, crying on them:

> 'Ere, mind me shirt', says Alfie to Annie, with obvious care and attention *for the shirt*!

In fact in promotional material for the film Michael Caine is photographed with two tailor's dummies suggesting he is as stylish (but perhaps as empty) as they are.

As well as music and fashion, Alfie shares the same need for freedom and independence as the Beatles in *A Hard Day's Night*. He is the loveable rogue, funny and charming, not wanting to be pinned down but wanting to be free to enjoy the fun on offer in the swinging sixties, just like John, Paul, Ringo and George.

However, there is a side to this film that is not apparent in *A Hard Day's Night*. As well as portraying the fun Alfie appears to be having, the film injects a sense of reality that brings with it some serious social messages that are to some extent glossed over in *A Hard Day's Night*.

Alfie and class

Alfie is, just like the Beatles, a working-class protagonist. But unlike the Beatles he is neither wealthy nor famous. Instead he experiences some of the practicalities of everyday life that the working-class audience could identify with rather than escape from.

analyse this

Lewis Gilbert (director) in an interview with *The Guardian* in 2001 spoke about the need for working-class representation on British cinema screens.

> 'When we first screened it in America – to 400 people at Paramount – my anxiety was that they wouldn't understand the cockney. The chief of distribution said, "When we open the film in America, we ought to dub it. What about Tony Curtis?" I said: "No, you mustn't do that! It's the fact that it's cockney that makes it interesting."
>
> At that time, there had never been a cockney film. In cinema, the cockney was the man who said: "Guvnor, your car's outside." You never saw a cockney family with real problems. In the 60s, we were beginning to make films that reflected something of the British way of life. Before *Alfie* and its contemporaries, British film was all Noël Coward and drawing rooms.
>
> *Source*: Edited from 'All About Alfie', *The Guardian*, 4 May 2001.

Gilbert says that, "it's the fact that it's cockney that makes it interesting".

Do you agree with this? Could the same story be told from a middle-class perspective or set elsewhere?

talking point

Look at the 2004 remake of *Alfie* starring Jude Law, which is set in the USA. How does it compare with the original?

Alfie has a strong working-class, London accent, and although it is authentic and charming like those of the Beatles (and was a refreshing sound in cinema of the 1960s) it carries with it certain social limitations that the film and Caine's character acknowledge rather than ignore.

analyse this

Look at the scene in the flat where Gilda and Alfie discuss having their son adopted.

What comments are made about the child's well-being and reasons for him being adopted?

The mise en scène in the film also serves to portray *two* sides of London and not just the famous tourist sites that are the setting for so many British films. Using real locations the film shows its (international) audience many famous landmarks such as Tower Bridge, The Embankment, Festival Hall and Hyde Park, but it also shows the back streets of working-class south London and the run-down areas of the riverside around Battersea to its domestic audience who would possibly identify with this realistic portrayal.

analyse this

Look at the scene where Alfie and Gilda are walking down the street where they live.

Also look at the setting of the interior of their flat.

Describe the mise en scène of both in detail and try to explain the meaning it conveys about working-class life in sixties Britain.

Realist style

When trying to portray the realities of working-class life it helps to use cinematic techniques which convey reality or authenticity, and just as *A Hard Day's Night* tries to do this with its style of filming (as mentioned earlier) so *Alfie* employs similar details and techniques to give a sense of the 'real'.

Apart from real locations and colloquial dialogue the film adds narrative detail – for example, Alfie having to borrow the money for the abortion – to show the complexities, not the simplicities, of everyday life.

Michael Caine also introduces himself as 'Alfie', again confusing reality with fiction in the same way that the Beatles play themselves but are also characters. In fact the advertising for the film on its release read, 'Michael Caine *is* Alfie'.

Another unusual technique is the way that Alfie speaks directly through the screen to the audience.

talking point

What effect does the direct address to camera have? Why do you think it was filmed this way?

Alfie and the sexual revolution

One of the main differences between *A Hard Day's Night* and *Alfie* is its representation of women and the sexual revolution. Whereas *A Hard Day's Night* glosses over the true position of women in sixties society, *Alfie* deals with it head-on and it is this theme which underpins the whole film.

Alfie is a womaniser and, accompanied by the jaunty score of the soundtrack, he appears to be the living embodiment of the swinging sixties. He picks up women and drops them like playthings, then moves on to the next one. He even refers to women as 'it'.

analyse this

What does Alfie's attitude towards women indicate about their social status in sixties Britain? Do any of the women appear to be enjoying the same freedoms as Alfie? How are the others represented?

Anna Billson in *My Name Is Michael Caine*, (Muller, 1991) says:

> 'The main trouble with the film is that all Alfie's women, with the notable exception of Shelly Winters as the older woman, are such pathetic specimens that one almost ends up sympathising with Alfie's wayward behaviour.'
>
> *Source*: Anne Billson, *My Name Is Michael Caine* (Frederick Muller, 1991).

Women in films of the sixties were often portrayed in subservient positions or where they were objectified in a sexual way. The sexism that exists in *Alfie* is an accurate portrayal of the position women held in sixties society and it was one of the reasons for the call for women's equality and rights which would eventually be made law in the early 1970s.

With this in mind, is the message of the film to confirm these stereotypes or is it to challenge them?

talking point

Do you think Anna Billson is right? Are the women in *Alfie* pathetic?

MESSAGES AND VALUES: BRITISH AND IRISH CINEMA (FS3)

Activity

Look again at each main female character in turn and follow her story from her entrance in the narrative to her exit.

- the married woman having an affair at the beginning
- Gilda (the single mum)
- Annie (the runaway)
- Vivien (the older, married housewife)
- Ruby (the American)

How many of them ultimately take control of their own lives and make the decision to leave Alfie?

The abortion scene: consequences and a call for change

The abortion scene appears to be the turning point of the film; the point at which Alfie's philandering ways catch up with him. Is he ever the same character again after this point?

talking point

Look at the abortion scene in *Alfie* and consider your responses to it. How does Vivien come across in the scene?

How do you feel about Alfie after this scene?

analyse this

Watch the conversation Alfie has with his friend immediately after the abortion scene in which he describes his reaction. What do you understand to be the messages behind such dialogue? Note the interesting mise en scène that is playing out in the background of the scene.

His eyes, and those of the 1960s audiences, have been forced open to look at the consequences of casual relationships.

Alfie was made in 1966 when abortion was still illegal in Britain. However, hundreds of women were dying each year from the effects of 'back street' abortions.

Activity

Read the following article to gain insight into the reasons why abortion was eventually made legal in 1960s Britain. Consider the role of the film *Alfie* in terms of messages and values in the light of this information.

Continued

Reasons contributing to the introduction of the 1967 Abortion Act

Paul Ferris estimates that 10,000 west end legal abortions were taking place per year, where women with the economic means were paying Harley Street physicians. Meanwhile, women who could not afford these excessive fees were forced to resort to criminal and dangerous 'backstreet' abortions. Glanville Williams in his introduction to A. Jenkins' book, *Law for the Rich*, remarked that 'cases have been known where she [the aborted woman] has been made a complete cripple'. Indeed, it was estimated that 35,000 women were being treated annually after botched abortions, which was a considerable strain upon the National Health Service. Moreover, reports into maternal deaths in England and Wales 1952–1966 found that by the mid-1960s, unsafe abortion was the leading cause of avoidable maternal death.

Even the minimal estimate was sufficient evidence of a serious social problem. The horror surrounding back street abortions was one of the most powerful arguments used by proponents of new legislation, and was crucial in shaping public and parliamentary opinion.

The historian Stephen Brooke has described the 1967 Abortion Act as a 'symbol of permissive Britain'. Indeed, rather than a unique phenomenon, the legalisation of abortion should be viewed in the wider context of the radical relaxation of sexual mores and legal changes during the 1960s. The public were becoming more openly engaged in debates over sexuality and morality, which is witnessed by films, books, plays and TV programmes dealing with hitherto forbidden subjects such as homosexuality, mental illness and abortion in a frank way, for example the film *Up the Junction* in 1965. The change in the law was a response to prevailing liberal attitudes and behaviour that also led to the radical reappraisal of legislation over capital punishment, divorce, homosexuality, drug use and juvenile delinquency.

Source: Edited from The Abortion Act 1967, www.bris.ac.uk/Depts/History/Sixties/Feminism/abortion.htm

Although on the surface it may seem as though the film itself is supporting the submissive role of women in society when we look a little closer it appears that the film is actually highlighting their predicament(s) and is perhaps offering possible solutions. Just because a film represents a character in a certain way does not mean that it is in agreement with that representation, and in fact the film's overall messages and values can be very much the opposite.

All the women in the film decide eventually that they do not need Alfie and he is ultimately left on his own. Perhaps this is a comment on the growing independence of women throughout this decade?

One thing is for sure and that is that unlike the Beatles and James Bond, Alfie's lifestyle in the 'swinging sixties' comes with consequences and complicatons. Alfie is where the swinging sixties meets social reality, a genre that many other New Wave directors of the time took up in earnest.

To get this film made, the film-makers struggled against the social and moral conditions of the time. Several famous actors turned down the part of Alfie before Caine accepted the role, because it dealt with the taboo and illegal subject of abortion and they did not want to be associated with it.

Once the film was cast and shot, the film-makers had to deal with censors particularly in getting the abortion scenes 'passed'. The scene was only passed on condition that it included the line by the abortionist referring to the 'crime against the unborn child'.

The messages and values, which derive from this film, are twofold.

On the surface it may look as though the scene is merely warning about the immorality of casual relationships and the consequences of them, with Alfie representing both the upside and downside of the 'permissive' society.

However, on further investigation the film and this scene in particular sends out a much wider message than this.

Activity

Look at the abortion scene again. Describe the mise en scène of the setting and the abortionist. How does the mise en scène convey horror, deceit and crime?

The film's judgement seems to be reserved for the abortionist and his illegal money-making ways. He comes across much worse than Alfie in terms of morals and is given no likeable qualities; he is certainly not portrayed as the saviour of the hour. The woman on the other hand is portrayed very sympathetically and we cannot help but feel her pain and lack of control over the situation. When Alfie insensitively gives her the teddy bear we become acutely aware of the differences between male and female responsibilities in the 1960s.

From this the scene's message gets even wider. Not only does it condemn the illegal actions of the abortionist, it is also criticising the moral and political restraints of the era for putting young people in this position in the first place, particularly the woman. Vivien's character highlights women's predicament in the 1960s (not having control over their biology) and the film, which at first seems sexist and misogynistic (anti-women), actually appears to be pushing for changes in society so that women can gain equal rights.

Darling (Schlesinger, 1965): the female equivalent of Alfie

An interesting comparison with *Alfie* is the film *Darling* and the character of Diana Scott. She appears to be the female equivalent of Alfie in that she is liberated in terms of sexual relationships and epitomises the 'swinging' aspect of the genre. Unlike the female characters in *Alfie* who seem submissive and restrained by their gender and class, Diana is a woman who is in control of every aspect of her life including her career and her biology; you might say a precursor to the modern female of today. As in *Alfie*, fashion and music are dominant. Diana is a fashion icon (both on screen and off) and symbolises the youth-orientated consumer-driven society of the time. The film-makers portray this lifestyle as shallow and selfish and, again like Alfie, ultimately punish her for it by showing how lonely she is as a consequence.

In terms of class, Diana gives us a middle/upper-class perspective on life on the London scene which contrasts sharply with the working-class accents and mise en scène of *Alfie* (as well as the 'kitchen sink' dramas of the sixties).

The style of the film shares elements with both *A Hard Day's Night* and *Alfie* in its use of new and unusual camera techniques: freeze frames, jump-cuts, etc, and the use of voiceover. Although there is no direct address to camera, both films use a voiceover but, unlike Alfie's painfully honest account of his bad behaviour, Diana's narration often contradicts the image on screen. For example 'I always encouraged Robert to see his children…I wasn't the jealous type' which precedes a scene where she quite clearly is. Using similar techniques, the structure of each film portrays the swinging side of life for some people in the sixties but shows that ultimately both Alfie and Diana pay for their behaviour, and audiences are unsympathetic to their plight. The permissive society the films depict may create new freedoms but with that comes a whole new set of problems.

One such problem is that of unwanted pregnancy. *Darling* highlights the difference in freedoms between lower-class and upper-class women.

Activity

Compare the abortion scenes in *Alfie* and *Darling*. One is an illegal backstreet abortion and the other a procedure which is paid for privately. Compare the mise en scène of the scenes and the responses from the two female characters involved. What are the messages of each? Do you suppose they are both supporting women's rights and calling for change?

Conclusion

The world was changing in the 1960s and Britain was at the forefront of that with its swinging attitude. Films like *A Hard Day's Night* and *Alfie* reflected some of those changes. The range and diversity of British cinema in the 1960s reflected the range and diversity within British life. These developments and how they affected different sectors in society could not be summed up with one, uniform type of film-making and hence variety came in the shape of the New Wave (social realism), the commercial (*Bond* and *Carry On* films), the historical epic, the Hammer horror and the swinging sixties genre, each reflecting and commenting in some way on a new post-war Britain. The films made in Britain at this time would become some of the most well-known and critically acclaimed of its history.

In this chapter we are going to examine the work of an individual British director, Ken Loach, and focus on one of his films, *Sweet Sixteen* in close detail. We will review Loach's career as a film-maker, discuss some of his working methods and then analyse specific key sequences in the film.

Close study: Sweet Sixteen **directed by Ken Loach**

Loach's career

Ken Loach is arguably the greatest living British director. At least this is the view presented by the directors, Michael Apted, Alan Parker and Stephen Frears in the BFI documentary, *Typically British*.

Now in his mid-sixties Loach began his work as a director in television working on the police series *Z Cars*. He then worked for the innovative producer Sydney Newman on his series of Wednesday plays that introduced new writers like Dennis Potter and were noted for their focus on contemporary life and issues.

He began to really come to public attention, however, with his work with the producer, Tony Garnett, and their energetic, experimental adaptation of Nell Dunn's portrayal of teenage life in South London, *Up the Junction*. Loach began to develop here his distinctive style of film-making, influenced by developments in documentary film-making, getting out of the studio and filming on location with newly developed lightweight 16mm cameras. *Up the Junction*, although drama, was intended to be a conscious, clear contribution to the debate that was then going on in society about abortion and reforming the law to make it legal. At a crucial point in the narrative when the central character is recovering from the pain of an illegal, or as it was then called, 'backstreet', abortion, Loach breaks the basic conventions of television drama to introduce a voiceover, a real doctor, giving the figures for the number of women who have undergone such illegal operations and the deaths and injuries that have resulted. As we shall see with *Sweet Sixteen*, Loach has always felt it important to challenge as well as entertain his audience.

Cathy Come Home, made with Garnett in 1966 was, if anything, an even more powerful dissection of a social problem, homelessness.

Loach's documentary style, and forensically precise depiction of the way uncaring landlords, council officers, bailiffs and social services officers slowly destroy the family at the centre of the drama had many of the audience believing they were seeing a real documentary. There was public outrage and in the wake of the drama the law was changed so that homeless hostels run by local councils no longer separated husbands and wives. The homelessness charity, 'Shelter', was formed. In similarly hard-hitting vein in 1969, he made what is widely regarded as his finest film *Kes* (see fig 12.1), based on a book that is still widely used in schools and with which you may well be familiar.

Figure 12.1 ▶

After the successes of the 1960s, the 1970s and the 1980s were a more difficult time for Loach with the political mood having shifted away from progressive socialist views under the Labour government of Jim Callaghan, but accelerating sharply away with the election of the Conservatives with Mrs Thatcher as Prime Minister in 1979. It became almost impossible for Loach to raise money for his feature films. He responded in typically determined fashion by making more politically engaged non-fiction films. *A Question of Leadership* (1981) attacked Mrs Thatcher's government, and *Which Side Are You On?* (1984) firmly backed the miners in their year-long dispute with the government. Later in the 1980s he directed television advertisements to generate some income.

In the 1990s his career underwent a second great period. In 1990 his film about Northern Ireland, *Hidden Agenda* won a Jury Prize at Cannes, and this renewed interest in his work. With *Riff Raff* (1991), *Raining Stones* (1993) and *Ladybird Ladybird* (1994) he was able to explore again the lives of working-class people put under enormous strain by poverty and low expectations. In the mid-1990s he made *Land and Freedom* about the Spanish Civil War, and *Carla's Song* about the military and political struggle in Nicaragua. Although *My Name is Joe* (1998), about an alcoholic, was a critical success it is still difficult for Loach to get his films seen. His 2001 film *The Navigators* about the privatisation of the rail industry had only one screening in the UK before it was shown on Channel 4. In contrast it was a small-scale box office success in France.

Sweet Sixteen was made in 2002. He also directed the UK segment of a left-wing response to the attack on the twin towers in New York, *11'09'01-September 11*, reminding audiences that that date was also the day in 1973 that the CIA inspired a coup against Chile's democratically elected government that led to the deaths of 30,000 people.

> ## talking point
>
> What do you think are the major social issues today that a committed, political film-maker might take as his/her subjects for a film?

Influences on his cinematic style

Naturalism

There are a couple of key influences on Loach's style. After the Golden Era of British film-making immediately after the Second World War, British cinema in the 1950s had largely been dominated by genre films: horror, science fiction, or war films. The first really interesting film movement was called Free Cinema and was initially a documentary movement, focusing on working-class life and the growth of teenage culture, in films such as *We are the Lambeth Boys* (1958) directed by Karel Reisz. These documentary makers attempted to present their subjects realistically but also sympathetically through a close observation of the detail of everyday life.

This focus on close attention to the detail of everyday life, creating a highly realistic mise en scène and using 'ordinary' people as opposed to kings and queens or the rich and famous as subjects was part of a broader cultural movement that is called naturalism. You might compare it with the kind of mise en scène used in Hollywood in the studio era, what we have referred to as verisimilitude. In Warner's films of the 1930s the sets needed just enough detail to keep the audience convinced it was a realistic setting while the audience kept focused on the narrative. In naturalism there must be lots of attention to detail because we need to believe completely in these characters and locations as real people and places. It is also because, as we shall see, in naturalism the places, the environments where people live play a crucial role in how they feel about themselves and what kind of life chances they have.

To illustrate this we can hear Ken Loach's commentary on the DVD of *Sweet Sixteen* where his first comments very specifically locate the film where it has been shot in Greenock on the banks of the Clyde near Glasgow in Scotland, and give a quick summary of the area's long term economic decline.

Free Cinema directors went on to make feature films which also foreshadow Loach's concern with social issues. Karel Reisz's *Saturday Night and Sunday Morning* (1960) showed with harsh realism a factory worker's life in the East Midlands. Tony Richardson's *A Taste of Honey* (1961) showed interracial relationships and, sympathetically, a gay man.

talking point Some people argue that soap operas are naturalistic. Certainly when *Coronation Street* started in 1960 it was regarded as a great achievement in naturalistic drama. Would you agree that soaps are still valuable in presenting the difficult realities of modern-day Britain in contrast to the escapist fantasies of Hollywood?

A second great influence on Loach is the group of films known as Italian Neo-Realism.

Italian Neo-Realism

At the end of the Second World War as the Germans were retreating from Rome, the director Roberto Rossellini filmed with whatever scraps of film he could find the first Neo-Realist film, *Rome, Open City*. The film was absolutely contemporary, a dramatisation of the events going on as the film was being made. Part of the footage of the Germans fighting a rearguard action in the streets as they retreat is believed to be documentary footage of a real skirmish. Melodramatic at times and presenting some stereotyped characterisation, the film was intended to be a direct intervention in the political and military conflict it was presenting, encouraging its audience, whether Catholic or Communist, to see themselves as part of the same struggle against the Germans. We might see here a connection with Loach's engagement in social issues like abortion or homelessness.

The films that have arguably had the greatest influence on Loach's style though are those of Vittorio DeSica: *Bicycle Thieves* and *Umberto D*. Many of Loach's working methods such as using non-professional actors, were also used by DeSica, but perhaps most important is the way in which both film-makers use single figures in their dramas to give us a human understanding of social issues; in DeSica's case, of unemployment in *Bicycle Thieves* and poverty in old age in *Umberto D*.

Working methods

Loach's working methods are unusual, and would never be tolerated by one of the big studios. He sometimes works with inexperienced or non-professional actors and is often led to reshape and refine his story ideas when his casting gives him the right person to play his main character. In the case of *Sweet Sixteen* Loach saw 400–500 young men from whom he chose Martin Compston to play the central character Liam in the film. He shoots his films in sequence to enable the actor to stay close to the character's development and develops much of the dialogue through improvisation with the actors so their reactions are as natural as possible. He also gives the actors just the pages of the script that are necessary for that day's shooting, again to keep reactions as natural as possible.

Loach works with a regular team of collaborators that includes production designer Martin Johnson, and director of photography, Barry

Ackroyd, as well as producer Rebecca Wade. Based on his socialist beliefs his films have in the past been difficult and complex to finance. They are very much dependent on the kind of 'pack of card' financing deal that we have seen in previous chapters. Selling the distribution rights to different territories especially on the continent is often the key to generating enough money to make the film. As Wade has pointed out, when you have twelve or thirteen sources of finance, the deal-making becomes extremely complicated. *Sweet Sixteen*, to illustrate this, is a British, German and Spanish co-production, made with the support of BBC Films, Scottish Screen and the Glasgow Film Office.

Cinematic style

Loach has maintained an easily identifiable cinematic style throughout his career. His style as a director might be summarised as follows:

1 Concern with overtly political and social issues.
2 The use of improvised and highly colloquial dialogue.
3 The use of a mixture of professional and non-professional actors.
4 A thoroughly authentic and naturalistic mise en scène.
5 A documentary style of filming, apparently responding to the actions of the actors.
6 Realistic, but also melodramatic, plots.

We will now look at how this style works in a couple of specific sequences in the film.

Messages and values: Sweet Sixteen

Analysing the opening sequence

The opening sequence includes three scenes: Liam and Pinball looking at the stars with a group of kids with a telescope; the two friends selling cigarettes in the pub (see fig 12.2); and the trick played on the lorry driver so that he runs over the policeman's motorcycle.

Figure 12.2 ▶

The sequence is very successful in quickly characterising the two boys and their working-class environment. *Sweet Sixteen* is, of course, an ironic title – any initial impression we might have that the boys are showing the kids the stars for fun is quickly dispelled by Liam's telling the kids 'it's twenty-five pence a go. Give the money to Pinball.' Yet we can still see that the friends are not much more than kids themselves and a theme of the losing of innocence is established in the first few seconds. The idea of yearning for escape and for a different kind of life is also there in the stargazing. Setting the young people against this vast backdrop, while it makes them seem tiny and vulnerable also dignifies them, making them seem special, embodying a universal human experience of wonder.

As Loach has pointed out, this contrast between the tough social world the boys inhabit in Greenock and the sweeping beauty of the Clyde and the surrounding hills is a key motif in the film, pointing forward to Liam's isolation at the edge of the ocean in the final few seconds of the film. There's no romance here even so. The boys are after money, and the clothes, especially the baseball caps, immediately 'place' them in our minds as working-class lads, probably only interested in football, music, drinking and chasing girls. A key task for the film is to make us see how much more complex, troubled and courageous are the lives that they lead. The strong Scottish accents, of course, also indicate that this will be an authentic, realistic 'slice of life'.

This is powerfully reinforced in the next scene in the pub. In the commentary on the DVD, Loach describes the kind of industrial decline that Greenock has gone through and the very limited opportunities that now exist for people, and both the writing by Paul Laverty and the direction by Loach are terrifically economic yet effective. The economic decline is suggested by simple elements of the mise en scène, such as that the pub is quite full during the day. The customers are chatting quietly and do not seem rushed. There are no business suits, or work overalls. The customers are also pleased to get the option of some cheap 'fags'. Few other pleasures, of course, can be got so cheaply. Liam and Pinball's reaction to the publican throwing them out, that is to say verbally abusing him, shows them to be tough, what working-class people might call, 'hard-faced'.

That this toughness might border on recklessness is seen in the next scene. Liam's leadership qualities are suggested in his cool, opportunistic weighing up of the situation. Deliberately backing a driver into something has been done before on film, of course, most memorably by Woody Allen in his early film *Bananas*, but it works really well to suggest both the mischievous, irrepressible high spirits and good humour that we can all admire in young people, and a wildness and lack of respect for authority that might lead us to be anxious for the futures of such boys. Laverty, the writer, knows well that a well-chosen action is worth hundreds of lines of dialogue. The scene is very effective in clearly placing the boys as products of Greenock.

Activity

Go straight to the final sequences of the film and use the cinematic codes to compare Liam's position now with the sense of possibility that we have identified in the opening sequence.

Analysis of the end of Liam and Pinball's friendship

This is a crucial scene as it marks the first point at which events begin to get out of Liam's control and the central relationships start to break down. We see Liam approach some flats. The sense of the oppressiveness of the high-rise flats all around is clear. There are other children not much older than Liam just hanging around and he asks two passers-by, 'Are there any flats where the junkies might be?' They answer quite casually. Again, meeting here in a flat with drug addicts is a skilful choice: the dereliction of the flat, the damp walls and peeling paintwork make it clear that this is what they were trying to escape, and this is the prospect, drug addiction, by which they are always tempted as an easy way out. Liam and Pinball are connected not just by their exploits, but also by their family experiences, Liam's mother and Pinball's father both being 'junkies'.

When Liam approaches and enters the flat the camera is hand-held, a technique drawn from making documentaries, and unusual in this film. It gives a rawness and immediacy to the drama as Liam throws the junkies out. In the following exchange between Liam and Pinball the camera changes position. This gives us more angles and viewpoints from which to feel the deep, destructive confusion that is now taking over their relationship. Pinball is too hurt, really from a lifetime of hurt, to hear that Liam has no intention of hurting him and turns Liam's knife on himself.

Activity

The above is, we hope, a suggestive analysis, but is not exhaustive. Look again at the sequence and try to work out how Loach uses the cinematic codes to draw out the irony and the pathos, the sadness of the situation.

Alternatively choose a sequence that you feel in its drama and intensity illustrates Loach's skills as a director and analyse it in some detail.

Sweet Sixteen **and genre**

In one way, of course, *Sweet Sixteen* is clearly a social realist movie. Its main themes are how tough social conditions, unemployment and poor housing can present people with terrible choices. Loach's cinematic style is then all about making the situation feel as realistic and authentic as possible. However, having said that, an interesting way to look at *Sweet Sixteen* is as a gangster film.

Activity

It may be helpful to watch some gangster films. Try some early classics of the genre such as *The Public Enemy* or *Angels with Dirty Faces*, or later classics such as *Goodfellas* or *Scarface*.

In one way, of course, this should not be surprising. The gangster movie, like the western genre invented in the United States, is about the moral corruption that underlies modern, cosmopolitan society, an idea not that far from Loach's – that modern capitalist society is about greed for the few and not meeting the needs of all people.

Figure 12.3 ▶

If we compare *Sweet Sixteen* and Martin Scorsese's gangster film, *Goodfellas,* we see a number of similarities. Henry, the main character in *Goodfellas* and Liam both begin in relative poverty and in dysfunctional families. Within the first few scenes of both films we see them being beaten by their 'fathers'. However, both remain devoted to their mothers and wear smart suits as a sign of their success to impress them. Henry does this early in the film, and in a wonderfully ironic moment his mother opens the door to him and says, appalled, 'You look like a gangster'. Liam does this much later in the film when his mum comes out of prison (see fig 12.3). Both show initiative and determination in their exploits and prove their trustworthiness to the gang boss. Henry does this when he doesn't 'rat' on the others when he first goes to prison. Liam is tested by his boss when he is told to stab a man in a club while he is in the toilets. The scene is very reminiscent of the crucial sequence in *The Godfather* where Michael Corleone, the youngest brother of the gangster family, goes to the toilet to recover a gun with which he then kills a policeman with whom he is having a meeting in the restaurant. Both Liam and Henry enjoy the fruits of success, Liam gets his new flat for his mother and Henry's life becomes one long round of hedonism. However, their lives then start to come apart, Pinball, Liam's best friend, feels that he has betrayed him. One of Henry's two best friends is killed and the other becomes murderously paranoid. However, where Henry chooses to abandon all loyalty to his friends and join the witness protection programme, testifying against his former gangster colleagues, Liam's murder of his step-father leaves us feeling that his situation is hopeless and his young life may well be ruined. Refer back to your analysis of the final sequence of the film. How did you describe the audience's feelings as Liam is alone on the beach at the end of the film?

Ken Loach rejects any notion that the film has a very pessimistic ending and sees in Liam and his sister sources of hope and courage. However, isn't Liam a more morally compromised figure than this implies? Isn't he more like Henry a traditional gangster figure than the director may have wanted? The problem is most acute in the scene in the toilet where Liam is being 'tested'. Will he stab the man? It is highly tense and dramatic but isn't it also a moment when Liam is shown to be an immoral young man willing to take the life of someone he has never met on the orders of a criminal?

Interestingly the character who as Loach says became more important in the making of the film and who is a more reliable source of hope is Liam's sister. She, like the woman who tries to chase the pizza sellers/ drug dealers out of the flats, embodies more straightforwardly a sense of hope and courage for the future.

talking point

What kind of message do you think the film ultimately conveys? Is it one of hope for the future as Loach believes or would you see it as more pessimistic?

Activity

Hopefully this work on *Sweet Sixteen* will have enthused you for Loach's works. Try to see as many of his films as you can.

Conclusion

We hope that you have enjoyed both reading this book and doing the activities contained in it. One thing above all seems to be the key to doing well in studying film and that is forgetting that it is work! For film students there should be no boundary between going to the local multiplex with friends and reading *Empire* or *Total Film* and working on an analysis of a film sequence for coursework. Everything should be adding to your breadth of knowledge of the industry and the sophistication of your understanding.

Take pride in having an intelligent, intellectual, critical approach to film but without losing your enthusiasm for your favourite films, stars and directors. Let both of these elements come out in your writing about film. The information going into the book is up to date at the time of writing but things change in the industry very quickly. Use some of the sources below to keep your understanding and information absolutely contemporary.

Further reading
Books

Pam Cooke and Mieke Bernink (eds.), *The Cinema Book* (2nd ed. British Film Institute Publishing, 1999).

Peter Biskind, *Easy Riders, Raging Bulls: How the Sex, Drugs and Rock 'n' Roll Generation Saved Hollywood* (Simon and Schuster, 1998).

David Bordwell and Kristin Thompson, *Film Art: An Introduction* (3rd ed. McGraw-Hill, 1990).

Richard Dyer, *Stars* (British Film Institute, 1998).

Richard Maltby, *Hollywood Cinema* (Blackwell, 1995).

Steve Neale and Murray Smith (eds.), *Contemporary Hollywood Cinema* (Routledge, 1998).

Jim Smith, *Gangster Film*, Virgin Film series (Virgin Books, 2004)

Jill Nelmes (ed.), *Introduction to Film Studies* (Routledge, 2003).

Neville Langley, *Pulp Fiction*, York Film Notes series (York Press, 2000)

Nick Lacey, *Narrative and Genre* (Macmillan Press, 2000)

Patrick Phillips, *Understanding Film Texts: Meaning and Experience* (British Film Institute, 2000). Worth looking at as Phillips is the WJEC's Chief Examiner!

Newspapers and magazines

Empire magazine.

The Guardian newspaper on Fridays – intelligent reviews of the week's releases and the latest box office charts in both the US and the UK.

Screen International – weekly journal of the global film and television industries. Excellent for up-to-date industry case studies.

Sight and Sound – the monthly journal of the British Film Institute.

Websites

Internet Movie Database – www.imdb.com. You'll find just about every movie ever made here and each film has very useful sections of reviews, sources of finance and distribution patterns.

Try visiting the films unlimited section of *The Guardian* newspaper online, GuardianUnlimited. It has an excellent link to 'film sites we like'.

Also try downloading the meta search engine most favoured by academics, Copernic. There is a free version on the website and it will help you in chasing down information you may need for your research.

Also see:

www.exposure.co.uk
www.filmmeducation.org

Glossary

Action codes significant moves or gestures to indicate that a certain action will take place.

Arthouse audience film lovers who prefer more challenging and complex films than are often to be found in the multiplex. They prefer films driven by character or the director's artistic intentions rather than an appeal based on special effects or 'big' stars.

Aural relating to hearing/ears. Not to be confused with 'oral' which relates to speaking/mouth, as they are both have similar pronunciation.

Blind bidding business practice whereby cinema owners could not see the film before they bought it.

Block booking business practice whereby major studios required cinema owners to buy up to a year of the studios' films in advance.

Chronological arrangement of events in order of occurance.

Cinematic codes refers to the technical process of film-making (camera, editing, etc.) with each technical or 'cinematic' code carrying meaning for the audience.

Cover the amount of varied footage shot for one scene.

Cultural codes are codes that we use in everyday life to create and assess meaning. We make judgments and have responses based on our own cultural knowledge and experience. This can be based on how someone dresses, their body language, their accent, etc. We take these 'cultural codes' into the cinema with us and apply them to characters and situations in the films we watch and this affects our response.

Cut is the term used to mark the change of shot when editing. When editors worked on film they would literally 'cut and splice' the film with 'joining tape'. With digital editing, the same term is used as the shot 'cuts-out' or 'cuts-in' although the original footage is never actually cut at all, only a digital copy.

Digitised when media (images) are converted electronically from one format (e.g. film) and stored in a digital edit suite.

Director the person in charge of the shooting of the film itself. He or she must understand technically what is happening, the implications this might have for the budget, and still be creative in making a film that will be enjoyable and distinctive.

Distribution the process of making more copies or prints of the film, and transporting them to cinemas.

Enigma codes narrative devices which set up little puzzles or mysteries for the audience to solve.

Equity investor a person or company who puts money into the film and then recovers their investment when the film is released plus a share of the profits.

Exhibition the showing of the films in the cinemas and getting a local audience in to watch the film.

External cuts are whole scenes joined to other whole scenes, e.g. a scene in a pub followed by a scene in a shop.

External motivation some external event that makes the narrative agent act and start the chain of cause and effect. This could be anything relevant to your story but usually involves the hero's goal, e.g. to get the girl, find the treasure or win the race.

Film package is usually made up of a one or two page treatment, summarising the story and its appeal for its target audience. There will also be details of the 'talent' that is envisaged for the project, or who may have already indicated that they are interested.

Format relates to the different types of material that are used to create films or TV programmes, e.g., film, videotape, DVD, etc.

Genre French term meaning 'type' or 'kind'

Iconography iconic signs (especially of mise en scène when applied to genre) which typify a particular place or thing visually.

Internal cuts are cuts within a scene, using the various different angles and set-ups within that one scene.

Internal motivation something *within* the main character that drives the narrative (e.g. revenge, jealousy or love).

Linear in order or sequence.

Marketability is the ease with which the film will generate interest because of its stars or its director.

Mise en scène (setting the scene). It refers to the four basic elements that make up the visual language of the scene: setting, costume (including hair and make-up), props and figure expression (or performance).

Narrative a story or a description of a series of events. It is a word which is not specific to film but to other ways of storytelling also.

Non-linear not in order or sequence.

Obstacles things or events that get in the way of the hero reaching his goal and which have to be overcome. If the man gets the girl just by asking her then there is no story!

Oligopoly the control of a market for a particular product by a small group of companies in which no one company is dominant. They may well, however, work together as a group to keep other companies out of the market.

Paradigm an example/pattern/model with a *vertical* set of associations (from Saussure's theory of communication).

Parallel simultaneous, at the same time.

Playability is the degree to which a film will continue to attract an audience because audiences like it and it gets good 'word of mouth'.

Plot refers only to the actual events on screen including any non-diegetic material like titles or credits.

Post-production the phase in the process after production where the film is edited and music and effects are added.

Producer the person in overall charge of the film from conception to the delivery of the final finished film to the distributor.

Production the phase in the process where the actual shooting of the film takes place.

Props is the abbreviated term for 'properties' and refers to all the items within a scene that are placed to 'dress' the set.

Rental the proportion of the ticket price that the film exhibitor returns to the distributor for the right to show their film.

Run zone clearance system business practice whereby distribution of films was controlled by 'zone', with certain cinemas having the right to run the film first.

Scene a succession of shots.

Score the music specially written for the film.

Sequence a succession of scenes.

Sexual revolution a term that encompasses many changes in the sexual attitudes and freedom of young people including the introduction of the pill (liberated female sexuality); divorce laws; and the legalisation of homosexuality and abortion.

Shot is a 'set-up' within a scene. There may be many different set-ups (shots) to film a scene. For example, the same conversation may be shot from many different angles.

Social realism this genre, common in the 1960s, employed a cinematic style that attempted to construct an authentic 'realism' on screen through various narrative techniques and cinematic code use. One technique was to cast non-actors to play dramatic parts. This, coupled with handheld camera, authentic mise en scène and lack of editing, created a documentary 'look' that complemented the real life issues that the films were concerned with.

Soundtrack refers to any sound which accompanies the picture. When we talk about 'music soundtrack' we mean music which is added to the film from various artists but not specially written for the film.

Story refers to the actual events portrayed on screen *plus* those events which do not but which form part of the story. Events which do not appear on screen can be events which are implied or referred to and which we the audience need to know about to make the film make sense.

Structuralist a theorist who seeks to find order and pattern in communication.

Synchronisation running simultaneously at the same speed.

Synergy the way in which a single product, such as a film, can be used across a whole range of the company's interests to generate profit.

Synopsis a summary of your story that gives all plot events and twists including the final outcome.

Take a sample of one shot. A shot may need many 'takes' to get it right.

Transition a way of moving from one shot to another.

Transnational corporation a global company made up of many smaller companies throughout the world in a range of different markets.

Verisimilitude a mise en scène that has to approximate closely enough to a real setting as to be credible, without paying too close attention to detail so that too much money is not spent on the sets!

Vertical integration when a company owns all stages of the production, distribution and sale or, in the case of cinema, exhibition of its product.

Word of mouth other people telling you what a film is like and recommending it (or not!).

Index

Page numbers in italics indicate illustrations and photos.

abortion 202, 203, 204, 205
action codes 70
actors
    direction/description in screenplay 90
    figure expression 30
    see also stars
ADR (Automated Dialogue Replacement)
    43
advertising
    costs 147–8
    on television 124–5
aerial shots 14
Alamo, The (Hancock, 2004) 181
Alfie (Gilbert, 1966) 198–205
American Graffiti (Lucas, 1973) 125–6
ancillary rights 128
Angels with Dirty Faces (Curtiz, 1938)
    79, 111
angle, camera 10, *10*
Around the World in 80 Days (Coraci,
    2004) 173
arthouse audience 151
arthouse cinemas 169
aspect ratio 17
atmosphere, lighting and 18
Atomfilms 177
audience
    arthouse 151
    expectations 19, 44, 56–9, 60–3
    modern 130–1, 164–5
    research 165–7
    word of mouth recommendation 105
aural motifs 45
auteurism 55
Automated Dialogue Replacement (ADR)
    43

back lighting 20, 24, *24*
Barrymore, Drew 137–8
Battlefield Earth (Christian, 2000) 148
Beach, The (Boyle, 2000) 140
Beatles, The 194–8
Bevan, Tim 158, 159
Birthday Girl (Butterworth, 2001) 158
Bitzer, Billy 102
Blair Witch Project, The (Myrick and
    Sanchez, 1999) 7, 15, 177

blind bidding 107
block booking 107
blockbusters 135, 171–3
British film industry 140–2, 153–4
    Britishness and 190–1
    cinemas in Britain 167–70
    demise of FilmFour 157–8
    distribution 154–5, 160
    Film Council and 156–7
    independents 142–3
    Ken Loach and *Sweet Sixteen* 207–15
    National Lottery and 155–6
    sources of finance 141, 142
    the swinging sixties 191–206
    Working Title 158–60

Cagney, James 76
Cahiers de Cinéma (Journal of the
    Cinema) 27
Caine, Michael 199, 200–1
camerawork 5, 8, 18
    film formats 5–7
    and lighting 18–19
    moving frame 12–15
    shooting script directions 91
    special affects 16–17
    static framing 8–11
    technical terms 17
Captain Corelli's Mandolin (Madden,
    2001) 159
car-mounted shots 14
Carey, Jim 76
Cathy Come Home (TV drama) 207–8
celebrity, cult of 196
certification 147
Channel 4 157
characters roles 66
Charlie's Angels: Full Throttle (McG,
    2003) 136–39
cinemas
    decline in attendance 104, 113
    early 101
    Hollywood and 106, 107, 112
    ownership in UK 167
    and spectatorship 161–2
    types of 168–9

cinematic codes 3, 5
  analysis of two films 47–53
  cinematography 5–18
  editing 33–41
  lighting 18–26
  mise en scène 26–33
  sound 42–7
cinematic ideas 87–8
cinematography 5, 18
  analysis of 47–50
  common techniques 8–15
  film formats 5–7
  and lighting 18–19
  special effects 16–17
  technical terms 17
clapperboards 42, *42*
class and British cinema 190–1, 195,
    197–8, 200–1, 205
Collateral (Mann, 2004) 129, 130
colour, use in lighting 25, *25*
Columbia 106, 118, 124, 136
comedy 31, 58
community cinemas 169
computer games industry 152–3
content 3
  see also genre
continuity editing 34, 110
  rhythm 40
  space 35–8
  time 38–40
continuity persons 35
contracts, stars' 182
contrapuntal sound 45–6
costume 30, *31*
cover (footage shot) 41
crane shots 14, *14*
cross cutting technique 39
Cruise, Tom 181, 182–3
Crying Game, The (Jordan, 1992) 158
cultural codes 3, 18
cuts 34
  cut-aways 36
  external and internal 34
  transitions 41
  see also editing

dailies 6
Darling (Schlesinger, 1965) 205
Davis, Bette 109
de Havilland, Olivia 109, 112
De Niro, Robert 76
depth of field 17
DeSica, Vittorio 210
dialogue
  and genre 63
  recording 43–4
  in screenplay 90
Dialogue Editor 43
Diaz, Cameron 137
diegetic and non-diegetic sound 43

digital technology 5
  digital cinema 7
  digital projection 176
  DV cameras 6, *6*, 7
  DVDs 162–3
  Film Council and 156
  internet distribution 160
  small independents and 142, 160
Director of Photography (DoP) 17
directors 103
Disney 116, 178
dissolves 41
distance, camerawork 9
distribution 101, 104
  British film industry and 153–60
  computer games industry 152–3
  the first distributors 101–2
  marketing a film 147–50
  new technology and 160
  role of distributors 145–7
  today 128
documentaries, camerawork 15
dollies 12, *13*
Donnie Darko (Kelly, 2001) 47–50
DoP (Director of Photography) 17
Dreyfuss, Richard 124
drive-ins 165
Dubbing Mixer 43
Dutch angle 11
DV (digital video) 5, 6, *6*, 7
DVDs (digital versatile discs) 162–3

e-cinema 7
East is East (O'Donnell, 1999) 157
editing 34
  action codes 70
  continuity 34–40, 110
  home 164
  the process 34
  transitions 41, 95
English Patient, The (Minghella, 1996)
    148–50
enigma codes 70
equity investors 140
establishing shots 12, 14, 35
event movies 124–5, 161
exhibition 100, 104
  cinemas in UK 167–8
  Hollywood studio system and 106,
    112, 121
  media 128, 161–3, 175–7
  modern cinema audiences 164–7
  strategies 171–4
  The Godfather and mass exhibition
    121–2
  types of cinema 168–71
expectations, audience 19, 44, 58–9,
    60–5
eyeline matches 35

fade down/out 41
fade up/in 41
Fahrenheit 9/11 (Moore, 2004) 174, 178
fans 186–8
Fellner, Eric 158, 159
figure expression 30, 70
fill light 20
film, 35mm 6
film clubs 170–1
Film Council 133, 142, 156–7
film form 1–3
   micro and macro components 3
   see also cinematic codes; genre
film industry 99–100
   and ancillary rights 128–30
   annual revenues 145
   Hollywood 115–16
   Hollywood origins 102–3
   Hollywood studio system 1930–1949 106–11
   long decline of studio system 112–13, 121
   New Hollywood 121–7
   origins of 100–3
   sectors of 100, 103–6
   sources of finance 141–2
   Time Warner 117–20
   see also British film industry; distribution; exhibition; production
film packages 135
FilmFour 157–8
finance *see* funding of films
flashbacks 74
Flynn, Errol 109
focus 17
Foley Editor 43
Football Factory (Love, 2004) 143
Ford, John 108
formats 5–7, 8
formulaic films 60–3
   see also genre
Four Weddings and a Funeral (Newell, 1994) 158, 160
Fox 106, 116, 126
fractured narratives 72–4
frames and framing
   moving 12–15
   static 8–11
France, academic study of film in 27
Free Cinema movement 209
From Dusk to Dawn (Rodriguez, 1996) 56–8
funding of films
   in Britain 133, 140–1, 155–7
   outside Britain 141–2
   producers and 134, 135

gangster films 77–81, 213–15
genre 55–62
   expectation and 58–9

gangster films 77–81
Hollywood studio system 1930–1949 and 107–9
macro analysis 81–4
narrative and 65–72
repetition and difference 59–63
stars and 75–6
Sweet Sixteen and 213–15
'swinging sixties' 194–205
themes and ideology 75
Gilbert, Lewis 198, 199
Gladiator (Scott, 2000) 16, *16*, 25, *26*, 135
Godfather, The (Coppola, 1972) 19–20, 40, 80, 121–2, 214
Goodfellas (Scorcese, 1990) 13, 45, 64, 69, 214
Gosford Park (Altman, 2001) 156
graphic matching 41
Great Train Robbery, The (Porter, 1903) 102

hair and make-up 30
Halloween (Carpenter, 1978) 82–4
handheld shots 14–15
Hard Day's Night, A (Lester, 1964) 194–8
hard and soft lighting 20, 21
Harry Potter and the Prisoner of Azkaban (Cuarón, 2004) 172–3
Heaven's Gate (Cimino, 1975) 105
height, camera 10–11, *10*, *11*
Hidalgo (Johnston, 2003) 173
high and low key lighting 20
Hitchcock, Alfred 45, 110
Hollywood
   classic lighting 20–1, *21*
   New Hollywood 1970s onward 121–8
   origins of 102–3
   studio system 1930–1949 106–9
   studio system decline 112–13, 123
   today 115–20
horror 82, 83
hybrid genre 56

I Robot (Proyas, 2004) 148
iconography 27, 60
ideas
   cinematic 87–8
   story 86–7
ideology 75
If. . . . (Anderson, 1968) 195–6
Ifilm 177
In This World (Winterbottom, 2002) *156*, 157, 176
independent companies 140–1, 142–3, 154–5
Industrial Light and Magic 127
Institutional Mode of Representation 110

internet 160, 163, 176–7
interviews, research 166
Italian Job, The (F. Gary Gray, 2003) 51–3
Italian Neo-Realism 210

Jaws (Spielberg, 1975) 15, 45, 124–5

Keitel, Harvey 135
Kes (Loach, 1969) 208
key light 20
key props 28
Kill Bill (Tarantino, 2003) 46
Knightly, Keira 186–8

Laemmle, Carl 102, 103, 179
language, film 2, 18
Lawrence, Florence 180, *180*
level, camera 11, *11*
lighting 18
    classic Hollywood 20–1, *21*
    colour 24–5, *25*
    direction 22–4, *22, 23, 24*
    The Godfather 19–20
    high and low key 20
    quality (intensity) 21
    source 24
Liu, Lucy 137
Loach, Ken 207–11
    cinematic style 211
    influences on 209–11
    Sweet Sixteen 211–15
    working methods 210–11
Lord of the Rings trilogy (Jackson, 2001) 31
low and high key lighting 20
Lucas, George 125–7
Lumière Brothers 1, 100

Madagascar (Darnell and McGrath, 2005) 150–1, *150*
macro elements of film form 3
    analysis of 81–4
    genre and narrative 55–84
make-up 31
market research 165–7
marketability of films 146
marketing 147–8
    The English Patient 148–50
    on the internet 177–8
    Jaws 124–5
merchandising 125, 126–7
messages and genre 75
MGM 106, 117
micro elements of film form 3, 5
    analysis of 47–54
    cinematography 5–18
    editing 34–44
    lighting 18–26
    mise en scène 26–33
    sound 42–7

Miramax 178
mise en scène 26, *26*
    analysis of 47–50
    costume, hair and make-up 30–1
    figure expression 30
    and genre 63
    reading a scene 27–30
    realistic 209
    setting and props 28–30
    verisimilitude 111
montages 39
mood
    lighting and 18–19
    music and 46
Motion Picture Patent Company (MPPC) 102, 106
motivation of characters 87
Mr 3000 (Stone III, 2004) 129, 130
multiplexes 104, 168–9
multiscreens 169
music 44, 45, 46
    and audience expectation 62–3
    aural motifs 45
    pleonastic and contrapuntal sound 45
My Beautiful Laundrette (Frears, 1985) 157–8, 158–9

narrative 65–6
    cause and effect 64, *65*
    classic Hollywood 109–10
    devices 69–70
    gangster films 77–81
    macro analysis 81–4
    story patterns 65–9
    unusual use of 72–4
narrative agents 69
National Lottery and film funding 155–6
naturalism 209
Navigators, The (Loach, 2001) 208
Neo-Realism, Italian 210
nickelodeons 101, 103
1960s *see* swinging sixties
non-linear narratives 72–4

observation, participant 166–7
oligopolies 107
180 degree rule 36–8, *37–8*
overhead lighting 22, *22*

panning shots 12, *12*
paradigms 68
parallel cutting technique 40
Paramount 106, 116, 122
Paramount decree 1948 112
Pathe 102, 155
Pearl Harbour (Bay, 2001) 173
performance 30
Pitt, Brad 184–6
platform release pattern 173–4
playability of films 146

pleonastic sound 45
plot 64
Porter, Edwin S. 102
post-production 33
   editing 33–42
posters 149, *149*, 150–1, *150*
pre-production 133
   difficulties 133–4
   the producer 134–5
   risk reduction 136–9
   the story 134
producers 100, 103, 133–5
product placement 138
production 100, 103
   assembly line system 107–8
   new technology and independent
      142–3
   in the UK 140–1
   see also cinematography; post-
      production; pre-production
promotions 148
Propp, Vladamir 66
   analysis of stories 66–7
props 28–30
Psycho (Hitchcock, 1960) 41, 45
publicity 147, 148
Pulp Fiction (Tarantino, 1994) 72–6

qualitative research 166
quantitative research 165–6
questionnaires 166

Raindance film festival 140–1
Ratcatcher (Ramsey, 1999) 155–6
rentals 101–2
research
   forms of 165–6
   methods 166–7
   undertaking own 174–5
Reservoir Dogs (Tarantino, 1991) 46,
   135
restricted and unrestricted narrative
   69–70
RKO 106
Road to Perdition, The (Mendes, 2002)
   80–1
Roberts, Julia 181
romantic-comedy 56
Rome, Open City (Rossellini, 1945) 210
run zone clearance system 107
rushes 6

saturation release 171–3
Saturday Night and Sunday Morning
   (Reisz, 1960) 209
scene headings 89–90
scene, setting the 26–32
scenes 34
   editing 33–41
Schwarzenegger, Arnold 30, 76
science fiction 56, 60, 75

scores, music 44
Scream (Craven, 1996) 82–4
screenplays 86, 88
   scene direction 90
   scene headings/slug lines 89
   script layout 88, *93–5*
   transitions 92
screens, cinema and TV 17
scripts
   getting made into a film 133
   shooting 86, 88–92
setting 28–30, 60
Se7en (Fincher, 1995) 28–9, 71–2
sexual revolution 194, 198
   Alfie and 201–4
SFX (sound effects) 42
shooting galleries 176
shooting schedules 33, *33*
shooting scripts 86, 93–5
   layout 88, *89*
   scene direction 90–1
   scene headings/slug lines 89–90
   transitions 92
shot-reverse-shots 35–6, *36*
shots 33
   depth of field 17
   editing 33–41
   moving frames 12–15
   static framing 8–11
   storyboards 86, 95, *96–7*
Shrek 2 (2004) 171–2
side lighting 23, *23*
silence, sound of 45
Sky Captain and the World of Tomorrow
   (Conron, 2004) 129, 130
slug lines 89–90
social realism 195
soft and hard lighting 20, 21
Sony 116, 134
sound 42, 46
   detailing in screenplay 90
   diegetic and non-diegetic 43
   pleonastic and contrapuntal 45–6
   the process 42–4
   silence 45
   using creatively 44–6
Sound Effects Editor 43
soundtracks 42, 43
special effects 16–17, *16*, 127, 142
speech patterns and genre 63
Spider-Man (Raimi, 2002) 120, 134
Spielberg, Steven 124–5
Stallone, Sylvester 76
Star Wars films (Lucas) 41, 64, 124,
   125–7, 152–3
stars
   defining a star 182–6
   and genre 75–6
   history of the star system 179–80
   and Hollywood studio system
      1930–1949 107–8, 109, 112

stars (continued)
  importance to film industry 181–2
  and lighting 20
  and their fans 186–88
  see also actors
Steadicams 14–15, *15*
Steiner, Max 111
stereotypes 27
Stewart, James 112, 180
story
  analysis of 66–8
  distinct from plot 64
  ideas 86–7, 87–8
  importance of good 134
  see also narrative; screenplays
storyboards 86, 95, *96–7*
structuralists 66
style *see* micro elements of film form
Sweet Sixteen (Loach, 2002) 209, 210, 211–15
swinging sixties 191–4
  Abortion Act 1967 203
  Alfie 148–205
  Darling 205
  A Hard Day's Night 194–8
synchronisation 42
syndication 128
synergy 120, 136
synopsis 87

takes 34
Tall Guy, The (Smith, 1989) 159
Taste of Honey, A (Richardson, 1961) 209
television
  film integration with 176
  films advertised on 124–5
  impact on film industry 112–13
  selling films to 128
Terminator films 30
Terrorist, The (Sivan, 1998) 150–1
themes 75
35mm film 6
three point lighting system 20–1, *21*
tilt shots 13, *13*
time, editing and 38–9
Time Warner 117–20
Titanic (Cameron, 1999) 64, 104
titles 61–2
Todorov, Tsetvan 66
  analysis of stories 67–8

Topsy Turvy (Leigh, 1999) 173–4
tracking shots 12–13, *13*
Trainspotting (Boyle, 1996) 157
transitions 41, 95
transnational corporations (TNCs) 116
Trauma (Evans, 2004) 129
Travolta, John 76
treatment 135
Trust, the (MPPC) 102, 106
TV *see* television
12 Monkeys (Gilliam, 1995) 46
28 Days Later (Boyle, 2002) 7

UGC 154
UK *see* British Film Industry
under lighting 22, *23*
United Artists 105, 106
Universal 106, 116
  and *Jaws* 124, 125
  and Working Title 160
Up the Junction (TV drama) 207

values and genre 75
verisimilitude 111
Vertigo Films 143
video 6, 162
  playback 6
video-making project 85–6

Warner Brothers 101, 106, 109, 110–11, 116
Warner, Jack 109
websites 218
  film fan 186–8
  films' own 177–80
  gossip 178
  showing films 176–7
Webster, Paul 158
wild soundtracks 44
Williams, Robin 76
Wimbledon (Loncraine, 2004) 129, 130
Winchester '73 (Mann, 1950) 112, 180
wipes 41
Wizard of Oz, The (Fleming, 1939) 2
women, in 1960s Britain 193, 201, 202–4, 205
Working Title 158–60
writers 134

zoom 15